Detain and Punish

Detain and Punish

Haitian Refugees and the Rise of the World's
Largest Immigration Detention System

Carl Lindskoog

UNIVERSITY OF FLORIDA PRESS

Gainesville

23 22 21 20 19 18   6 5 4 3 2 1

Library of Congress Cataloging-in-Publication Data
Names: Lindskoog, Carl, author.
Title: Detain and punish : Haitian refugees and the rise of the world's
 largest immigration detention system / Carl Lindskoog.
Description: Gainesville : University of Florida Press, 2018. | Includes
 bibliographical references and index.
Identifiers: LCCN 2017060692 | ISBN 9781683400400 (cloth : alk. paper)
Subjects: LCSH: Haitians—Legal status, laws, etc.—United States. |
 Refugees—Legal status, laws, etc.—United States. | Detention of
 persons—United States. | United States—Emigration and immigration.
Classification: LCC KF4836 .L56 2018 | DDC 365/.4—dc23
LC record available at https://lccn.loc.gov/2017060692

University of Florida Press
15 Northwest 15th Street
Gainesville, FL 32611-2079
http://upress.ufl.edu

UF PRESS

UNIVERSITY
OF FLORIDA

For my parents

Contents

Figures

Acknowledgments

I have been extremely fortunate to have had outstanding mentors, colleagues, and friends during the years when this book was taking shape. Joshua Freeman, David Hernández, María Cristina García, Aviva Chomsky, Kevin Reilly, Thomas Kessner, Nancy Foner, Millery Polyné, and Amy Chazkel all offered critical guidance and encouragement at various stages of the project. The suggestions I received from Alex Stepick and an anonymous reader were most helpful. Susan Eckstein also offered valuable suggestions and encouragement. James Oakes, Alfonso Quiroz, Judith Stein, Rosemary Feurer, Barbara Posadas, and James Schmidt each helped get me to the point where I could even consider doing something like this. And Geoff Johnson, Brandyn Heppard, Antonia Levy, Lauren Braun-Strumfels, Michelle Brazier, Charlie Bondhus, and Neil Warrence offered both scholarly support and friendship.

Other individuals and institutions also provided valuable support. My editor at University of Florida Press, Stephanye Hunter, patiently answered all my questions and steadily steered this project to completion. Editors Marthe Walters and Kate Babbitt also provided much-needed assistance. I am also so grateful to photographers Gary Monroe, Carol Halebian, Michael L. Carlebach, and Jon Kral, first, for documenting the experience of detained people, and second, for allowing me to use the images they captured to help tell this story. I received assistance through faculty research and travel grants from Raritan Valley Community College. I was able to spend a year as Scholarship Fellow at the college's Center for Teaching, Learning, and Scholarship. I learned from the discussions I had at conferences and professional meetings where I presented this work, including the Feinberg Family Distinguished Lecture Series at the University of Massachusetts in Amherst, the Immigrant America Conference at the University of Minnesota in Minneapolis, and at the annual meetings of the World History Association in Costa Rica and the Florida Historical Society in Miami.

Lectures I delivered at the Lambertville Historical Society in Lambertville, New Jersey, and at a series of lectures in public libraries throughout New Jersey also forced me to explore my topic more thoroughly. I am grateful to the archivists and librarians at the Schomburg Center for Research in Black Culture, HistoryMiami Museum, the University of Florida, Florida International University, Duke University, the University of North Carolina at Chapel Hill, the University of Miami, the Florida State Archives, and the Ronald Reagan and William J. Clinton Presidential libraries. I am particularly indebted to Patrick A. Stawsky, human rights archivist at the Rubenstein Library of Duke University, and to Dale Buscher at the Women's Refugee Commission for granting me access to restricted materials. I am very grateful to librarian Abbe Mulroy at Raritan Valley Community College, who helped me locate and obtain an amazing amount of material.

At Raritan Valley Community College, I have been fortunate to be part of a community that believes in education as a public good. Teaching students and learning from them, from colleagues, and from community members have benefited this project immeasurably. What greater gift can a person receive than to have one's ideas taken seriously? I am particularly grateful to the members of my department, many of whom have taken time to offer a word of encouragement or to share ideas and ask questions about the project. Special thanks to Roberta Harmon for all her labor in support of the faculty and the department. Many others have assisted me even further, offering comments on my work, whether as individuals or as members of the Research Writing Group or through discussion and debate in the Critical Theory Reading Group. This long list includes John Cleary, Deborah Corbett, Megan Dempsey, Jaqueline Drummer, Karen Gaffney, Kevin Hinkle, Jack Coleman, Alexa Offenhauer, Isabelle Portelinha, Barbara Seater, Isabel Gutierrez, Jay Kelly, Andy Manno, Voichita Nachescu, Jamie Parmese, Lisa Tucker, Jessica Darkenwald-DeCola, Jennifer Pearce-Morris, Anita Rosenblithe, and Ronald Tyson. My students have also offered valuable feedback on these ideas. Thanks especially to Javier Acosta, Tatiana Bacchione, Karson Meckeler, Olga Rivera, Brenna Ruggiero, Michael Sandoval, Fatima Sheriff, Alexis Wlodowski, and Timothy Woody. I am deeply indebted to the amazing teachers and staff at the Children's Campus, whose labor enables faculty to write our books and teach our classes. And finally, thank you to my sisters and brothers in the Social Action Collective and Immigrant Defense Network.

Engaging in this sort of scholarship in community has helped me appreciate Hiroshi Motomura's reminder that "scholarship is a way of teaching[,] . . . teaching is a form of scholarship, and . . . both are essential if ideas are to make a difference." And while I bear responsibility for the content of this book, I hope that the many community members who contributed to this project can be proud of what we have accomplished together.

My family, near and far, offered much-needed encouragement and support over the years it took to complete this book. Michelle, Auguste, Marie, Tracy, Dex, Dennis, Celine, and Yoonique, thank you. My parents, Verna and Don, offered endless encouragement and every other kind of support I could hope for. My mother in particular lent me her keen editorial eye, helping me fix problems big and small, and this book is so much the better for it. And what can I say about my sons, Justice and Jean-Luc? They made it much harder to finish this book, but every distraction was a delight. I thank Justice especially for his unflagging enthusiasm, for insisting that baseball was sometimes much more important than research and writing, and for asking the probing questions that only a five-year-old can imagine. Writing this book while caring for these two wonderful boys, with all their joy and curiosity, strengthened my resolve to help build a world where children are not detained, families are not separated, and all people can live lives of freedom and dignity. And finally, Yves, I thank you. Your love, friendship, and solidarity mean everything to me.

Introduction

The United States incarcerates more than 400,000 people every year for immigration-related violations. It has the largest immigration detention system in the world. On any given day, tens of thousands of immigrant detainees, including asylum seekers and their families and children, are locked up in the United States' vast network of more than 200 detention facilities. More than half of these detention facilities are privately operated with virtually no regulation or oversight. By 2016, the cost of this immense detention effort was $2.3 billion, or $124 per individual detainee and $343 per family per day. The immigration detention system in the United States has grown so large that the number of individuals incarcerated in the federal penal system for immigration-related offenses has now surpassed the number of people imprisoned for drug-related crimes. In the most incarcerated nation in the world, immigration detainees are now the largest proportion of federal prisoners, historian Torrie Hester notes. In other words, immigration control and the war on drugs are now cornerstones of the carceral state."[1]

But it was not always so. This massive reliance on detention as a tool of immigration control is a relatively recent phenomenon. Our current immigration detention system has been in place only since 1981. This is not to say, however, that immigration detention was a new practice when it emerged toward the end of the twentieth century. In fact, immigration detention has a long history in the United States. Chinese immigrants in particular were subject to detention at the West Coast immigration station of Angel Island as part of the U.S. government's broader efforts to exclude them from the country entirely. Migrants crossing the U.S.-Mexico border were also often detained by border patrol officials. On the East Coast, European immigrants were sometimes detained at Ellis Island, although as part of a more targeted restriction rather than as an effort to enforce mass exclusion, as in the west. Prior to 1954, the immigration policy of the United States was to detain almost all those seeking to enter the United

States until a determination could be made on their admissibility, although this policy was unevenly applied. In 1954, the government ended its policy of detention, replacing it with a policy of "parole" for all but those who were deemed a flight risk or a threat to public health or national security. In the post-1954 period, although limited detention continued in certain places, particularly the short-term detention of Mexican migrants along the U.S.-Mexico border, immigration detention ceased to be a formal part of U.S. immigration policy. "The physical detention of aliens is now the exception," declared Supreme Court Justice Tom C. Clark in 1958. "Certainly this policy reflects humane qualities of an enlightened civilization."[2]

So what led to the return of immigration detention in the United States? And how did the detention system become the behemoth that it is today? These are the questions this book seeks to answer.

This book is a history of immigration detention in the United States from 1973 to 2000. It is also a history of Haitian refugees in the United States. By combining these two histories, this book does more than simply tell the story of immigration detention through the lens of Haitian refugees. It also reveals how the history of Haitian refugees and the history of immigration detention in the U.S. are so thoroughly intertwined that one story cannot be told without the other. The government's dealings with Haitian refugees were central to the rebirth of immigration detention and its early development, to the legal challenges and other forms of resistance to the detention system that soon emerged, to the government's project to expand its detention network beyond its territorial boundaries, and, indeed, to virtually every important element of this history. In fact, to try to tell the story of immigration detention without telling about the Haitians' experiences largely misses the story.

Haitian refugees were the central characters in immigration detention from the moment it reemerged in the early 1970s until the end of the twentieth century. They were the one group that consistently drove the government's detention program, and they and their allies required the government to modify and reinforce its detention program. Ironically, these efforts often led the government to enlarge and strengthen its detention regime. This book shows how the government's efforts to exclude Haitian asylum seekers in the 1970s cleared the way for the formal return of detention in 1981. An even greater impetus for the reinstitution of immigration detention was the mass arrival of Cuban and Haitian asylum seekers in the spring and summer of 1980. This unprecedented Caribbean refugee crisis provided the U.S. government with an opportunity to experiment with detention as a tool of immigration enforcement. When the Reagan administration formally reinstituted the policy of immigration detention in the spring of 1981 after it had lain dormant for more than two decades, it was applied exclusively to Haitians. Although Haitian refugees and their allies immediately attacked the program, the government issued a blanket detention order in 1982, extending immigration detention to all inadmissible aliens. This expanded detention program grew rapidly throughout the 1980s and soon ensnared asylum seekers and unauthorized migrants from all over the world.

From 1991 to 1994 Haitians were again at the center of the government's attempts to expand its immigration detention system when they occupied the United States' first detention camp at the U.S. naval base in Guantanamo Bay, Cuba. As the government's detention of Haitians at Guantanamo in the early 1990s was the United States' most ambitious attempt at the time to establish a detention system that extended beyond the country's territorial boundaries, the political struggles and legal challenges that centered on the Haitian detainees of Guantanamo are especially significant in the history of immigration detention, particularly because of the major place Guantanamo has occupied in U.S. history since September 11, 2001. The focus on Haitian detainees continued into 1995 as the government held hundreds of unaccompanied Haitian youth at Guantanamo Bay, a practice that generated substantial controversy.

By the late 1990s, the immense U.S. immigration detention regime that had developed over the preceding two decades had long ceased to be a Haitian-only system. But in many ways the underlying logic that had led to the reinstitution of the system continued to color and shape it. Even into the early twenty-first century, as many different foreign-born groups were affected by the government's response to the terrorist attacks of September 11, Haitians continued to be singled out for extraordinarily harsh treatment, just as they had been more than twenty years earlier, when detention was reborn.

In addition to providing the first in-depth history of immigration detention in the United States and revealing the central role Haitian refugees played in that history, this book offers a case study in social, political, and legal struggle. The story of immigration detention is also a story of ostensibly powerless people standing up to the state and its seemingly limitless power and resources. Studies of refugees and of immigration detention often tend to portray those who are displaced and detained as powerless in the face of the immense power of the state. Peter Gattrell has made this argument about historians' treatment of refugees, and Lucy Fiske makes a similar argument about contemporary studies of immigration detention. But both Gattrell and Fiske show that detained refugees and immigrants were not and are not powerless. Indeed, detainees resisted and continue to resist in a range of ways. Julie A. Dowling and Jonathan Xavier Inda call these acts of resistance "migrant counter-conducts," noting that such acts range from political and legislative campaigns to strikes, direct action, and occupations, all of which "speak to the political becoming of undocumented migrants and their enactments of citizenship."[3]

This book adds to our understanding of immigrant and refugee resistance by historicizing and documenting the many ways refugees and their allies pushed back against the power of the state. It also shows how Haitian detainees prefigured the current global resistance movement of detained people, demonstrating that the acts of resistance that immigrant detainees are now engaged in around the world, such as marches, protests, hunger strikes, and riots, were part of Haitian detainees' campaign of resistance decades earlier.[4] Patrick Ettinger has shown how state efforts to limit mobility and regulate border crossing in the late nineteenth and early twentieth centuries were compromised by people who insisted on the freedom of mobility. According to Ettinger, immigrants' success in using "inventive resistance," posing a "challenge to state power over human mobility," provides still more evidence of immigrant agency.[5] This story of Haitian refugees extends these findings, offering another example of the "inventive resistance" unauthorized migrants determined to enter the United States use to win their freedom once in the United States and to resist forcible return to their country of origin.

Resistance began at the very moment when U.S. officials started jailing Haitian asylum seekers in the early 1970s. This campaign of resistance was complex and multilayered, involving the action and leadership of detained people inside U.S. jails, prisons and detention centers and the activities of their allies and advocates on the outside. Family and community members' protests in the streets were part of the resistance, as were the lobbying and legislative campaigns of members of Congress. This activism is part of a much longer history of struggle and solidarity in the African diaspora of the Americas, in which black migrants from the Caribbean struggled alongside African Americans.[6] It is also part of a pantheon of resistance to imprisonment and state violence in which African American activists, civil rights groups and other organizations on the left, and black prisoners struggled mightily for freedom.[7] The activism documented in this book, which features Haitians in partnership with African Americans and left/progressive groups, represents a lesser-known chapter in this long history of black freedom struggles and black migrant activism in the United States and throughout the African diaspora. Once we recognize the number and range of individuals and organizations involved at various points in the campaign for Haitian refugees, it becomes clear that the Haitian solidarity movement of the 1980s and 1990s was one of the United States' major civil and human rights campaigns of the late twentieth century.

This history also highlights the critical role of legal resistance. Some of the most important battles over immigrant detention occurred in the courtroom.[8] But there is a paradox here. While legal challenges to the immigration detention system were sometimes successful in blocking or limiting the government's detention efforts, they also often enabled government officials to create a more resilient and all-encompassing system. Time and time again, court rulings that awarded a major legal victory to detained people and delivered a serious blow to the detention system turned into policies that expanded and strengthened the system. Successive administrations from the early 1970s onward refused to yield their powers to detain; they repeatedly took steps to circumvent both court orders and domestic and international law. Like blowing on a dandelion, a particular case or legal action that restricted detention in one area often contributed to its proliferation in many other areas and locations. As a result, the prisoners, lawyers, and activists in this story grappled with a question that retains its currency today: How does one resist state power that wields the law in its favor and at the same time refuses to accept limitations the law places on it?

Resisting violence and abuse by the state is especially difficult when those in power exercise their ability to legally define an institution such as immigration detention in ways that shield it from legal challenge. Critics of contemporary immigration detention practices point out that there is a distressing disjuncture between detention's status according to the law and the way it is carried out. As scholars Christina Elefteriades Haines and Anil Kalhan observe, "Unlike criminal incarceration, immigration detention is an administrative, or civil form of custody that is not meant to be punitive in nature." As an "administrative form of custody" it is "permissible only to facilitate the administrative function of immigration removal, not to impose criminal punishment." And yet, "the vast majority of detainees are held in jails or jail-like facilities, where they are subjected to similar treatment as criminal suspects and offenders."[9] Because the incarceration of immigrant detainees is related to civil rather than criminal procedure, the constitutional right to counsel and other matters of due process do not apply, leaving the majority of detainees with scant defense before the vast power of the state.[10]

A number of scholars have characterized this problem, in which a technically administrative procedure masks the punitive effects of the system, as a relatively recent phenomenon. Galina Cornelisse argues that "while in most countries immigration detention was originally intended as an individual measure of last resort (and was accordingly used relatively sparsely until the early nineties), contemporary practice shows that immigration detention has become a large-scale instrument—almost punitive in character—that explicitly targets categories of person, leaving ever less scope for the consideration of the individual circumstances of each and every case."[11]

A recent work by Amy Nethery and Stephanie J. Silverman traces the punitive origins of immigration detention back to Guantanamo Bay, Cuba, which they call "the first modern immigration detention centre." According to Stephanie J. Silverman and Amy Nethery, at Guantanamo, the U.S. government's attempt "to deter Haitians who were not seeking political asylum from attempting to come to the US without pre-authorisation" might be seen as the first of "a suite of policies designed to deter and deny asylum seekers access to a state's territory in which they can claim asylum and the potential of regularized status."[12] It was the beginning of detention with the goal of using punishment as deterrence. However, as later chapters demonstrate, the modern detention regime was designed with punitive intent from the beginning. While the detention of Haitians in the 1970s and of a growing number of other asylum seekers in the 1980s did serve an administrative function, its main purpose was to deter future asylum seekers and unauthorized migrants using a regime of punishing incarceration. Nearly two decades into the twenty-first century, immigration has been increasingly criminalized; unauthorized border crossers are now subject to escalating levels of state violence. The roots of our current moment go deeper and are more tangled than we might have thought.

An exciting amount of scholarly attention has been paid to immigration detention in recent years. Some of the most useful works have been produced by social scientists, legal scholars, and journalists.[13] Within this literature, an increasing tendency to adopt a global perspective has clarified that the history of detention in the United States is part of a much larger shift toward restriction and incarceration.[14] However, most of this scholarship does not prioritize historical perspective.[15] We are left wondering exactly how and why immigration detention made its return in the United States when it did and how the detention system assumed the size and strength that it has today. Drawing upon extensive archival research, this book fills the gaps in our historical knowledge of immigration detention in the United States while integrating the history of immigration detention into the larger story of a changing nation in the last decades of the twentieth century.

One of the most important developments in recent American history that historians are only beginning to assess is what Heather Ann Thompson calls "the dramatic postwar rise of the carceral state."[16] As the United States approached the turn of the twenty-first century, it became home to the largest prison population on the planet, both in terms of the proportion of the population behind bars and of the sheer numbers of prisoners. "When a nation chooses to police and cage many millions of people who reside within its border[s], the implications for everything else that takes place in that country are vast," write Kelly Lytle Hernández, Khalil Gibran Muhammad, and Heather Ann Thompson, observing that "policing and punishment and detention and deportation powerfully shape the U.S. economy and American democracy."[17] Even more troubling, Thompson notes, is the fact that the "unimaginable incarceration crisis" in which the United States found itself by the first decade of the twenty-first century "was also severely racialized mass incarceration." This has led to the fact that black and Latino prisoners constitute the majority of inmates in state prisons and nearly three-quarters of those in federal prisons.[18] This book asks how else examining the historical rise of racialized mass incarceration might shed light on the parallel rise of immigration detention and how the history of immigration detention might help us unravel the problem of the carceral state. Some of the answers to these questions lie at the intersections of race, migration, and citizenship in American history.

In the United States, blackness has historically been a marker of alienage, which, as one group of scholars representing the Africana Cultures and Policy Studies Institute observes, has forced black migrants to remain "distinctly alien and illegal when they attempt to mainstream themselves as citizens."[19] And it has not just been the foreign born that have suffered because of race. African Americans have been treated as foreign because of their race, as have Asians Americans, Mexican Americans, and Native Americans, producing what Mae Ngai has called "alien citizens."[20] Other characteristics such as gender, socioeconomic status, and political beliefs are sometimes used to cast women, the poor, and political minorities as foreign and thus limited in the rights and protections to which they are entitled. And while the post–World War II social movements in which African Americans and other marginalized groups demanded their civil rights began to expand the boundaries of citizenship, Kunal M. Parker demonstrates that these immensely important movements for civil rights also drew a sharper line between citizen and alien. As communities of color pressed for civil rights, forcing the state to recognize and protect them because they too were citizens, the vulnerability of noncitizens grew. The civil rights campaigns of the postwar period, then, seem to have contributed to the current condition in which a growing number of noncitizens are deemed detainable and deportable.[21] Focusing on deportability, Nicholas De Genova and Nathalie Peutz point out that "inasmuch as citizens in most nation-states today cannot legally be deported, the deportable are similarly pressed to 'serve the state' as 'the citizen's other,' marking an apparently absolute and durable separation between the security of one condition, aligned with the state, and the other, indefinitely if not permanently expelled from its grace."[22]

But even for those who could claim civil rights through citizenship, the gains of the postwar period were not secure. And this is where the durability of race and racism becomes most clear. As the rights revolution of the 1960s and 1970s receded, new forms of racial subjugation emerged, leaving racialized migrants doubly vulnerable, with neither citizenship nor whiteness to protect them. Both of these developments—the increasing vulnerability of noncitizens and the continuing burden of race—helped lay the groundwork for the emergence of a heavily racialized immigration detention system in which the vast majority of detainees are brown and black. Nonwhite noncitizens who are deemed detainable are also deemed deportable, Torrie Hester notes, and race deeply influences "who is defined and policed as deportable."[23] David Manuel Hernández observes that the racialized detention regime was made possible by "genealogical precursors and judicial and legislative precedents" that invented and reinvented Latino "criminality" and "illegality." The targeting of black Haitians, along with the "racialized episodes of immigrant detention" that targeted Latinos, laid the foundation for the current racialized detention regime.[24]

Indeed, this history of Haitian refugees and immigration detention corroborates and extends the findings of other scholars who have discovered the intersecting histories of brown and black prisoners with the convergence of the immigration and non-immigration wings of the carceral state. In her study of the rise of the United States Border Patrol, Kelly Lytle Hernández explores "how the path of Mexican Browns and black Americans cross in the carceral era."[25] And in her subsequent work, *City of Inmates*, Hernández adds to our understanding of how U.S. immigration control became "the most highly racialized police and penal system in the United States today."[26] Placing Haitians at the origin of the modern detention regime and documenting their imprisonment and resistance alongside those of Central Americans, Cubans, African Americans, and others adds to our understanding of the historical foundations of the modern racialized carceral state.

We live in a country that imprisons and removes those who dare to cross our borders without permission. This is the story of how that practice came to be.

Overview of the Book

A new phase in Haitian migration to the United States began at the end of 1972, when Haitian asylum seekers began arriving on American shores by boat. Chapter 1 examines the U.S. government's response to the Haitian "boat people" from 1973 to 1980. The government immediately began a policy of denying asylum and implemented a set of practices, including detention, meant to deter Haitian asylum seekers. This chapter also chronicles the earliest resistance to detention by detained refugees and their allies and the advocacy campaign for Haitian refugees that included political mobilization and legal resistance. The most notable achievement of the resistance was the decision in the landmark case *Haitian Refugee Center v. Civiletti*, which struck a lethal blow to the government's Haitian Program, which involved the detention and expedited removal of Haitians. Despite this victory for the refugees, the government's efforts to exclude and deter Haitian asylum seekers during the 1970s cleared the way for the return of immigrant detention in the following years.

Chapter 2 examines the Caribbean refugee crisis of 1980 and the government's response. After more than 100,000 Cubans and tens of thousands of Haitians arrived on American shores in a matter of months, the Carter administration implemented a policy of detention for both groups. But this temporary response mutated into a more permanent policy of long-term detention for Haitians (and several hundred Cubans) and ultimately into the more widespread use of detention for asylum seekers. This chapter also explores the origins and early history of the Krome Avenue Detention Center in Miami, a site that was central to the history of immigration detention, and also documents the government's attempts to create its first refugee processing center and detention facility outside the mainland United States, in Fort Allen, Puerto Rico. Ultimately, the Carter administration's treatment of Haitian asylum seekers at this critical moment in 1980 made it possible for the succeeding administration to dramatically expand the use of detention as an immigration control policy.

Immigration detention was formally reborn in the United States when the Reagan administration reinstituted a policy of detention in 1981. At that moment, the new detention policy applied exclusively to Haitians. Chapter 3 documents how and why Haitian asylum seekers were the first targets of the revived detention program. It considers how the Reagan administration's concerns about surging numbers of asylum seekers and anxiety over mass migration to the United States influenced its decision to redeploy immigration detention. The chapter also documents the government's early efforts to construct its new detention system and the movement that emerged to resist it.

Chapter 4 explains how the government's blanket detention policy came about and why the Haitian-only detention policy was subsequently expanded to include all inadmissible aliens. It charts the growth of the new detention system in its first decade, including the introduction and use of the first private prisons in the United States. The chapter also illustrates the wide-ranging movement that developed in response to the growing detention system, led by detainees and their allies in the streets, in courtrooms, and in the halls of Congress. Many of the most important legal challenges to the burgeoning immigration detention system came from Haitians.

Chapter 5 examines the government's first detention camp at the U.S naval base in Guantanamo Bay, Cuba, and the experience of the Haitian refugees— the original Guantanamo detainees—held there from 1991 to 1994. An important part of this history involves the government's detention of HIV-positive Haitians in the world's first and only "HIV prison camp." This chapter illuminates the history of the legal struggle over the government's authority to detain in such extraterritorial facilities and debates over how far the U.S. Constitution might reach beyond the territorial boundaries of the United States.

Haitian detention at Guantanamo Bay continued to focus attention on U.S. detention practice in 1995 as the government's detention of hundreds of unaccompanied Haitian youth generated enormous controversy and loud calls for their freedom. Chapter 6 documents this struggle over child detention. It also examines two key pieces of legislation in 1996 that had a decisive impact on the history of immigration detention in the United States. The Antiterrorism and Effective Death Penalty Act (AEDPA) and the Illegal Immigration and Immigrant Responsibility Act (IIRIRA) were measures that consummated the marriage of immigration restriction and mass incarceration, devastated immigrant communities, and led to an enormous expansion of the immigration detention system. Finally, this chapter illustrates what the immigration detention system had become by the late 1990s and how, despite the extraordinary power and cruelty of the system, detainees continued to resist.

The conclusion examines U.S. detention practices in the wake of the terrorist attacks of September 11, 2001, and the global spread of immigration detention as countries around the world constructed their own detention regimes based on the U.S. model. It then conducts a brief examination of the problem that emerges at the intersection of state sovereignty and universal human rights. It closes with a survey of the contemporary movement against immigration detention, asking what future there might be for a world in which liberty and freedom of movement are treated as inalienable human rights.

1

Making a Path for the Return
of Immigrant Detention, 1973–1980

In February 1974, Jean-Paul George was thrown into jail in Port-au-Prince for publicly criticizing Jean-Claude Duvalier. "We cannot tolerate a young playboy to be President," George had said about the Haitian president for life, who had inherited his position from his father, François Duvalier, at the age of nineteen and was known for his lavish lifestyle. For his public criticism of Duvalier, George spent three months in the notorious Fort Dimanche prison, where he was frequently beaten and tortured. After his release, George went into hiding, and in April 1975, he finally managed to escape by boat to the United States. Once in the United States, George was put in jail for ten months because he was unable to produce the $500 bond immigration officials required. "I seek refuge in the U.S.," George declared, "and instead of freedom, security, justice, I find worse repression here."[1]

At the same time that Jean-Paul George was fleeing Haiti, Emanuel François was complaining to a group of friends about how unhappy he was that he couldn't find work that would enable him to support his family and send his four children to school. François was unaware that one of the men listening to him was part of the Tonton Macoute, the Duvalier government's paramilitary force. Claiming that François was speaking against the government, members of the Macoute struck him, knocking him out. Then they arrested him and took him to a Port-au-Prince jail, where he spent more than three weeks enduring brutal torture and interrogation. After François was released, he and his family received repeated threats to their lives. Finally, on October 26, 1975, François made his escape from Haiti by boat, stopping briefly in Cuba and sailing on to Miami, which he reached on November 6. In a ten- to fifteen-minute interview with immigration officials, François made his case for asylum, insisting that if he were forced to return to Haiti he would be killed, as his uncle and three of his friends had been. Immigration officials put François in detention. On January

10, 1976, he lamented, "I have been in jail in this country for two months and four days for no crime."[2]

The stories of Jean-Paul George and Emanuel François represent the experience of many Haitians who fled violence and imprisonment in Haiti in the 1970s, only to be jailed in the United States. In response to the arrival of Haitians such as George and François, the U.S. government issued a blanket denial of asylum for the Haitian migrants and instituted a set of harsh practices in an effort to speed their removal and to deter others from trying to reach the United States from Haiti. Members of the Haitian community and their allies repeatedly challenged these practices, which included detention, the denial of work permits, and expedited exclusion and deportation hearings, most notably in the landmark lawsuit *Haitian Refugee Center v. Civiletti*. But the U.S. government was determined to continue its campaign to exclude Haitian asylum seekers. As a result, immigrant detention reemerged as an instrument of U.S. immigration enforcement. The 1970s Haitian Program of the Immigration and Naturalization Service (INS) cleared the way for the expanded use of detention in 1980 and its formal reinstitution in 1981.

Haitian Migration and the Denial of Asylum

The first boatload of people from Haiti arrived in the United States in September 1963. The twenty-five Haitians claimed to be fleeing persecution and violence in Haiti. All were denied asylum and deported. Attorney Cheryl Little, a longtime advocate for Haitian refugees, observes that this treatment of the first Haitian boat people "signaled the wave of rejection that was to come."[3] Nine years later, another group of Haitians seeking asylum in the United States arrived by boat. This group of sixty-five included Yvon Bruno, a barge operator from Port-au-Prince. He had escaped from a Haitian prison and had embarked on a treacherous three-week ocean voyage. The vessel he and his companions were on landed in Cuba and the Bahamas before it finally arrived safely in Florida. Observing the Haitians' arrival, the *Miami News* wondered how these asylum seekers would be treated by "our local immigration officials who so casually go about their almost daily task of processing Cuban citizens landing in South Florida after having escaped the Castro regime. Should the procedure be any different for the dark-skinned Haitians? The action taken on this day will be watched by people across the country and even around the world."[4] The government's response in this case was indicative of what was to come. Each of the forty-two men, twenty women, and three children who made up this second group of Haitian boat people was ultimately denied asylum.[5]

The arrival of the sixty-five Haitians in December 1972 marked the beginning of a new phase in Haitian migration to the United States in which increasing numbers of Haitians traveled by boat to U.S. shores in order to seek asylum. These Haitian "boat people" were not the first Haitians to migrate to the United States in significant numbers, however. An earlier phase of Haitian migration to the United States had been triggered by the rise of François "Papa Doc" Duvalier in 1957. Duvalier's use of violence and terror to consolidate his power sent his key political rivals and other members of the Haitian elite into exile. In the 1960s, this group was followed by growing numbers of the Haitian middle class who fled the Duvalier regime's intensifying repression and their dimming economic prospects. However, in contrast to the boat people, the vast majority of the more than 130,000 Haitians who arrived in United States from 1957 to 1970 had permission to enter the country as tourists, not as refugees or permanent residents. Many overstayed their tourist visas and joined the large community of undocumented Haitians.

In this earlier period, the U.S. response to Haitians was benign neglect. As Christopher Mitchell notes, although Haitian immigrants arriving in the 1950s and 1960s "often experienced great difficulties in adapting to reduced social status in a society with harsh and unfamiliar racial attitudes, neither the sending nor the receiving governments paid great attention to this immigrant group."[6] Because their arrival was much less visible than the arrival of those who came by boat and who attempted to "enter without inspection," Haitian migration to the United States from 1957 to 1972 did not precipitate the same crisis that the growing number of boat people after 1973 precipitated.[7]

The wave of refugees who began fleeing Haiti by boat in December 1972 was driven by several factors. After François Duvalier's death in 1971, his nineteen-year-old son, Jean-Claude Duvalier became Haiti's president for life. Although he promised a more liberal society, in fact he continued many of the most repressive practices of his father. The most significant changes the younger Duvalier introduced were economic. He partnered with the United States Agency for International Development and other international finance institutions to reorient Haiti's economy toward commercial agriculture and export-oriented manufacturing. The result was the mass displacement of Haitian peasants and increased misery among Haiti's working class and urban poor. The combination of the fierce repression of the Duvalier dictatorship and economic hard-

Figure 1. Haitian refugees at sea, 1981. Caribbean Sea Migration Collection, David M. Rubenstein Rare Book & Manuscript Library, Duke University. Used by permission.

ship resulting from the restructured economy forced a new wave of Haitians to seek refuge abroad. The Haitians who traveled to the United States by boat in the 1970s were poorer than many of their compatriots who had made the trip earlier. Unable to afford airfare or obtain the documents that had enabled the earlier group to enter the United States legally, these refugees fled Haiti in overcrowded vessels that they hoped would carry them to Florida, where they planned to disappear into the Haitian community safely and without detection. Some succeeded in this endeavor. Many others did not.[8]

Despite substantial evidence that many of those who fled Haiti for the United States in the 1970s had a well-founded fear of persecution, U.S. officials immediately adopted a policy of denying asylum to Haitians, which they justified by claiming that they were economic migrants rather than political refugees. "Ninety percent of the Haitians come here looking for work," argued INS deputy district director in Miami Richard Gullage. "Most of the political asylum applicants do not even come close to meeting the United Nations definition of a refugee."[9] Responding to an appeal for asylum for Haitians the National Council of Churches (NCC) lodged in 1974, Assistant Secretary for Public Affairs Carol C. Laise made a similar argument. Whereas the NCC and other organizations believed that Haitians should be granted refugee status,

> We do not agree. For example, some of the boats came to Florida from the Bahamas and carried people who lived in the islands for many years and were leaving because their work permits had been revoked. Are all these people refugees? Further, others enter the United States as tourists bearing Haitian passports, find illegal employment, and then claim to be refugees when faced with deportation. Are all these refugees? We do not believe so.[10]

Based on this position that Haitians were not refugees, the U.S. government implemented a policy of blanket denial of asylum for Haitians. Fewer than 100 of the approximately 50,000 petitions for asylum that Haitians filed from 1972 to 1980 were granted.[11]

International relations and Cold War considerations factored significantly in the U.S. government's classification of Haitians as economic migrants rather than as political refugees. The Duvalier government was a useful anti-communist ally for the U.S. government as it sought to contain the threat of communism posed by Cuba, Haiti's neighbor to the west. Accepting those fleeing Haiti as refugees would be a formal acknowledgement that the Haitian government had committed human rights violations, which would seriously harm U.S.-Haiti relations. U.S. officials reasoned that they could not afford to alienate the government of Haiti, which had a key anti-communist vote in the Organization of American States.[12]

In fact, the United States had a well-established policy of giving preference to refugees and asylum seekers from communist countries. The mechanism that allowed the U.S. government to do this was the parole authority, which gave the U.S. attorney general the discretion to parole any alien into the United States temporarily. Thus, in the same period when the U.S. government was implementing its policy of blanket denial of asylum for Haitians, it was also using its parole authority to facilitate the entrance of other groups from its Cold War enemies. From 1962 to 1979, more than 600,000 Cuban refugees were paroled into the United States, and more than 200,000 Indochinese refugees entered the country under the parole authority in the period 1965 to 1979. According to the practices of the INS and the U.S. State Department, Cubans and Vietnamese were legitimate refugees, but Haitians were not.[13]

But geopolitics was not the only factor that determined the U.S. policy toward Haitian refugees. Local political pressure and concerns in the United States about race, economic competition, and the impact Haitians might have on U.S. culture also shaped the federal government's policy for Haitian refugees. The prospect of large numbers of poor black refugees frightened many residents of South Florida. Christopher Mitchell notes that as "poor black migrants entering a U.S. southern city less than twenty years after the advent of the Civil Rights movement," the Haitians had to contend with racism and xenophobia.[14] In addition, as the number of Haitian arrivals increased, a tuberculosis scare swept South Florida and the perception took hold that Haitians were likely to spread the disease to the general population. Alex Stepick, who was among the first to observe and document the experience of Haitian boat people in the United States, points out that throughout the 1970s "negative stereotypes and fears of Haitians became firmly embedded in the general South Florida population. Haitians were perceived by many to be not only disease-ridden, but also uneducated, unskilled peasants who could only prove [to be] a burden to the community." As a result,

> Local political groups goaded national authorities into an unparalleled campaign to repress the flow of Haitians into Miami and to deport those Haitians already in Florida. Members of south Florida's political elite—including Democratic party members, elected officials and some Cubans—believed that the boat people were a disruptive force, destroying the community and draining resources. They appealed to their local members of Congress, who apparently pressured the INS into a response. The INS thereafter began to expend a far greater effort in controlling the flow of Haitians than was expended on nearly any other group of illegal immigrants.[15]

Goaded to action by local and state officials, Washington moved to implement a policy of detention and removal for Haitian boat people.[16]

As Gil Loescher and John Scanlan observe, the U.S. government quickly introduced "a series of reinforcing practices" to buttress its policy of denial for Haitian asylum seekers. According to the U.S. Committee for Refugees, these practices included detention "in local and state jails and prisons. If released after posting bond, [the Haitians] were denied work permits," and "once apprehended, they were immediately processed for exclusion or deportation."[17] The processing involved a perfunctory 20-minute interview, for which the Haitian person had inadequate language translation services and usually no legal counsel. The result was denial of asylum in almost all cases. As the Miami district director of the INS quite candidly explained, "We feel that any relaxation of the rules could produce a flood of economic refugees from all over the Caribbean."[18] As a result, from the arrival of the first Haitian boat people, the U.S. government employed a program of detention and curtailed due process to discourage Haitians and other refugees from coming to the United States.[19]

As soon as U.S. officials began their program of blanket denial of asylum, deterrence through detention, and denial of work authorization, the Haitian community in the United States and their allies began a program of resistance. The coalition was able to form quickly because it grew out of activist networks that already existed in the Haitian exile community that had formed in the late 1950s and the 1960s. Made up of exiled politicians, activists, and students, and based in New York City, the Haitian opposition in exile sought to decrease U.S. support for the Duvalier regime and to topple the dictatorship so Haitians could return home. Although Haitian activists in the United States focused primarily on the political situation in Haiti in the late 1950s and the 1960s, they incorporated solidarity with the newly arrived boat people into their political campaigns in the 1970s.[20]

The National Council of Churches of Christ in the United States was an early ally from outside the Haitian community. In 1973 the NCC and other religious, community, and labor organizations funded the creation of the Haitian Refugee Center (initially called the Haitian Refugee Information Center). The center quickly became the hub for activism concerning Haitian refugee issues in South Florida; it was the organization that launched the most important legal challenges to the government's abusive treatment of Haitians.[21]

The NCC contributed to the public advocacy campaign on behalf of Haitian asylum seekers. A February 28, 1974, resolution adopted by NCC's governing board stated that "all Haitian refugees arriving by boat in Florida . . . were, with the exception of women and children, jailed or paroled under $1,000 bonds. As of February 21, 1974, there were 120 males imprisoned, some for periods exceeding four months." In addition, "Fifty detainees have been removed from Miami for further detention in Port Isabelle, Texas, and another thirty-six to Collier County, Florida, an act which in itself reflects the continuing insensitivity of federal agencies to the cruel and unusual punishment which such removal visits upon detainees and their families." Condemning the detention of Haitian refugees as a "violation of [the] United Nations Protocol on the Status of Refugees" and the denial of due process as a violation of the INS's own Operating Instruction 108.1, the NCC called upon its members to support the campaign in support of Haitian refugees and created a task force that focused on the treatment of Haitian refugees.[22]

Members of the movement on behalf of the Haitian boat people recognized detention as one of the worst examples of discrimination on the part of the U.S. government. The Rescue Committee for Haitian Refugees was one of the organizations that attacked the government's Haitian detention policy as part of its broader campaign against the U.S. government's treatment of Haitians. At its founding in 1974 in New York, the committed declared that its main purpose was "to save Haitian refugees from deportation to Haiti . . . [where] they face torture and even murder by the terrorist Tontons-Macoutes [*sic*] of President-for-Life Jean Claude Duvalier." The new group also dedicated itself to ensuring "due process under the Refugee Law" and "fair treatment" for Haitian refugees, which included the right to an attorney and to a full hearing before an immigration judge, the right to work while awaiting a ruling on asylum applications, and "the release, without bond, of those risking their lives to come here.[23]

The U.S. government's practice of imprisoning Haitian asylum seekers struck the Haitian exile community as especially abhorrent because it appeared to be a mirror image of the Duvalier government's practices. One flyer that promoted a protest that was to be held in front of the State Department's office in midtown Manhattan in February 1974 featured a *New York Times* report placed next to an Amnesty International quote. The quote described Haiti's prisons as "filled with people who have spent many years in detention without ever being charged or brought to trial." The *New York Times* reported the jailing of the male members of a recently captured boat of Haitian refugees. Drawing the parallel between Haitian and U.S. detention policies, the flyer noted that "the United Nations Protocol and U.S. immigration rules provide for due process hearings for refugees. Why not for Haitians? Cubans arriving by plane are given residence. Why jail for Haitian refugees?"[24] The Haitian Refugee Center produced a pamphlet that used a similar tactic. Responding to the question "Why are the Haitian refugees here?" the pamphlet described the role of imprisonment and torture in Duvalier's Haiti:

Many prisoners are arrested and tortured in Port-au-Prince's "Caserne Dessalines," replacing the infamous Fort Dimanche, without ever having charges filed against them. Frequently relatives are not allowed to visit the "prisoners," and must rely on rumors to determine if relatives are still alive, and if so, where they are being held.[25]

And "instead of being helped," those who managed to escape Haiti and make it to the United States "have been incarcerated." The pamphlet argued that both the Haitian and the U.S. governments were victimizing innocent people in distressingly similar ways, citing a *Miami News* editorial:

The Haitians aren't criminals. Their reasons for leaving their homeland are as valid as those of Cuban, Vietnamese, and Eastern European refugees. Yet the federal government, for all its tarnished trumpeting about human rights, goes on behaving toward the Haitians like the villain in a grade B political prisoner movie. With the exception of the Haitians, the U.S. has never made it a policy to detain people seeking political asylum.[26]

Highlighting the disturbing parallels between the Haitian and the U.S. governments' use of detention not only provided refugee advocates with a powerful argument that Haitian asylum seekers should be released from U.S. jails and prisons; it also lent credence to their broader argument that Haitians were fleeing a repressive regime and thus deserved to be treated as legitimate refugees.

In the spring of 1974, the death of a Haitian man in a Florida detention facility focused attention on the U.S. government's detention and deportation policy. On March 14, just hours before his scheduled deportation, 27-year-old Turenne Deville hanged himself in a Dade County jail. The members of the Haitian refugee movement seized upon Deville's death as a "tragic ending" that might befall any of the other "700 Haitians [detained in the Dade county jail who were] faced with the same fate—deportation at the hands of the U.S. government." The scores of Haitians in Texas jails, "the Dade County stockade, [or] various work camps around the state of Florida or in Texas" were at risk of a similar fate. In New York, demonstrators memorialized Turenne Deville's death with a picket line in front of the State Department offices and a march to the United Nations. In Miami, members of the Haitian refugee movement carried Deville's lifeless body through the streets in protest.[27]

As the case of Turenne Deville elevated the profile of the Haitian refugee movement, activists cultivated an increasing number of supporters from the ranks of labor, religious, and civil rights organizations. Although these connections with labor and civic organizations were certainly strengthened by the fact that many Haitians already in the United States were members of labor unions and an active Haitian left was present in New York City, the conduit for involvement for many of these groups was most likely immigration and human rights attorney Ira Gollobin. Gollobin was already a well-established advocate for refugees and immigrants when he became involved with the Haitian refugee campaign in the early 1970s. In the 1930s and 1940s, he had represented refugees fleeing fascism in Spain and Germany. In 1937, he co-founded the National Lawyers Guild, and for two decades, starting in 1967, he served as general counsel for the American Committee for the Protection of Foreign Born. Gollobin was thus well situated to connect the cause of Haitian boat people with progressive and left communities and organizations. He began cultivating such connections as soon as he began work as legal consultant for the NCC in 1974.[28]

In the summer of 1974, labor leaders from a variety of organizations appealed to U.S. officials on behalf of the Haitians. Patrick E. Gorman, secretary-treasurer of the Amalgamated Meat Cutters and Butcher Workmen of North America, wrote to President Nixon to urge asylum for the Haitian refugees. The president of the Dade County Federation of Labor issued a statement of support for fair asylum hearings and work authorization for Haitians. Cesar Chavez, the president of the United Farm Workers, sent letters to California senators John V. Tunney and Allan Cranston, urging them to support asylum for the Haitians. Solidarity with imprisoned refugees was spreading far beyond its origins in the Haitian neighborhoods of New York and Miami. The leaders of the Illinois chapter of the American Indian Movement offered their support in securing freedom and asylum for jailed refugees, suggesting that the Anishnawbe nation (Ojibwa-Chippewa) might be able to grant the Haitians asylum if the United States would not.[29]

By the summer of 1974, the protests over U.S. treatment of Haitian asylum seekers were growing so loud that that INS and State Department officials felt compelled to respond. After receiving a telegram protesting the death of Turenne Deville from U.S. Representative Bella Abzug of New York, INS commissioner L. F. Chapman Jr. issued a telling response. He claimed that a series of interviews had revealed that Deville was not a refugee but an economic migrant. He also claimed that Deville had not been denied due process. Finally, he argued that it was Deville's prolonged detention, not his pending deportation, that led him to take his own life. "He had grown dissatisfied during the long wait for a decision in his case. In fact, on the day of his scheduled departure, prior to his attorney's filing an appeal in the United States court, he gave every indication that he was willing, even pleased, to be going home." And lest this revelation cause Abzug and others to focus their scorn on the Haitian detention policy, Commissioner Chapman offered this defense:

> It is the policy of the service to hold an alien in detention under deportation proceedings only 1) when his freedom at large would clearly represent a present danger to public safety of security, or 2) when his lack of funds or fixed address support a finding that he is likely to abscond. Mr. Deville was detained in lieu of $1,000 bond. Each case, whether he be Haitian or other nationality, is judged on its individual merits. In fact, to date over 100 of the Haitians have violated the conditions of their release and have absconded and are being actively sought by this Service.[30]

Despite U.S. officials' claims that the detention of Haitians was justified and their assurances that only economic migrants were being sent back to Haiti, the protests over the detention and mistreatment of Haitian refugees grew. In March 1975, a growing number of labor, civil rights, and Haitian community groups staged demonstrations in front of the New York City offices of the U.S. State Department.[31] In addition, the Haitian refugee movement began to garner support from members of Congress. In August 1976, eight members of Congress, including Claude Pepper, William Lehman, and Dante Fascell from Florida; Shirley Chisholm, Edward Koch, and Frederick Richmond from New York; and Charles Rangel and Charles Diggs from Michigan, wrote to Joshua Eilberg, chair of the House Subcommittee on Immigration, Citizenship, and International Law, asking the subcommittee "to urge the State Department and the Immigration Service to cease all deportation of exiles to Haiti" until the U.S. government could obtain reliable evidence that returnees were not being persecuted and until new procedures for Haitian asylum hearings "that will allow for greater fairness and objectivity" could be implemented. The members of Congress urged the subcommittee to pressure "the State Department and the Immigration Service to allow those Haitians that have been incarcerated to be released and to allow those persons to seek employment in order to support themselves and pay for legal counsel." The U.S. government's treatment of

Haitian asylum seekers did not "lend itself to the traditions upon this nation was founded," the members of Congress pointed out.[32]

In the spring of 1977, jailed refugees added their voices to the protests of U.S. Haitian policy. Writing from the Collier County Stockade Detention Center in Florida, a group of thirty-three who called themselves "the Haitian Refugees at Immokalee" issued an appeal to the INS district supervisor. "We, the Haitian refugees, detained at the Stockade Detention Center, are willing to stay under the discipline of the institution. However, placed under such unfair treatments inflicted to us by the guards and administrators, we decided to inform you of our life conditions at Immokalee jail," the letter began.

We left our native country and came here to solicit the political asylum, because of the injustices we encountered with the brutal police corps of Duvalier, the tontons-macoutes [sic]. But as you know, we have been put in jail upon our arrival in the United States. Now that we are retained here without clear knowledge of our crime, the jailers have forced us to do all kinds of heavy jobs. We are forced to paint, carry rocks, paint the walls of the cells, dig big holes for dogs, cut grass, clean the yards, by the order of the immigration office. . . . When we try to protest, we have been punched and beaten with sticks or they even put us in those small cells (dungeon), where we cannot move.

The Haitian Refugees at Immokalee wanted the INS district supervisor and all others to know that they were a people stuck between the violence of Duvalier and the imprisonment and violence of the U.S. government. "We know that if we have to face those unfair treatments [in the Collier County Stockade], that's because the Haitian government cannot guarantee our rights. But, we want you to know that our lives in this jail will remain for each of us a unique souvenir during our terrible sojourn in the United States," the Haitian prisoners concluded.[33] In a press release publicizing the refugees' protest, the Rescue Committee for Haitian Refugees asked why the Carter administration kept Haitians "languishing in prison for over a year" while extending a welcome to Cubans and Vietnamese. And because it was addressing an administration that claimed a special commitment to human rights, the committee offered a pointed rebuke: "An espousal of human rights that begins abroad and not at home becomes suspect as hypocrisy."[34]

Haitian prisoners in the El Paso Alien Detention Facility also sought their freedom by appealing to supporters on the outside. The group of forty-six in

Texas, who had been transferred from a South Florida detention facility, faced deportation in February 1977. "We already have 15 months in jail," the "Haitian prisoners in El Paso camp" wrote.

> We [are] asking for a political [asylum] . . . because we have some kind of political [persecution] home in haiti, we know if we go back to Haiti we will [be] executed . . . with our family on the public place. Please save us from that great dangerous we in now. We ask you please to show this letter to the rest of the peoples to help us in that great dangerous we in now.[35]

The detention and pending deportation so terrified one of the detainees in El Paso that he attempted to take his own life. Forty-four-year-old George Pierre was found by another detainee shortly before 1:00 a.m. on February 8, 1977. He had attempted to hang himself with a mattress cover that he tied around a steam pipe running along the ceiling of his cell. Although Pierre reported that he had been a part of organized anti-government activities in Haiti and that he bore the scars of two severe beatings by the Tonton Macoute, he and the other Haitians had been denied asylum "on the grounds that any persecution they might have suffered was economic rather that racial, religious, or political."[36]

As the imprisoned refugees and their supporters continued their protests, the NCC led a series of legal challenges to the U.S. government's treatment of Haitian asylum seekers. Ira Gollobin reported that several cases winding their way through the courts sought to ensure due process for the Haitians and the right to work. Among the cases was a "prison suit" that challenged the government's practice of requiring between $500 and $1,000 bond for the release of Haitian detainees. "Practically all of them are indigent and have no way of securing the amount fixed for bail," Gollobin observed. "In not ruling on their affidavits while continuing to detain them the [Immigration and Naturalization] Service deprives them of due process of law and other rights."[37]

The key legal challenge to the government's Haitian detention policy and its practice of denying work authorization and hearings to Haitians was *Sannon v. United States*. In May 1976, U.S. District Judge James Lawrence King decided in favor of Marie Sannon and the other plaintiffs, ruling that the government had violated the Haitians' right to due process. He ordered the INS to grant the plaintiffs new asylum hearings, where they could present whatever evidence they possessed to document their petitions for asylum.[38] The House Subcommittee on Immigration, Citizenship, and International Law also supported the NCC's efforts to ensure due process and to secure the Haitians' release from detention. The government, however, appealed the court's ruling, and the case went to the Supreme Court in November 1977.[39]

Under growing pressure from a wide range of sources that included religious and civil rights organizations and members of Congress and facing the possibility that the Supreme Court might strike down key elements of its Haitian policy, the INS reached an agreement with the NCC and the Haitians represented in *Sannon*. INS commissioner Leonel Castillo acceded to the three major demands the refugees and their allies had been making: Haitian refugees would be released from detention without bond, the 1,000 Haitians who had applied for asylum would be given authorization to work, and INS regulations would be changed to provide "excludable" Haitians with a hearing before an immigration judge at which they would be represented by an attorney. The Department of Justice publicly characterized the settlement as a practical measure that would save time and money, citing a statement by Commissioner Castillo, who observed that the government's policy toward Haitians "had not discouraged asylum applicants from coming to the United States over the last several years, and the detention of a significant number of aliens is an unnecessary expense to the government."[40] Haitians and their supporters believed that they had forced the government to accede to their demands. Among the chorus of voices celebrating the victory was National Urban League president Vernon Jordan, who declared that "pressure from religious, civil rights, social service agencies, labor and community groups" had succeeded in forcing the government "to end the odious practice of forcing these refugees to either post bonds ranging upward to $1,000, or face being sent to jail."[41] Mobilization and legal action had worked, it seemed, to shield Haitian asylum seekers from the worst abuses by immigration officials and to win their freedom from detention.[42]

The Haitian Program

While freed refugees and their allies were celebrating the softened stance toward Haitians, others were reacting with anger. Some residents of South Florida were concerned about the increasing strain on social and medical services the refugees posed, worried that Haitians were spreading tuberculosis and other diseases in their communities, and were resentful about the decision to grant Haitians the right to work. Residents and local officials in South Florida who were worried about a new influx of Haitians also pointed out that recent steps by authorities in the Bahamas to arrest and deport Haitians were likely to create a new wave of asylum seekers, adding to the growing backlog of applications for asylum. In July 1978, a confidential cable from the American embassy in Nassau, Bahamas, to the U.S. secretary of state noted that the Bahamian government "is really interested in getting Haitians out of the Bahamas." While Bahamian officials "were careful to deny and disclaim U.S. press reports and allegations that the [Bahamian government] is encouraging a Haitian alien exodus to the U.S.," they "acknowledged that roundups, arrests, and public statements against the illegal aliens result in many of these aliens leaving." Bahamian authorities "also agreed that a logical destination for these fleeing Haitians is Florida." The State Department cable concluded that "underlying this is a deeply held Bahamian prejudice against Haitians in general[,] whom they perceive to be inferior."[43] A similar hostility to the arrival of Haitians in South Florida drove immigration officials in Miami to protest the liberalized stance toward Haitians and to pressure the U.S. attorney general to reverse the new policy.[44]

In response to the backlash in Florida and motivated by the fear that the actions of Bahamian authorities and the recently liberalized policies in the United States would draw many more Haitian refugees to American shores, U.S. policy toward Haitian refugees swung back in the other direction.[45] The result was a policy that was much harsher than anything that had preceded it. Surveying the growing backlog of Haitian asylum cases, which by that point exceeded 5,000, a high-ranking INS official concluded that "the most practical deterrent to this problem [was] expulsion from the United States."[46]

In response, INS and State Department officials introduced the Haitian Program.[47] The Haitian Program was formulated in a series of meetings between the heads of the INS and the State Department. In a July 19, 1978, meeting attended by Commissioner Leonel Castillo and Deputy Commissioner Mario Noto of the INS and the Carter administration's general counsel, Noto reported that border patrol was being beefed up in South Florida to guard against the arrival of new boatloads of Haitians. In addition, the immigration service had obtained additional immigration judges and hearing rooms to speed up the deportation and exclusion hearings for Haitians. According to Noto, "The number of Haitians scheduled for hearings each day has been increased to ten and as soon as the detailed immigration judges report for duty, a minimum of fifteen hearings per immigration judge will be scheduled." To ensure this increased pace of the removal of Haitians, "the Chief Immigration Judge will direct that Immigration Judge productivity be at least tripled to 15 hearings per day for each judge," Noto said. The INS also directed Miami officials to obtain additional "non-criminal detention space" to ensure that Haitians would be available when the day of their deportation arrived.[48] Once he was instructed by INS and State Department officials in Washington, Acting District Director in Miami Richard H. Gullage informed his staff of what was expected of them under the Haitian Program:

> 1. All newly arriving Haitians, true abscondees and those in illegal status coming to the Service's attention for the first time will be placed in detention. 2. No work permits will be granted to any Haitians. 3. Any deviation from the above will be only for the most unusual and meritorious reasons and the decision will be made solely by the District Director or Acting District Director.[49]

The Haitian Program reinstated the detention policy for Haitians and revoked their authorization to work. It also introduced expedited deportation hearings, increasing the number of hearings from an average of 5 to 15 per day in early 1978 to 100 to 150 per day by September of that year. All the cases were scheduled to be heard by no more than five immigration judges. Although Haitians who appeared at these expedited hearings were entitled to have a lawyer present, the court often scheduled simultaneous hearings involving the same attorney in an effort to limit the asylum seekers' access to counsel. When attorneys could be present at a hearing, they were barred from speaking on behalf of their clients. And when asylum seekers were allowed to speak for themselves, inadequate translations often reduced lengthy, complex statements to one or two sentences. Sometimes no translation was provided at all. At the conclusion of such hearings, the asylum applicants received a form presenting a denial of their applications for asylum that had been prepared in advance and pre-signed by the INS district director.[50]

When the Haitian Program was introduced, jubilation over the briefly liberalized policy toward Haitian asylum seekers turned to outrage among the refugees and their allies. As in the years leading up to the implementation of the Haitian Program, the government's practice of detention and denial of due process further energized the community working in defense of Haitian refugees. Identifying the shared culpability of Bahamian, U.S., and Haitian governments in this most recent chapter of the Haitian refugee crisis, the New York City–based Ad Hoc Committee Against Mistreatment of Haitian Refugees and allied civil rights groups organized a demonstration in New York that began at the Bahamian consulate, moved to the U.S. State Department offices, and ended at the Haitian consulate. A flyer advertising the demonstration declared that Haitians were in a "struggle for their lives." It condemned "the mistreatment of Haitians in the Bahamas and the threat of deportation from the U.S.A." It also demanded "political asylum for the Haitian refugees[,] . . . total and unconditional amnesty for Haitians and all 'illegal aliens,'" and "an end to U.S. aid to Duvalier's dictatorship."[51]

In December 1978, a shocking discovery in a West Palm Beach city jail presented another opportunity for the Haitian Program's opponents to castigate the U.S. government's treatment of Haitians. As he was conducting a routine visit to the city jail, Father Gerard Jean-Juste discovered a crying child alone in one of the cells. Eight-year-old Rosiline Dorsinville, who had fled Haiti with her father, had already been jailed for two weeks and would have remained so had she not been discovered. After Father Jean-Juste negotiated with immigration officials for several hours, they released the child into his custody, along with Sister Marie Pierre, but officials insisted that her father and sole surviving parent, Minfort Dorsinville, remain in detention without bond. In a joint statement, Dr. Paul Lehmann, chair of the American Committee for the Protection of Foreign Born, and Father Antoine Adrien of the Haitian Fathers cited the Dorsinville family's case as another example of the systemic abuse of Haitian refugees. "Such flagrant disregard, not only of the refugee law (the protocol relating to the status of refugees), but of the most elementary human norms cannot be attribute to mere bureaucratic 'error' by local authorities," they observed. "It is part and parcel of the new harsh policy toward Haitian refugees dictated by Associate Attorney General Michael Egan, the Superior of Immigration Commissioner Leonel F. Castillo." More and more Haitians were being detained under the policies of the Haitian Program, Lehmann and Adrien observed:

Before July, under Castillo's more humane policy, Haitian refugees were released without bond and given employment authorization. Since then they have been detained without bond; 48 are in West Palm Beach City Jail and about 20 in Immokalee, a county prison for criminals. This is done at the very time that more than 25,000 Vietnamese refugees are being brought over 10,000 miles at U.S. expense! Haitians fleeing the repressive regime of President-for-Life Jean-Claude Duvalier are entitled to the same hospitality.[52]

The campaign against the detention policies of the Haitian Program continued to grow. Two months after the discovery of little Rosiline in the West Palm Beach city jail, more than seventy Haitian refugees detained in jails in Immokalee and in Belle Glade, Florida, launched a hunger strike to protest their ongoing incarceration and poor treatment in detention. According to a press release by the Rescue Committee for Haitian Refugees,

> The Haitians are protesting the contaminated, bad-smelling water, poor food, and one set of clothing—when laundered and until their clothes are dry, the Haitians have to lie around naked in a chilly room—all of which have resulted in skin diseases, respiratory ailments and other illnesses. Typifying this inhumane treatment, indigent and sick Hubert Mezador, who fled to the United States in August 1978 and was hospitalized for four months, remains in jail for lack of the $1,000 bail demanded by Justice Department authorities in Washington.[53]

Representatives of the Miami-based Haitian Refugee Center charged that the bond requirement was punitive, and the Rescue Committee for Haitian Refugee agreed: "Having failed in their efforts to coerce the Haitians who fled 800 miles in flimsy sailboats to leave 'voluntarily,' the authorities are making good on their threat to jail them indefinitely."[54]

As important as activism was in building the political opposition to the Haitian Program, the most effective form of resistance occurred in the courtroom. In May 1979, Haitian refugees filed a class action lawsuit against the U.S. government and its attorney general, Benjamin Civiletti. James Lawrence King, the same judge who had ruled in favor of the Haitian plaintiffs in *Sannon v. United States*, heard the case. In *Haitian Refugee Center v. Civiletti*, the plaintiffs charged that the Haitian Program violated the refugees' constitutional rights and that the government had unfairly and illegally prejudged Haitians' applications for asylum, ignoring evidence of Haitians' legitimate fear of persecution in Haiti. The government had denied the applications for asylum of each of the more than 4,000 Haitians represented in the suit.[55] Presenting extensive evidence to document immigration officials' abuse of Haitian refugees, the plaintiffs also presented the court with the first-hand experience of Haitian asylum seekers such as Patrick Lemoine. Lemoine had been arrested in Haiti and accused of participating in a communist plot to overthrow the government of Jean-Claude Duvalier. After a brutal six years in two of Haiti's most notorious prisons, Cassernes Dessalines and Fort Dimanche, Lemoine was among the 104 political prisoners released by the Haitian government after the newly elected Carter administration sent its ambassador, Andrew Young, to visit Haiti. After his release, Lemoine fled Haiti for the United States, where he joined the many other Haitian refugees who could attest to the reality of political persecution in Haiti.[56]

After a three-week trial, on July 2, 1980, Judge King issued his decision. "This case involves thousands of black Haitian nationals, the brutality of their government, and the prejudice of ours," King's ruling began. "The plaintiffs charge that they faced a transparently discriminatory program designed to deport Haitian nationals and no one else. The uncontroverted evidence proves their claim," he ruled. Although the Haitians had established that the INS had discriminated against them on the basis of national origin, there seemed to be something else motivating the government's treatment of the Haitians, King suggested.

The plaintiffs are part of the first substantial flight of black refugees from a repressive regime to this country. All of the plaintiffs are black. In contrast, for example, only a relatively small percent of the Cuban refugees who have fled to this country are black. Prior to the most recent exodus, all of the Cubans who sought political asylum in individual 8 C.F.R. Sec. 108 hearings were granted asylum routinely. None of the over 4,000 Haitians processed during the INS "program" at issue in this lawsuit were granted asylum. No greater disparity can be imagined.[57]

The Haitian Program violated the plaintiffs' right to due process and was clearly designed to carry out the mass expulsion of Haitians, the judge continued. "Their asylum claims were prejudged, their rights to a hearing given second priority to the need for accelerating processing. . . . Virtually every one of these violations occurred exclusively to Haitians. The violations were discriminatory acts, part of a program to expel Haitians," Judge King observed. And although *Haitian Refugee Center v. Civiletti* focused on the recently created Haitian Program, these abuses had been occurring since the arrival of the first boat people in the 1960s, Judge King continued. "Over the past 17 years, Haitian claims for asylum and refuge have been systematically denied, while all others have been granted. The recent Haitian Program is but the largest-scale, most dramatic example of this pattern." The judge concluded, "The manner in which the INS treated the more than 4,000 Haitian plaintiffs violated the Constitution, the immigration statutes, international agreements, INS regulations and INS operating procedures. It must stop." Haitian refugees and their supporters celebrated Judge King's ruling as a victory for their movement. They also recognized the historic ruling as a landmark decision in immigration and refugee law, a conclusion that legal scholars and historians have since affirmed.[58]

The ruling in *Haitian Refugee Center v. Civiletti* gave the government's program of detention, exclusion, and deportation unprecedented public exposure. The *Washington Post* drew upon documents made public during the trial to report to its readers what Haitian refugees and their supporters already knew. "U.S. Formulated a Haitian Refugee 'Solution' 2 Years Ago," read the headline of the article. The article stated that State Department and immigration officials had partnered to "set up a program aimed at speedy wholesale deportation of Haitian refugees from South Florida," despite officials' "doubts about the legality of what they were doing." The article also revealed the "intense interest by the State Department and the White House in dealing with the increasing flow of Haitians." The revocation of work permits and a "propaganda campaign" to discourage Haitians from coming to the United States were designed to buttress the process of mass expulsion, even though INS associate director Charles C. Sava claimed that these practices were "the best, most practical deterrent to this problem." Not only did the ruling in *Haitian Refugee Center v. Civiletti* threaten the Carter administration's Haitian Program, it also helped precipitate a growing public relations disaster.[59]

Instead of accepting their obligation to comply with Judge King's order or to submit to public pressure to reform its policy toward Haitian asylum seekers, however, Carter administration officials developed a plan to circumvent the landmark ruling. Judge King's ruling in *Haitian Refugee Center v. Civiletti* applied only to Haitians in the jurisdiction of the Southern District of Florida. If Haitians seeking asylum in the United States could be processed outside that district, they would not enjoy the protection afforded by Judge King's ruling. Toward that end, the Carter administration announced that it would begin processing Haitians at Fort Allen, a U.S. army base in Puerto Rico.[60] At the same time, those opposed to Judge King's ruling began to raise the prospect of eliminating federal court jurisdiction over applications for asylum. Supporters of this proposal claimed that preventing federal judges such as James Lawrence King from adjudicating asylum claims was a necessary step in "streamlining the process." But U.S. Representative Shirley Chisholm denounced the idea as a transparent effort "to cut Haitians' access to the courts," adding that "this action is in direct response to the success of the Center's lawsuit and other lawsuits brought on behalf of Haitian asylum claimants."[61]

As the U.S. government's actions in the wake of the *Civiletti* ruling demonstrate, the court-ordered halting of the Haitian Program in South Florida was just one battle in the ongoing struggle between Haitian asylum seekers and policy makers who sought to keep them out. This debate, and the *Civiletti* ruling itself, occurred as the United States was experiencing a refugee crisis unlike anything it had ever experienced before. Carter administration officials chose to deal with the unprecedented refugee crisis by relying even more heavily on detention. Although the government's treatment of Haitian asylum seekers in the 1970s cleared the way for the return of immigrant detention, the refugee crisis of 1980 drove government officials to begin using detention as a key tool for regulating immigration.

2

The Refugee Crisis of 1980

Forging the Detention Tool

By the spring of 1980, the U.S. government had been using a range of facilities to detain Haitians for years, from locally administered jails to federally run detention centers. The 1954 policy change that had replaced the mandatory detention of illegal aliens with a policy of parole had already been significantly compromised. In March 1980, the federal government took another important step away from the policy of parole and toward the reinstitution of immigrant detention.

On March 5, 1980, an agreement among the Bureau of Prisons (BOP), the U.S. Public Health Service, and the INS went into effect that authorized the INS "to [utilize] Bureau of Prisons Facilities to screen, process, and detain aliens who are in the United States illegally." The five-page agreement illustrated the increasingly close collaboration among the agencies. For example, the INS would provide a duty deportation officer and an immigration detention officer to each federal correction institution where aliens were imprisoned. INS officials would be chiefly responsible for the imprisoned immigrants, but BOP and INS officials on site would share certain decisions pertaining to the prisoners, such as determining whether "the arriving alien" would be required to shower after being photographed and fingerprinted. The agreement, signaling the government's growing embrace of incarceration as a tool of immigration control, was signed in Miami, Florida, the frontline of the effort to block unauthorized migration from Haiti. Requiring that at least one of the four INS personnel at each federal prison where illegal aliens were held had to be a Creole interpreter, the agreement was clearly aimed at Haitian refugees.[1]

At the same time that the Carter administration was merging the functions of the BOP and the INS, it was creating new facilities that could detain and process Haitians in South Florida. On March 7, 1980, the Southeastern Regional Federal Council established the Haitian Processing Center at the Federal Correction Institute "upon the request of the White House." An administration document outlining this creation of the new detention and processing center for Haitians noted that "in the month of March a total of 1,401 Haitians arrived in South Florida. Nearly 750 of them were detained in the National Guard Armory at Homestead; the remaining refugees were at FCI [Federal Correction Institute] and at local jails to await processing." The wide range of facilities detaining Haitians included "FCI, Holley Hospital at Lantana, Miami Salvation Army, Palm Beach County Jail, Lee County Jail, Collier County Stockade, and the Harvest for Christ Church in Delray."[2]

The timing of these actions was significant. The authorization for the INS to use federal prisons to detain immigrants was put in place more than a month before the refugee crisis of 1980. In addition, the creation of the Haitian Processing Center at the Federal Correction Institute preceded the crisis. This shows that the Carter administration was expanding its use of immigrant detention even before it was engulfed by a refugee emergency in the spring and summer of 1980. The flight of more than 100,000 Cuban and nearly 15,000 Haitian asylum seekers to the United States, all arriving within just a few months, thrust American officials farther down the road toward the formal reinstitution of immigrant detention.

The Caribbean Refugee Crisis

In April 1980, Cuban president Fidel Castro, submitting to pressure from those clamoring to leave Cuba, announced that his government would allow Cubans to leave the country. Thousands of Cubans wanted to leave, and Cuban Americans in South Florida began sailing to the port of Mariel, Cuba, to bring their compatriots to the United States. This began the Mariel boatlift, a period of mass emigration from Cuba that stretched from April to October and brought nearly 125,000 Cuban *marielitos* to the United States in search of asylum.[3] The mass influx of Cubans occurred just as thousands of Haitians, fleeing a deteriorating human rights situation, were sailing to the United States. Approximately 15,000 Haitian asylum seekers joined the more than 100,000 Cubans who arrived in the spring and summer of 1980, placing the United States in the unprecedented position of being a country of mass first asylum and presenting the Carter administration with a refugee crisis for which it was unprepared.[4]

Based on past practice, the Cuban émigrés might have expected a warm welcome while the Haitians might have foreseen the exclusion, detention, and deportation that awaited them. Legislation such as the Cuban Adjustment Act of 1966, which gave Cuban refugees a path to permanent residence, and a refugee policy that favored those fleeing communist countries offered a major advantage to the Cubans. More than 750,000 Cubans had entered the United States under these provisions in the period 1959 to 1980.[5]

But just before the refugee crisis, U.S. lawmakers had passed the Refugee Act of 1980, a law designed to restructure how the United States handled refugees and do away with the ideological bias that had favored those fleeing left-wing countries while barring those fleeing nations controlled by right-wing governments. As María Cristina García notes, by 1980, there was growing concern among members of Congress that "the overuse of the parole authority," which had become a primary tool government officials used to admit those fleeing communist countries, "was providing a 'back door' to the United States, allowing hundreds of thousands to enter, without congressional input, on the assumption that those fleeing communist countries were more worthy of admission than other immigrants."[6] The Refugee Act of 1980 was intended to correct this problem. In addition, as Gilburt Loescher and John Scanlan note, the Refugee Act of 1980 "clearly committed the United States to adhere to international legal standards and made asylum (or its statutory equivalent) available as a matter of right . . . to any individual demonstrating that he or she was in fact a refugee." The act put in place a refugee policy that was supposed to apply the single standard of a "well-founded fear of persecution" for determining who was a legitimate refugee and required the U.S. government to recognize the rights of asylum seekers. Haitians arriving in the spring and summer of 1980 appeared to have more security in the United States than they had previously known. However, the scale of the refugee crisis coupled with Americans' anxiety over the mass arrival of Cuban and Haitian refugees ensured that the Refugee Act of 1980 would not be implemented in the way lawmakers had intended.[7]

In response to the arrival of tens of thousands of Caribbean refugees, the Federal Emergency Management Agency created a Miami-based coordinating team that converted the Orange Bowl stadium into an ad hoc refugee shelter and established refugee processing centers at Eglin Air Force Base in Florida, Fort Chaffee in Arkansas, Fort Indiantown Gap in Pennsylvania, and Fort McCoy in Wisconsin.[8] Both Cubans and Haitians were detained until a sponsor, such as a family member or an institution, could be located. When detainees had no family, friends, or institution willing to sponsor them, they remained in detention.[9]

Since the government's detention policy applied to both Cubans and Haitians, one might conclude that the government had adopted a policy of evenhanded and equal treatment of the two groups. President Carter even stressed that it was his administration's policy "to treat the Haitians now here in the same, exact, humane manner as we treat Cubans and others who seek asylum in this country."[10] Unfortunately, as an internal administration memo observed, a policy that released those with families and held others until a sponsor could be located would result in the disproportionate detention of Haitians, since, "unlike the Cubans, most of the Haitians do not have families that can assure placement." Further complicating the possibility for equal treatment, the voluntary agencies that might have agreed to secure Haitians' release through sponsorship wanted some assurance that the people they would sponsor would receive "permanent legal status that assures they will not be deported after they are placed somewhere." These voluntary agencies, the memo observed, "seem to feel relatively assured that . . . Cubans will not be deported, but they do not feel similarly assured for the Haitian arrivals."[11] The potential for unequal treatment soon emerged. In the initial phase of the refugee crisis, each Cuban was given an application for political asylum (and sometimes cash) while Haitians were given nothing and were not even considered potential asylees but were simply classified as undocumented entrants. In the eyes of the government, the Cubans were in the asylum process from the moment they arrived. The Haitians, in contrast, were classified as being in exclusion proceedings.[12]

The Haitian community and their allies immediately pressed for more equity in the government's response to the refugee crisis. A campaign of demonstrations, marches, petitions, and letters, aided by the Congressional Black Caucus and an often-sympathetic media, applied pressure on the Carter administration to make the treatment and status of the Haitians equal to that of other refugees. A senate judiciary committee hearing on the Caribbean refugee crisis held in May 1980, gave them another opportunity to challenge the Carter administration about its treatment of Haitians.[13]

At the opening of the hearing, the chair of the committee, Senator Edward M. Kennedy, described the problem. "We are concerned today about the chaos surrounding boat refugees" and "the steps that our government has taken and should take to deal with this crisis," he said. "This desperate flight of humanity on the high seas endangers the lives of thousands of men, women, and children each day. It also threatens to disrupt the economy of Florida and other states and is undermining the integrity of our nation's immigration laws. Indeed, as a nation of refugees, we take pride in America as a haven of those seeking freedom from oppression in other lands and a better chance at life." However, Kennedy observed, "the American people must ask what more is expected of them. We must know what the number of new refugees will be, and what our government is going to do to cope."[14]

In the first testimonies, which featured Catholic Church officials from South Florida, the unequal treatment of Cubans and Haitians emerged as a powerful theme. "For seven years, the church in South Florida has been pleading, along with many others, the cause of our Haitian boat people," declared Archbishop Edward A. McCarthy. "Repeatedly we have pointed out the discriminating practices of the U.S. government and the consequent impact on our community." And while recent steps to equalize treatment of Haitians and Cubans were welcome, the archbishop observed, the action was "inadequate and falls far short of the treatment accorded to previous influxes of Cubans."[15]

While the archbishop urged the U.S. government to go further in equalizing treatment of Cubans and Haitians, others were opposed to doing away with the long-established distinction that cast Cubans as legitimate political refugees but categorized Haitians as economic refugees. Senator Bob Dole, for example, reasserted the government's traditional position by asking if those working in the South Florida Haitian community had "had an opportunity to determine how many of the Haitians . . . are here for economic reasons as compared to persecution." Monsignor Bryan Walsh, director of Catholic Charities for the Archdiocese of Miami, pushed back against Dole's suggestion: "I don't think anybody falls into a neat category, economic or political. There are definitely mixtures in the whole lot, as they are of the Cubans coming in. . . . I don't think we can easily separate people into those two categories." The government's distinction between political and economic refugee "really doesn't make sense," Monsignor Walsh concluded.[16]

A later exchange between Senator Kennedy and Victor Palmieri, ambassador at large and U.S. coordinator for refugee affairs, shed light on the Carter administration's ambivalence about equalizing the treatment of Cubans and Haitians, despite the mandate the Refugee Act of 1980 imposed. "Does the open door that the President talked about . . . include the Haitians or doesn't it include the Haitians? Can we have that answer?" asked Senator Kennedy.

Ambassador Palmieri evaded the question and instead provided a review of U.S. policy toward Cuba and Cuban refugees. In response, Kennedy tried again.

SENATOR KENNEDY. That is fine. But does "open arms" mean we accept the Cubans and not the Haitians? I just want to find that out.

MR. PALMIERI. What it means is we treat applicants for asylum—whether they are from Haiti or from Cuba or from anywhere else—in exactly the same way under the new act. This is your own mandate. You had a big hand in the Refugee Act of 1980.

SENATOR KENNEDY. That is right.

MR. PALMIERI. Yes.

SENATOR KENNEDY. I know what the law is. It says that you can let them in. Parole them in today, after consultation with the Congress. I know that you have the power and the authority to do that today. Now we are back to the other question about whether you are prepared to do it. The President made the statement of an open arms policy. We have had the Haitian situation here for a period of time. We know that we can resolve it. We are just trying to find out what the administration's position is. Evidently from your answers, you are not prepared to make that recommendation.[17]

The Senate Judiciary Committee received more evidence that the passage of the Refugee Act of 1980 had not reshaped U.S. policy in a way that would revise its view of Haitian refugees in a statement submitted by Michael H. Posner, executive director of the Lawyers' Committee for International Human Rights. "The administration continues to contend that the Haitians are so-called 'economic refugees,'" Posner argued, noting that in its April 15, 1980, report to Congress, one month after the Refugee Act of 1980 was passed, the administration admitted that it was continuing its policy of prejudging Haitians' applications for asylum. Posner quoted from the report: "We are not proposing to admit any Haitians as refugees because we do not expect that a significant number of those outside of the U.S. will meet the eligibility requirement of the Refugee Act definition and demonstrate that they are subject to political persecution in their homeland." The Lawyers' Committee for International Human Rights submitted a 50-page report documenting the atrocious human rights situation in Haiti in an effort to urge the administration to change its stance toward Haitians.[18]

Representative Walter Fauntroy, a member of the Congressional Black Caucus, rebuked the Carter administration for its stance toward Haitians. Testifying at the Judiciary Committee hearing with a group of Haitian refugees, Faun-troy said, "The Congressional Black Caucus has been watching with shock, outrage, and indeed, increasing anger, the treatment of Haitian refugees—the black boat people." From 1972 until that moment, Fauntroy noted, the govern-ment's policy toward Haitians had remained the same. "Shamefully, our gov-ernment's response has been jailings, starvation, and deportation of more than 1,000 Haitian refugees to Haitian jails, where they face torture and death . . . in violation of the U.N. protocol relating to the status of refugees." It was unaccept-able that an administration "which has talked so loftily about human rights . . . was continuing to vacillate" in its position on Haitian refugees to refuse to use its parole authority to admit Haitian refugees into the country. Failure "to ad-dress this issue immediately in a humane and rational way, by granting politi-cal refugee status" to the Haitians, Fauntroy concluded, "would condemn the administration" to a legacy of "gross hypocrisy and racism."[19]

While the Carter administration was under substantial pressure to reform its policy toward Haitian asylum seekers, it must have also felt political pressure from the nativist reaction welling up in South Florida and across the country. Growing support for immigration restriction was, in part, a reaction to the changing demographics of those arriving on American shores. As David M. Reimers observes, "white Europeans, who had dominated the historical pat-terns of immigration to the United States, came in much smaller numbers after the 1965 immigration act went into effect. By the 1980s Europeans made up only about 10 percent of the migrant stream." Like the Haitians, "most of the latest migrants were not white; they were people of color from the so-called third world nations."[20] Joseph Nevins observes that beginning in the late 1960s and early 1970s, "national and local state politicians and officials played a key role in raising the profile of the boundary and associated matters in the national imagination."[21] Anxiety over immigration led to the creation of the Federation for American Immigration Reform in 1979, an organization that had significant influence among lawmakers who favored immigration restriction. In Miami in 1980, anxiety about immigration and the changes it was bringing to South Florida crystalized in the nation's first anti-bilingualism/English-only move-ment. According to Max Castro, Miami's English-only campaign was "a vehicle for the expression of mass native white resistance to Latinization" and "a po-litical project aimed at symbolically reestablishing Anglo dominance." Those who favored restrictionist politics in South Florida and across the nation were gathering strength by the early 1980s.[22]

While the Congressional Black Caucus and Haitian advocacy groups were calling for a more open door, particularly for the Haitian asylum seekers, another portion of the American populace was calling on its members of Congress and the Carter administration to close the door completely. Rumors that Fidel Castro had emptied his jails and allowed the freed prisoners to join the Mariel exodus gave credence to claims that the United States was being invaded by criminal aliens and other undesirables. The Ku Klux Klan openly began to hold anti-refugee demonstrations and protests. Local and state officials declared that they would not allow refugees into their cities and states.[23]

On June 20, 1980, the Carter administration announced its solution. Cubans who arrived in the United States between April 21 and June 19, 1980, and were in INS proceedings as of June 19 and all Haitians who were in INS proceedings as of June 19, 1980, would be paroled into the country, renewed for a six-month period as "Cuban/Haitian Entrants (status pending)."[24] According to this policy, the Cuban and Haitian "entrants" were not refugees. Their final status would be determined after a review of their applications for asylum. Labeling the Cubans and Haitians as "entrants" allowed administration officials to claim that they had not even legally "entered" the United States, despite the fact that the detention centers they were sent to were clearly within US boundaries. "Instead," Jana K. Lipman explains, "the refugee camps at Krome and on US military bases were legally equivalent to being stopped at border control or an immigration checkpoint in an airport." With a "linguistic trick that taxes one's imagination," Lipman observes, applying this legal category had major implications for the government's ongoing use of detention as tool to regulate unauthorized migration, since it "created a material contradiction between Cubans' and Haitians' legal status and their physical status."

> Even if they waited for weeks or months on US soil, legally Cubans and Haitians were not in the United States until they were paroled with a sponsor (hence the "status pending" designation). As they had not "entered" the United States, Haitians and Cuban marielitos could be *excluded* from the United States, rather than *deported*. This distinction had material consequences, as excludable alien detainees have far fewer rights than immigrants slated for deportation, and since 1981, courts have ruled that they "have virtually no constitutional rights" and can be detained indefinitely.[25]

The Carter administration announced that it was seeking legislation that would regularize the status of Cuban-Haitian entrants so that they would be allowed to remain in the United States and be eligible for certain benefits, though they would not be granted the status or benefits accorded to refugees and those granted political asylum.[26] At the same time, the administration stressed that "persons who arrive illegally after June 19, 1980 [later extended to October 10, 1980] will not be eligible for the program and will be subject to exclusion or deportation in accordance with U.S. immigration laws."[27]

Despite the ongoing uncertainty of the entrants' status in the United States, for Haitians and their advocates their inclusion in the program was victory. They had forced the U.S. government to give them the same status as Cuban refugees had. Many of those who qualified for the program did ultimately achieve permanent residence in the United States, which was no small feat for Haitian asylum seekers arriving in the United States after 1972. But the Cuban-Haitian Entrant Program proved to be a brief and anomalous departure from U.S. policy toward Haitian refugees.

Even as Carter administration officials were determining how exactly to implement the new program, they were preparing a vigorous return to the previous policy for all Haitians not afforded protection as entrants. In an August 12, 1980, memo entitled "Action Plan for Haitian Entrant Program," Roger C. Adams, general counsel for the Carter administration's Cuban-Haitian Task Force, urged the task force's director, Christian R. Holmes, to "announce that the INS is taking steps to deport those who arrive after June 19." Doing so would "provide several advantages," Adams wrote. It would send a strong message "that the post-June 19 Haitians risk exclusion and deportation [which] may discourage more from coming," Adams continued. "It simply puts future Haitian arrivals on notice that in the future they will be treated like other illegal aliens such as Mexicans, Nicaraguans, etc. and is a declaration that our immigration laws mean something."[28] In other words, the Cuban-Haitian Entrant program was not to serve as a precedent for any future equal treatment of the two groups.

The Carter administration was also quietly preparing to appeal the ruling in *Haitian Refugee Center v. Civiletti*, which had ordered the government to halt its Haitian Program of mass detention and deportation. In doing so it was carefully crafting its public statements about the protection afforded those Haitians arriving before June 19 so as not to "impair the government's chance for a successful appeal in the *Haitian Refugee Center* case."[29] As Roger C. Adams explained, "What must be avoided in a statement giving an absolute assurance that the Haitians in INS proceedings on June 19 will not be deported since such a statement might cause the Fifth Circuit to treat the appeal as moot. If we guarantee they can stay in advance of a decision there is no issue left for the court to decide."[30] At the same time, Carter administration officials were not publicizing their intent to appeal the *Civiletti* ruling because doing so would jeopardize their relationship with the Haitian community organizations they relied on to help resettle Haitian refugees held in detention. This danger was apparent in a letter the Haitian Coordinating Committee for Refugees wrote to Victor H. Palmieri, U.S. coordinator for refugee affairs, that demanded to know whether the Carter administration intended to appeal the court's ruling in *Civiletti*. The letter asked, "How can you expect the Haitian community to trust the U.S. government if it seeks to overturn King's decision?"[31]

There was a sign of things to come for Haitian refugees in the unequal treatment of Cuban and Haitian entrants, who were supposedly afforded the same status and protection. As Jana K. Lipman astutely observes, "It was the policies the US government directed at Haitian refugees in 1980 and 1981 . . . that created powerful precedents and framed future US policy."[32] This was nowhere clearer than at the government's new detention facility in Miami: the Krome Avenue Detention Center.

The Krome Avenue Detention Center

Carter administration officials were well aware that despite the existence of an entrant program that appeared to treat Haitians and Cubans equally, the government's treatment of Haitians remained troublingly unequal. An August 5, 1980, memo titled "Policy Issues for the Haitian Entrant Program" to members of the Cuban Haitian Task Force admitted as much:

> Newly arriving Haitians are either housed in inadequate, unsafe facilities, such as Krome South, or detained in jails and prisons. Cubans are being sent to army camps or being reunified with their families. Grants of $300 per person have been provided to the [voluntary agencies] for the Cubans. The CAA, if it "resettles" the 18,000 Haitians which the grant covers, will be given $27 per person for resettlement. The Cubans have been and are being resettled while the Haitians have not. Cubans are still being processed by INS as applicants for political asylum while Haitians are not. The INS processing itself is done differently for both groups.[33]

The Krome Avenue Detention Center was a converted Nike missile base located in the Florida Everglades, just outside the city of Miami. In June 1980, the Carter administration opened Krome as a refugee processing center for Cubans and Haitians. The significance of the government's choice to transform this missile site into a refugee camp should not be overlooked, Jana K. Lipman argues, as it was indicative of "how the US government reimagined structures that had secured nuclear missiles to later house and 'secure' undocumented migrants."[34] Krome was divided into two parts. Cubans occupied the drier and more habitable Krome North and Haitians were held in the former army barracks of Krome South, which was enclosed in barbed wire and infested with mosquitos and snakes. More than 1,000 Haitians were housed in a facility built for 150.[35]

The conditions at Krome South were dreadful. When Larry Mahoney, a State Department spokesman who later resigned in protest over the government's treatment of Haitians at Krome, first visited the facility in June of 1980, he was appalled by what he saw:

I saw women sleeping under blankets so soiled and threadbare I mistook them for the contents of vacuum cleaner bags; guards so indifferent to suffering that they snickered at the helpless; sanitary facilities so squalid that they turned your stomach. Above all, there was the crippling boredom. The people just slept and ate, ate and slept.[36]

In addition to having to endure detention in conditions not fit for human life, the Haitians held in Krome South were also subjected to brutal treatment by the facility's staff, some of whom were themselves Haitian. Attorney Ira Kurzban, an advocate for the Haitian refugees, reported that "serious abuse by Haitian refugees by Haitian INS employees has been reported not only by refugees but by staff members of voluntary agencies. Such mistreatment and abuse permeates everyday treatment."[37] The Haitian Coordinating Committee for Refugees also detailed such abuse at Krome and other facilities, suggesting that the Haitian employees committing the abuse might be acting as agents of the Duvalier government. "Persons expressing displeasure with Duvalier have been chastised by said INS employees and have been arbitrarily, suddenly, and without the slightest provocation, subjected to serious verbal and physical abuses."[38] Ira Kurzban described a frightening incident in July 1980:

Figure 2. Women detained at Krome, 1981. Gary Monroe Photographs, David M. Rubenstein Rare Book & Manuscript Library, Duke University. Used by permission.

A group of Haitians, frustrated by their hazardous conditions of detention, tried to escape Krome South. Upon their capture and return, a Haitian INS employee named Ramon, handcuffed them and secured them to a tree, arms over their heads, for hours during the night, subjecting them to attack by snakes, rodents and insects. They were taken down only through the intervention of other refugees and INS employees.[39]

Deadly threats to the Haitian prisoners also came from outside Krome. One female prisoner was struck by a bullet that INS authorities speculated must have come from the stray shot of a hunter somewhere outside the facility's fences.[40]

By August, Carter administration officials were beginning to recognize the grave situation and the potential scandal of Krome South. Secretary of Health and Human Services Patricia Roberts Harris, the first African American woman to serve as a cabinet head, expressed her "serious concern" over the treatment of the black refugees in Krome South.[41] In letters to the U.S. coordinator for refugee affairs and to the White House, Harris detailed the "deplorable conditions in which Haitians live."

> For example, no running water is available in the open housing area, water from the temporary showers remains stagnant in pools near the tents, toilet facilities are inadequate and stench permeates the air. The Haitians were not provided sheets, towels, soap, toothbrushes or toothpaste. Women and children are housed in an overcrowded administrative building where many of the women sleep on soiled mattresses placed directly on the floor. The males sleep outdoors in open, dirty tents in areas where both mosquitos and coral snakes are prevalent. Housing Haitians, or any other people, in such an intolerable and unsanitary environment is totally unacceptable from the perspective of both health and human decency.[42]

The Department of Health and Human Services, which shared responsibility for the care of those held in detention, found its resources straining under the burden of the newly arrived refugees. Members of the department also wanted to know where the administration's detention policy might be leading. "How long can the INS maintain detention of the aliens?" HHS officials asked the immigration officials. "There is no time limit expressed in the section which give the above [detention] authority," responded an INS statement. "Detention can continue indefinitely."[43] Perhaps sensing the unsatisfactory nature of this reply, INS deputy general counsel Paul W. Schmidt followed up with a letter to Undersecretary of Health and Human Services Nathan J. Stark. Schmidt explained that the agency drew its authority for indefinite detention from sections 233(a) and 235(b) of the Immigration and Nationality Act. "This authority was confirmed by the Supreme Court in *Shaughnessy v. Mezei*" (1953), which, Schmidt argued, affirmed the legality of indefinite detention.[44]

Christian R. Holmes, director of the administration's Cuban-Haitian Task Force (CHTF) urged the administration to resolve the crisis at Krome South. The CHTF was a body created in July 1980 to coordinate the processing and resettlement of Cuban and Haitian Refugees. It reported directly to the U.S. Coordinator for Refugee Affairs, an office of the State Department, and to the assistant to the president for intergovernmental affairs, and was later transferred to the Department of Health and Human Services. The fact that the CHTF had an interagency profile made its already challenging work even more complex.

In August 1980, the task force was working to improve conditions at the

Krome detention camp, including arranging for 24-hour access to medical care and additional food and addressing issues related to water supply, pest control, and sanitation.[45] However, the CHTF also wanted support from the Carter administration for a proposal that would have dramatically changed the terrain of Haitian detention. "There has been a tendency not to view the Haitian situation as a crisis," wrote Holmes in a memo to Carter aide Eugene Eidenberg. "However, I and my staff believe that the Haitian situation has now reached emergency proportions which in turn requires the federal government to utilize its emergency funds." Holmes proposed that the administration use these emergency funds to create a "consolidated facility" to which Haitians in Krome South and six other detention centers in South Florida would be transferred. Based on a report from an INS field team, Holmes suggested that a possible "site for Haitians" was another former Nike missile site, this time in Key Largo. Centralizing Haitian detainees in the Florida Keys would give the government "enough space" to "consolidate all processing, health care, etc." for Haitian detainees, wrote Holmes. There were drawbacks to the site, however. Key Largo was a two-and-a-half-hour drive from Miami and, like Krome South, had an enormous mosquito problem.[46]

The proposal to consolidate the facilities holding Haitians in one location on Key Largo did not come to fruition. But Carter administration officials did not abandon the idea of relocating Haitian detainees to one facility far from the U.S. mainland. On September 12, 1980, the CHTF assumed control of Krome South and initiated a series of improvements to the site. At the same time, the CHTF began upgrading Krome North. As Jana K. Lipman observes, this marks the point when Krome began its evolution from "a makeshift refugee camp into a more permanent facility designed to discipline and to hold unwanted refugees." Carter administration officials denied that the new and improved Krome would be a permanent refugee camp or a long-term detention facility. Instead, Krome was to be a short-term "turnaround" center. As they saw it, the solution to the Haitian detention problem lay off the shores of the United States.[47]

Toward a Caribbean-Wide Detention and Refugee Policy

By the fall of 1980, the Carter administration's biggest refugee problem involved Haitians still being held at Krome South and other detention sites. The CHTF sought to close the refugee camps at Fort McCoy in Wisconsin, Fort Indiantown

Gap in Pennsylvania, and Eglin Air Force Base in northwest Florida and to detain the remaining Cubans and Haitians in a smaller number of facilities. Krome North would be the central site for refugee processing. Fort Chaffee would also remain open temporarily and would receive some of those transferred from Fort McCoy, Indiantown Gap, and Eglin Air Force Base.[48] But the key to the government's consolidation plan lay in a proposed new site at Fort Allen, a decommissioned U.S. military base on the southern coast of Puerto Rico.

A detention and processing center in Puerto Rico that could house refugees currently held in detention and receive future unauthorized Caribbean migrants held great potential for the Carter administration. A detention center outside any state and distant from the mainland seemed a promising solution to the politically sensitive issue of U.S.-based refugee camps and immigrant prisons. If the Pentagon operated the facility, as was initially proposed, that would ease the pressure on the INS and State Department, which still oversaw the CHTF.[49] Furthermore, those held at Fort Allen would be outside the Southern District of Florida, where Haitian refugees were afforded some protection as a result of Judge King's ruling in *Haitian Refugee Center v. Civiletti*. In addition, centralizing the Haitians currently held in Krome South and in far-flung networks of jails and facilities would enable Carter administration officials to claim that the move was being made on humanitarian grounds, as conditions at Fort Allen could be characterized as an improvement over Krome South.[50]

But while the Carter administration anticipated that this move would deescalate some of the political conflicts over refugee camps in the states, it correctly anticipated other sources of political resistance. After details of the negotiations over the conversion of Fort Allen into a detention and processing facility leaked out, spokespersons for the CHTF tried to assuage the fears and concerns of Puerto Ricans who worried about the effect of hosting a new U.S. refugee camp on the island. According to the *San Juan Star*, U.S. officials initially informed Puerto Rican officials that only 1,000 to 1,500 refugees would be sent to Puerto Rico. At one point, administration officials said that 591 Cubans and 1,085 Haitians would be transferred from Krome North and South. They added that as many as 4,000 could be sent to Fort Allen in the event of another emergency. Later, however, a spokesman for the CHTF informed Puerto Rican officials that he "couldn't hazard a guess" as to how many Cubans and Haitians would end up at Fort Allen. To ease concerns about the deleterious economic impact thousands of refugees might have on the struggling Puerto Rican economy, U.S. officials initially said that none of the refugees would be permanently relocated on the island. But later, administration spokespersons allowed that some might be resettled in Puerto Rico. U.S. officials attempted to reassure Puerto Ricans such as those in the nearby community of Pastillito Prieto who were worried that their security might be jeopardized by the arrival of the refugees. Surrounded by barbed-wire fences and fields of sugarcane, the facility would be tightly guarded, administration officials promised. The detention center at Fort Allen would be "absolutely secure," declared Deputy Assistant to the President Tom Higgins. "No Puerto Rican will ever even see these people."[51]

However, the promises of the Carter administration failed to convince many Puerto Ricans that Fort Allen should be the new center of the U.S. government's refugee detention and processing program. Politicians across the political spectrum lined up against the plan. Members of the Puerto Rican Independence Party, the Puerto Rico Socialist Party, and many others demonstrated against the Fort Allen plan. In Puerto Rico, the Teamsters Union called on the entire labor movement to mobilize against the proposal. Opponents voiced concern over the economic impact the presence of refugees might have, sometimes characterizing the Fort Allen plan as more evidence of the island's ongoing colonial relationship to the United States. As Jana K. Lipman notes in her analysis of the episode, "the unilateral decision to transfer Haitian refugees to Puerto Rico inched too close to explicit imperial control and disrespect," provoking action by "hundreds of local residents in nearby Juana Diaz" while "thousands more marched in San Juan."[52] And while some, like Pastillito Prieto resident Benjamin Cruz Mangual, claimed to be "not afraid of the refugees coming," arguing that "all are humans and we have to share," others worried about the kind of people the United States would be transferring to Fort Allen. "Puerto Rico is not a garbage can," declared Sylvia de Jesus, president of the National Conference of Puerto Rican Women, warning that if Carter pressed forward with the plan she might withdraw her support for his reelection bid.[53]

The Carter administration also ran into resistance to the Fort Allen proposal in the United States. Haitian refugees and their supporters protested the plan as yet another effort by the U.S. government to circumvent the *Civiletti* ruling and facilitate the exclusion of Haitian refugees from the United States. Members of the Congressional Black Caucus saw the same sinister motive in the Fort Allen plan, charging that "the administration's plans to send Haitians to Puerto Rico" were "only the latest example of a continued determination to deport Haitian refugees without fundamental legal protections to an uncertain fate that Federal courts have found inevitably awaits them in Haiti."[54] Amnesty

International noted recent reports that those trying to leave Haiti had been harassed, imprisoned, and even killed for trying to flee. "The people who may be sent to Fort Allen may have legitimate claim to political asylum and, under international and U.S. law, should not be treated as prisoners," the human rights organization insisted.[55] Members of the Congressional Black Caucus also argued that sending detainees to Fort Allen would subject refugees to "grossly inadequate housing and hazardous health conditions," stating that they were "gravely concerned" that, once again, "only Haitians will be subjected to these inhuman conditions."[56]

Puerto Rico's residents and civil society groups turned to the courts to stop the conversion of Fort Allen into a detention and processing center. On September 29, opponents of the Fort Allen plan, including thirteen labor unions and residents of San Juan and Juana Diaz, filed two separate injunctions in federal court. The injunction the unions filed maintained that the Fort Allen project violated federal environmental statutes, the Refugee Act, and the United Nations Charter. The Commonwealth of Puerto Rico soon joined the action as a third party in the suit to halt the conversion of Fort Allen, citing violations of environmental regulations the Carter administration had attempted to waive, invoking a refugee emergency as its justification.[57] When the court heard the case, the arguments against the establishment of the Fort Allen detention and processing center received a favorable response. District Judge Juan Torruella ultimately ruled against the government, upholding the injunction against the Fort Allen refugee center on environmental grounds.[58]

Although the government's plan was derailed by the legal challenge, its attempts to distance its detention and processing of unauthorized Caribbean migrants from the mainland persisted. Carter's successor, Ronald Reagan, briefly revived the facility at Fort Allen. But the more lasting Caribbean detention project would be the prison at Guantanamo Bay, Cuba. Like Fort Allen, Guantanamo was initially created as a way of dealing with the problem of unauthorized Haitian migration.

The Lasting Impact of the Caribbean Refugee Crisis

By January 1981, when Reagan took office, the number of Haitian arrivals in the previous year alone had reached 20,748. Even as the number of Cuban arrivals had dropped off in the last quarter of 1980, the influx of Haitians increased. Approximately 5,000 of these asylum seekers from Haiti arrived after the October

10, 1980, deadline established by the Cuban-Haitian Entrant Program and were thus classified as "subject to exclusion."[59] Thousands more arrived from Haiti throughout the spring of 1981, and halting the influx of Haitians became priority number one for officials of the new administration.

Still, as officials in the CHTF looked back at their response to Caribbean refugee crisis of 1980, they celebrated the new power they had asserted in the area of immigration and refugee policy. "It is not currently expected that a new migration of Cubans and Haitians, of the magnitude of the exodus last spring and fall, will occur in the future," one report observed. But "contingency plans are being developed by [the Cuban-Haitian Task Force] and Dept. of State, in the event that a large influx of migrants to the U.S. does occur." Even if the detention facility at Fort Allen was out of service, the detention sites at Fort Chaffee, Krome Avenue North and South, and Richmond Naval Air Station could house future unauthorized migrants, the report noted. And despite the challenges of finding detention space, the Caribbean refugee crisis had allowed the federal government to assert its right to detain asylum seekers at these designated facilities. The authority to take such steps to manage another "immigration emergency" derived from a November 15 presidential executive order that delegated power from the president to the secretary of health and human services. In the event of another crisis like that of 1980, the CHTF memo asserted, "the Secretary's authority in this respect is virtually unlimited."[60]

President Reagan not only expanded these powers but also asserted new powers in the area of immigrant and refugee detention. Building upon the Carter administration's practices (most notably the Haitian Program of the 1970s and the detention policies developed during the Caribbean refugee crisis of 1980), the Reagan administration significantly extended the government's efforts to deter and even block asylum seekers and other unauthorized migrants from U.S. shores, leading to the formal reinstitution of immigrant detention as a U.S. policy. And this monumental transformation of immigration policy under Reagan resulted from the U.S. government's attempts to contain a single group: Haitian refugees.

3

Immigration Detention Reborn, 1981–1982

On April 2, 1982, a group of Haitian women who were imprisoned in a facility in Alderson, West Virginia, launched a hunger strike to protest their ongoing incarceration. In a letter to their supporters in the Haitian Refugee Project, they explained their reasons. "Here in West Virginia we now face a very black life. They treat us like animals for no reason at all. They give more importance to a garbage can than they do to us. We face a terrible situation. They treat us like crooks." The prisoners, some of whom had been incarcerated for ten months, struggled to make sense of their ordeal. "Are we not human beings like other human beings? Just because we fled our country to the U.S. is that why we are not considered human? Or is it because we are black? Don't we have a personality like all other human beings? What did the Haitian refugees do that was a crime so that they would get treated in such a way like this?"[1]

The prisoners in West Virginia occupied one site in a growing network of immigrant detention centers. In the spring of 1982, more than 2,000 Haitian refugees were being held in prisons across the country.[2] Their incarceration was part of the Reagan administration's attempt to staunch the flow of unauthorized Haitian migration to the United States and to keep undocumented Haitians already in the United States from obtaining freedom. In Reagan's first year in office, administration officials also developed a policy to block vessels filled with Haitian refugees before they could reach American shores, a process it called interdiction.

"An Immigration Emergency"

On July 31, 1981, officials from across the country appeared at a hearing of the Subcommittee on Immigration and Refugee Policy of the Senate Judiciary Committee to call for a tougher response to unauthorized immigration to the United States. The hearing's title, "The United States as a Country of Mass First

Asylum," suggested that it might be devoted to questions about how policy-makers could most effectively help the United States fulfill this role. But most who offered testimony made it clear that they were decidedly hostile toward the notion that America might have some legitimate responsibility to asylum seekers. Their perspectives were part of a growing backlash against refugees and illegal immigrants in the summer of 1981. The Reagan administration capitalized on this shifting political ground as it revived the long-dormant policy of immigrant detention and introduced the new practice of interdiction.

The chair of the Subcommittee on Immigration and Refugee Policy, Wyoming senator Allen Simpson, opened the hearing by describing an unprecedented challenge to American institutions and the American people.

> Seldom has the United States been galvanized into more active thinking on immigration issues as it was last year by the influx of Cubans and Haitians into South Florida. This was the initial time that the country was to find itself as a country of mass first asylum, and it was soon evident that we had very little within our laws or within our administrative procedures or in our national preparedness plans to provide any clear direction on the handling of this extraordinary situation.[3]

Simpson invited those testifying before the subcommittee to address the question of what was to be done when America found itself in the position as a country of mass first asylum. Many who testified supported policies such as interdiction, long-term detention, and speedy administrative procedures that would lead to mass deportation.

Assistant Secretary of State for Inter-American Affairs Thomas O. Enders laid out the Reagan administration's position. If Congress wanted to deter future mass arrivals of refugees, Enders argued, it would need to grant the president the authority "to declare an immigration emergency and take the necessary actions to respond to it." Enders also urged Congress to grant the president the authority "to interdict on the high seas those vessels that we have reasonable cause to believe may be engaged in transporting illegal aliens to the United States in violation of our laws." He argued that the policy toward Cubans and Haitians who successfully made it to U.S. shores "must be one of immediate detention and prompt exclusion for those found to be inadmissible to this country."[4]

The acting commissioner for the INS, Doris Meissner, proposed legislation that would "streamline asylum and exclusion procedures" and strengthen penalties against those "bringing undocumented aliens into our country." Meissner also asked for legislation that would "vest the president with special authority in a declared immigration emergency" and would clarify the president's authority to carry out interdiction. In addition, she argued, the government needed more "resources for the development of additional facilities to be used for temporary detention of illegal aliens pending their exclusion or grant of asylum."[5]

Others offering testimony at the hearing affirmed the basic positions of Enders and Meissner in more sensational terms. Kentucky senator Walter Huddleston declared that "we are reaching the end of our rope." He suggested that if the U.S. government could not find the space or resources for more detention facilities, it should develop "extracontinental holding centers" to incarcerate those attempting to reach the United States.[6] Illinois representative Robert McGlory argued that "we should use the military to interdict any persons who are undertaking to reach our shores and enter our country illegally. They should be interdicted, they should be deterred, they should be returned to the place whence they came."[7]

The senators from Florida added their support for a stronger program to stop the arrival of new refugees, describing a grave threat to their beleaguered constituents. Senator Lawton Chiles expressed frustration over the Reagan administration's lack of response to the refugee crisis, declaring that implementing an interdiction program "would be the best of all news for Florida." The senator urged members of the committee to consider the Huddleston-Chiles bill, which proposed to go much further to enforce detention and exclusion of undocumented immigrants. "There is a new bumper sticker that you will see on more and more cars in the Miami area," Chiles observed. "It says, 'Will the last person to leave please bring the flag.' That sums up a lot of the feeling of frustration that is down there presently."[8] Paula Hawkins added to the sense of crisis by painting a sordid picture of life in South Florida amid wave after wave of refugee arrivals. She referred to "reports that diseases have been brought into this country by the entrants" and cited one report that claimed that 80 to 90 percent of Haitian refugees were infected with parasites. Hawkins also claimed that a Cuban intelligence report "tells us that these groups are infiltrated with subversive activities also." Senator Hawkins warned, "The greatest concern to Floridians is the increase in crime that has accompanied the arrival of the Cubans and Haitians in this latest influx." The solutions to protect Florida and America from this threat of disease and crime, Hawkins concluded, were "legislation that would speed up the exclusionary hearing process" and a campaign to find "new holding facilities which will prevent illegal aliens from wandering the streets."[9]

Although it had been just over a year since the passage of the Refugee Act of 1980, the sentiments expressed at the congressional hearing of July 1981 could hardly have been further from the ideals the new refugee law expressed. When the Refugee Act became law, Congress had declared it "the historic policy of the United States to respond to the urgent needs of persons subject to persecution in their homelands." The law made a commitment "to provide a permanent and systematic procedure for the admission to this country of refugees of special humanitarian concern to the United States, and to provide comprehensive and uniform provisions for the effective resettlement and absorption of those refugees who are admitted."[10] A mere sixteen months later, however, a growing number of lawmakers seemed prepared to slam the door on would-be refugees and to consider interdiction and detention as methods for deterring future refugee arrivals. The refugee crisis of the previous year had persuaded some Americans that the United States should no longer extend asylum to those in need.

The sharp reaction on display at the congressional hearing can also be explained, in part, by the fact that at the moment of the refugee crisis, the American system was ill equipped to respond to the challenge of large numbers of asylum seekers. The process refugees generally followed was to apply for admittance to the United States in their home country and then await the government's ruling on their application. In contrast, the Cubans and Haitians who arrived in 1980 and 1981 came to the United States and then submitted their applications for asylum. Peter Schuck observes that prior to 1972 the United States received relatively few asylum claims; the INS did not even "establish procedures and standards for resolving asylum claims until January 1975." And while the Refugee Act of 1980 created "a legislative basis for an asylum status and a systematic basis for determining it," Schuck notes, overall the legislation "had little to say about asylum" and proved wholly inadequate to deal with the 53,000 asylum claims that were filed between March 1980 and July 1981.[11] In addition, as Michael J. Churgin notes, while refugee status "is adjudicated overseas" with "no judicial review of the overseas determination," asylum status was adjudicated in U.S. courts "with an elaborate process of administrative and judicial review of the asylum determination."[12] For this reason, the arrival of large numbers of asylum seekers were a substantial challenge for the legal system, not to mention the burden that local communities would face if tens of thousands of people were admitted while awaiting the ruling on their claims. This led, as Naomi Flink Zucker has observed, to "a profound fear of uncontrolled numbers of refugees."[13]

As lawmakers grappled with the difficult problem of asylum, a host of other factors contributed to opposition to the refugees. As Gil Loescher and John A. Scanlan have noted, the mass asylum crisis of 1980 came at a time of "deep economic and political malaise." They argue that Carter's "confused federal response . . . engendered a widespread belief that the United States had no refugee policy, that refugee admissions were completely out of control, and that Congress lacked effective means of regulating administrative discretion."[14] In fact, for those most concerned about the U.S. government's inability to control the latest influx of Cubans and Haitians, the very sovereignty of the nation seemed at stake. As Mae Ngai has observed, "nationalisms' ultimate defense is sovereignty—the nation's self-proclaimed, absolute right to determine its own membership, a right believed to inhere in the nation-state's very existence, in its 'right of self-preservation.'"[15] Unrestricted mass migration, especially on the scale of the Caribbean refugee crisis of 1980, posed a fundamental challenge to notions of state sovereignty based on immigration regulation.

Maxine S. Seller notes that the Cuban and Haitian refugee crisis occurred amid an increasingly negative reaction to the admission of Vietnamese refugees in the previous decade and rising concern over unauthorized immigration from Mexico. The image of tens of thousands of Cubans and Haitians arriving on American shores also stung "a nation still smarting from its long and humiliating inability to extricate its citizens in Iran," which made American leaders "sensitive to charges of weakness" in "dealings with foreign states." Each of these elements created fertile ground for the Reagan administration's tough new policies toward refugees and unauthorized migrants. Indeed, when Attorney General William French Smith declared in 1981 that "we have lost control of our borders," he was expressing a belief that seemed to be growing among lawmakers and their constituents who desired a strong response to such foreign threats and he was sending a signal that the United States intended to reassert its sovereignty in the area of immigration control.[16] The revival of immigration detention and the policy of interdiction, both originally aimed at stemming the tide of Haitian refugees, was the Reagan administration's first show of strength and an important symbol that the United States was once again prepared to exercise its sovereignty.

The Reagan administration's demonstration of strength in immigration affairs also played on the anxieties and fears many Americans had of a nation and a world that was dangerously out of control. As Julilly Kohler-Hausman observes, in the late 1970s, "the national media closely covered the violence, property destruction, and disorder" of the previous decade's urban rebellions. "For many present or watching on television, the scenes looked eerily like a war zone. Indeed, the uprisings at home and political insurgencies in Africa, Asia, and Latin American collapsed into each other. Politicians, law enforcement, and activists with different agendas identified an interconnected global rebellion underway challenging colonialism, racism and capitalism."[17] In the eyes of many South Floridians and others across the country, this alarming situation became a full-blown crisis with the mass arrival of Cubans and Haitians in the summer of 1980 and the specter of even more poor black Haitians flooding American shores in subsequent months.

A New Haitian Program

Although in 1980 and 1981 some viewed Cubans and Haitians as a dual threat, the Reagan administration made the case that the Haitian and the Cuban cases were very different and thus required a different response. Thomas O. Enders pointed out that "although the domestic impact of migration from [Cuba and Haiti] is much the same, the foreign policy significance is quite different." The influx of Cuban refugees into the United States was the result of "a totalitarian state that has suddenly decided to permit emigration from a society where it is normally not tolerated." Haitians, in contrast, were leaving a nation controlled by "a friendly government" that was "interested in enforcing its laws and in enforcing the laws of its neighbors." Furthermore, Haitian "emigration occurs as the result of separate decisions by private individuals without the support or sanction of their government."[18]

Because of these critical differences, Enders announced, "the steps we take to halt illegal immigration to the United States, and to arrange the return of citizens of these countries who are not eligible for admission, will obviously be different in these two very different circumstances." For Cuban refugees, Enders called for "legislation to prohibit and prevent U.S. residents, and U.S. registered, owned, or chartered vessels from helping aliens to travel illegally to the United States," as had happened during the Mariel boatlift. But the Haitians were "a significant social and economic problem for the United States particularly in the State of Florida," and the Reagan administration wanted much more, including legislation authorizing the president "to interdict on the high seas . . .

vessels suspected of attempting to violate U.S. immigration laws." Furthermore, in order to immediately return the captured Haitians, Enders stated, "we also need legislation to expedite exclusion and asylum procedures to allow for expeditious screening and processing of any asylum requests at sea so aliens who are not legitimate candidates for asylum can be returned promptly to their country aboard interdicted vessels." While these proposed laws might eventually be applied to any migrant "attempting to violate U.S. immigration laws," when they were created these policies were meant exclusively for Haitians. Since it was the Reagan administration's goal to bar Haitians from entering the United States, the proposed policies "may be the least expensive and most effective way to slow the Haitian migrant outflow."[19]

There were other reasons why the Reagan administration chose to target Haitians with the extraordinary policy of interdiction. Ever since the dramatic increase of Haitian migrants seeking asylum in the late 1970s and first years of the 1980s, the U.S. government had been searching for a way to issue a blanket denial of asylum and to carry out mass deportations of the Haitians. This had been the purpose of the Haitian Program of the 1970s. In fact, according to Naomi Flink Zucker, the policy of interdiction was first considered (though it was not implemented) in the earlier Haitian Program. After the ruling in *Haitian Refugee Center v. Civiletti* made the government's Haitian Program illegal and the Refugee Act of 1980 outlawed the traditional preference given to refugees from communist countries, the Reagan administration implemented interdiction as a way to circumvent the law. Correspondence prepared by the administration's Immigration Task Force candidly articulates this purpose:

> The purpose of an interdiction program would be both to deter directly further unlawful migration by expeditiously returning migrants to Haiti, and incidentally, to curtail the flow of aliens into administrative and judicial proceedings in the United States. Although required by the U.N. Protocol and Convention to adjudicate refugee claims prior to returning a claimant to his homeland, if interdiction occurs outside of U.S. territorial waters, the determination would not be governed by the Immigration Act.[20]

As it was developing the new program, the Reagan administration presented interdiction to the public as a legitimate and legal way to stop the influx of Haitians. But privately members of the administration were expressing considerable doubt about the legality and constitutionality of such a program. A March

13, 1981, memo to the president from his chief of staff James A. Baker conveyed the scope of the problem as the administration saw it:

> You should be aware that a boat with 107 Haitians on board landed last Monday night at Boca Raton and another boat with 140 Haitians arrived yesterday. These boats are being seized and the Haitians detained in temporary camps. There is evidence that additional boats of this type are being built in Haiti. For every boat apprehended, more get through. The Haitian population in South Florida is probably now increasing at rate of 1,500–2,000/month. This could increase as the weather improves.[21]

The problem was, Baker claimed, that "in the view of Justice, there is no clear legal authority to take persons without valid visas on such boats back to their country of origin, even though the country is willing to receive them and there is no evidence of political persecution."[22] Furthermore, Reagan administration officials acknowledged that the Haitian interdiction program had no legal precedent. "We have been unable to find any precedent for such an operation," a Justice Department memo reported. "Nor have we found any example of the President's using inherent executive authority to regulate immigration in the years before Congress first enacted extensive immigration legislation." Perhaps if President Reagan asserted his authority "in the field of foreign affairs" and obtained "the permission of the Haitian government," an argument for the authority to interdict could be made. But the president's ability to introduce interdiction would be much stronger if he had legislation from Congress that explicitly authorized this action. That is why Assistant Secretary of State Enders was making just such a request in testimony before the Senate in July 1981.[23]

As aware as Reagan administration officials were of the potential legal and constitutional problems surrounding interdiction, they concluded that these obstacles were not insurmountable. A memo from the Office of Legal Counsel advised the attorney general that it had concluded that the president did have the authority to interdict Haitians and that it came from two sources: "the power delegated by Congress to the President, through the Attorney General, to guard the borders . . . and the President's authority in the field of foreign relations." Because "the breadth of the President's authority in the field of foreign relations is extremely broad," the memo advised the president to frame interdiction and "the arrest of Haitian citizens as an aid to Haiti's enforcement of its emigration laws."[24] Toward this end the Reagan administration negotiated an agreement with the Duvalier government to allow the United States Coast

Guard to enter Haitian waters in order to board Haitian vessels and return those attempting to leave Haiti.[25] However, the Department of Justice acknowledged that the Haitian interdiction program might be seen as a violation of Article 33 of the UN Convention Relating to the Status of Refugees, "to which the United States is a party." That article "provides that 'no contracting state shall . . . return (*"refouler"*) a refugee in any manner whatsoever to the frontiers of territories where his life or freedom would be threatened.'" Under the rule of this international convention, individuals who claimed they had been persecuted were to "be given an opportunity to substantiate these claims." But, the Office of Legal Counsel observed, "the Convention does not . . . mandate any particular kind of procedure."[26] The State Department suggested that in order to be in compliance with a minimal interpretation of the Convention Relating to the Status of Refugees, "one individual from the Immigration and Naturalization Service should be on board for the purpose of making any amnesty determinations required."[27]

By the time the Reagan administration had worked out its legal argument for interdiction, it had also concluded that it could proceed without the authorization of Congress. In September 1981, President Reagan issued Executive Order 12324, "Interdiction of Illegal Aliens." A presidential proclamation marking the occasion declared that "the entry of undocumented aliens from the high seas is hereby suspended and shall be prevented by the interdiction of certain vessels carrying such aliens."[28] Nowhere in the executive order or the president's proclamation did the president specify that this was an action aimed at Haitians, although all of the internal correspondence confirms that "the continuing illegal migration by sea of large numbers of undocumented aliens into the southeastern United States" referred to Haitian immigrants.[29] Although the policy was conceived and initially implemented as way to block Haitians from reaching American shores, however, it would subsequently be used much more broadly. In the two decades that followed the Reagan administration's first use of interdiction, the United States Coast Guard halted more than 180,000 migrants attempting to reach the United States by boat. Fifty-five percent of these interdictions were implemented to stop those fleeing from Haiti. But in the years after 1981, interdiction was also used to halt the arrival of would-be migrants from many other countries, including the Dominican Republic, Cuba, Mexico, Ecuador, and China.[30]

Even before the Reagan administration issued the executive order, its Haitian interdiction program had created a firestorm of criticism, led by members of the Congressional Black Caucus. Testifying before a senate subcommittee in July 1981, New York representative Shirley Chisholm, the chair of the caucus's task force on refugees, remarked, "My colleagues in the Congressional Black Caucus and I view such proposals with the utmost horror." Comparing the forceful return of refugees to Haiti with the United States' earlier refusal to accept Jewish refugees fleeing Nazi Germany, Chisholm characterized interdiction as a violation of "the principle of refugee movement" and said that it was "in direct contradiction to the Universal Declaration of Human Rights which protects the right of a person to emigrate, a right which we constantly press upon the Soviet Union in an effort to force them to allow more Jewish and dissident emigration. . . . We cannot hope to retain the respect and admiration of the world if our immigration and refugee policies are discriminatory on the basis of ideology or skin color."[31]

Other refugee and human rights groups agreed that the new policy of interdiction set a troubling precedent and sullied the United States' image among nations. The U.S. Committee for Refugees observed,

Perhaps more than any other aspect of U.S. asylum policy, the Haitian interdiction program is a serious blow to international refugee protection. For it not only discourages people from seeking asylum; it actually prevents them from reaching the United States and returns them to their country without a chance for a fair hearing of their claims to refugee status. The image this projects is not lost on the rest of the world.[32]

These critics recognized interdiction as unprecedented and claimed that the policy broke dangerous new ground in the treatment of asylum seekers. In a letter to the president, Walter E. Fauntroy, chair of the Congressional Black Caucus, argued that "interdiction, as this country's response to the Haitian influx, raises serious questions about a double standard regarding first asylum issues," particularly for black refugees. In a press release that called interdiction "racist and inhumane," Fauntroy stated that "interdiction not only violates international and domestic law but is a racist response to prohibit black refugees from entering this country." He warned that the asylum hearing and exclusion process the interdiction policy established set a troubling precedent:

The problem of adjudicating asylum claims on the high seas without prejudice is insurmountable. No independent body, such as the United Nations High Commissioner for Refugees, has indicated an interest in participating in an operation which would require "on the spot" judgments about asylum claims. Without such an independent group involved in interdiction it would obviously be impossible for Haitians to have a "fair opportunity" to assert their asylum claims as required by the U.N. Convention and Protocol.[33]

In a brief response to Representative Fauntroy's concerns, David Crosland, general counsel for the president, retorted, "There is no legal impediment to interdiction. . . . The United States is not trying to deny asylum to anyone with a valid claim. On the contrary, each individual request is being treated on a case by case basis."[34]

There was good reason to fear that interdiction would serve as a tool of mass exclusion for the Haitians. According to the U.S. Committee for Refugees, in the first five years of the interdiction program, only two of the 9,146 Haitians who were stopped as they tried to reach the United States "were brought to the United States because of an expressed fear of what would happen to them upon their return to Haiti." The virtually complete exclusion of Haitians continued despite the fact that "U.S. State Department reports during this period contin-

Figure 3. United States Coast Guard on Haitian interdiction patrol, ca. 1981. Caribbean Sea Migration Collection, David M. Rubenstein Rare Book & Manuscript Library, Duke University. Used by permission.

ued to portray Haiti as an abuser of the most basic human rights."[35] In the first ten years of the interdiction program, only 28 of 25,000 people intercepted as sea were allowed to continue to the United States to pursue asylum claims. The rest were returned directly to Haiti after their vessels were burned.[36]

In the months after the interdiction policy began, it seemed to accomplish its goal. According to Associate Attorney General Rudolph Giuliani, only forty-seven Haitians had been apprehended on Florida's shores in November 1981, almost 1,000 fewer than one year earlier. He claimed that interdiction represented "a fair but firm decision on how the law should be applied" and that it excluded Haitians who "came to the United States in search of better jobs and housing, not to flee political persecution."[37] Other evidence suggests that the policy succeeded in deterring Haitians from seeking asylum in the United States. Christopher Mitchell notes that "in 1980 alone, 24,530 undocumented Haitian migrants—mainly boat people—were arrested in South Florida; over the succeeding eight years, a total of only 21,906 were apprehended there."[38] Interdiction, however, was only one piece of the Reagan administration's program to deter Haitians from pursuing asylum cases in the United States. The administration reinstituted a policy of detention for Haitians who made it past the Coast Guard and for those already in the United States.

The Formal Reinstitution of Immigrant Detention

Even while the Reagan administration was publicly calling for interdiction and formally announcing its new policy in September 1981, it was quietly introducing a practice with even more far-reaching consequences that targeted Haitian asylum seekers. In May 1981, four months before Reagan's interdiction order, immigration officials began detaining all undocumented Haitians without the possibility of bond. Under the Carter administration, Haitian detention had been somewhat more sporadic and detained Haitians had been able to secure their release through bond. The Reagan administration's blanket detention policy without the possibility of bond for all Haitians represented "a quantum leap forward," Gil Loescher and John A. Scanlan observe.[39] With this launching of a mandatory detention policy for all unauthorized Haitians, the Reagan administration formally reinstated the policy of immigrant detention, completing the reversal of U.S. immigration policy that had ended the use of detention more than two decades earlier.[40]

In reinstituting the immigrant detention policy, the Reagan administration's Haitian detention program accelerated the shifting role of detention in US immigration policy. Timothy J. Dunn has observed the detention program represented "an insidious turn," whereby "detention came to be seen instead as a punitive means of deterring undocumented immigration." In fact, this punitive turn in immigration policy preceded Reagan. But Dunn, who has examined the experience of Central American asylum seekers who came after the Haitians, is correct in recognizing the "ominous precedent" that the Reagan administration's "use of detention as a punitive measure to deter Haitians from migrating and applying for political asylum" set for Central American refugees.[41] Indeed, the implications of the return of immigrant imprisonment as a central tool in U.S. immigration policy would have troubling consequences for undocumented people from around the world in subsequent decades.

The Reagan administration sought to justify its use of mandatory detention by arguing that it would be a deterrent to Haitian asylum seekers, though it denied that Haitians were legitimately in need of asylum. According to Rudolph Giuliani, by November 1981, far fewer Haitians were trying to reach the United States not only because they were aware of the interdiction program but also because they knew that if they reached the United States, they would be detained rather than paroled into the community while their asylum requests were litigated. In other words, detention was meant to be a deterrent to future Haitian migration. But it was also a way to keep Haitians already in the United States from entering society. "The Haitians' history shows that they don't show up for asylum hearings once they are let go," Giuliani claimed. Giuliani argued that the cost of tracking Haitian asylum seekers would be prohibitive. "It would cost just as much to set up a parole officer system within the INS to keep track of them as it does to detain them." Although Giuliani acknowledged that the number of Haitian detainees was relatively low, he rejected this factor as an argument against detention. "If you look at a number like 2,000 or 2,500," you might "say 'Let's release them, what does it matter?'" But what about next year, and the year after and the year after that?" Giuliani pointed out that releasing detainees is "pretty much the philosophy that prevailed for the last two years and that is why the number got up as high as it did. . . . We don't have the space to take care of the two-thirds of the world which has severe economic problems. We have to take care of our own people."[42]

In a memo to INS commissioner Alan Nelson, Attorney General William French Smith reviewed the first year and a half of the administration's efforts to improve the enforcement of the nation's "long-neglected immigration laws." In July 1982, the Reagan administration had expanded the imprisonment policy that had originally included only Haitians in order to mandate the detention of all unauthorized migrants. This move enabled the administration to claim that detention "is done even-handedly with aliens of all countries." Smith conceded that people from Haiti were the principle occupants of the newly constructed detention system, but he attributed the fact that Haitians were the original immigrant detainees to their legal challenges.[43]

In most cases, an alien is detained only briefly, usually a few days, before it is decided whether he can stay. Regrettably, however, the Haitians have continued in detention considerably longer than other groups because most of them have filed claims for political asylum here, and because litigation brought on their behalf has stalled already slow processing of their cases. Under current court orders, each Haitian in custody is required to be represented by counsel in connection with the asylum hearings.[44]

The legal challenges detained asylum seekers from Haiti presented were such a vexation to the Reagan administration that officials began to search for creative solutions to the problem. Behind closed doors, Reagan administration officials sought a strategy that would allow them to rapidly move Haitian refugees through asylum hearings and toward deportation without giving the appearance that they were violating their rights. Reagan administration counsel Mike Horowitz claimed that the problem was that "a small coterie of Haitian defense lawyers has contrived to tie the exclusion process up in knots, preventing their exclusion and transportation back to Haiti. The cost to the taxpayer in fiscal 1982 to operate three detention facilities for Haitians is conservatively estimated at $70 million—and the cost rises with every day and every boatload." Prisons were overflowing with Haitians, and a new detention facility in Glasgow, Montana, had been proposed. But that was "a temporary solution, at best," Horowitz argued.

Without efficient exclusion procedures, our detention camps will be full by spring. The present policy is the worst of all possible options. We create inhumane and politically unpopular quasi-concentration camps, and produce a new fugitive class of undocumented aliens. Unless we are to change our immigration policy and admit the Haitians as refugees, the only long-range solution is to get fair exclusion hearings underway, with enough due process to withstand court challenges.[45]

The solution Horowitz offered drew upon Ronald Reagan's experience as governor of California. In 1970, welfare rights organizations had fought Reagan's welfare reform program by tying up the administration's hearing process. "The state broke the offensive by using modern case management techniques, increasing hearing personnel, and providing full and speedy due process for all claimants," Horowitz explained. The same strategy could be used to speed the Haitian refugees toward exclusion and deportation. "By giving the refugees all the due process in the world—and fast—we can avoid our problems with the courts, and spare ourselves the budgetary and political problems involved in massive detention centers."[46] While not all members of the Reagan administration were convinced by Horowitz's proposal to "smother [Haitian] claimants with due process," it was one solution that officials were seriously considering in the late summer and fall of 1981.[47]

Because long-term immigrant detention was a new policy, the Reagan administration was forced to build a detention system virtually from scratch. In July 1981, Reagan administration officials were searching for a suitable site to establish a high capacity, long-term detention center that could hold the thousands of Haitians currently in custody plus "950 Cubans" with "problems that prevent their release into the community (250 mentally ill and retarded; 400 antisocial; 100 homosexual; 100 alcoholics and drug users; 100 women, babies, elderly, and handicapped)."[48] According to Thomas R. Maddux, when the White House reviewed the recommendations of the Task Force on Immigration, it devoted more time to the detention issue than to any other immigration question, "dedicating a discussion at a cabinet meeting on July 1, 1981, and an entire cabinet meeting on July 7 to the issue of [the detention camp] at Fort Chaffee and alternative facilities.[49] The government was seeking "placement into state and private facilities" for Cubans who were being held at Fort Chaffee in Arkansas. The Haitians presented a bigger problem. "Haitians are arriving in Florida at a rate of 1,000 to 1,500 a month," the attorney general wrote in a memo to the president. "Existing facilities in Florida are overflowing. A detention policy requires facilities for up to 10,000."[50] The government was considering the Naval Training Center in Bainbridge, Maryland; the Ellington Air Force Base in Houston, Texas; and the Port Isabel Service Processing Center in Los Fresnos, Texas (a location that would subsequently became a major center for the detention of refugees from Central America).[51] The government even considered (but ultimately ruled out) the Fort Jefferson Monument off the coast of Key West, the famed Ellis Island immigration station, and the notorious Alcatraz prison in the San Francisco Bay. Ultimately, Bainbridge or Port Isabel were the best choices, in part because they were "both in relatively isolated areas" where "community opposition is likely to be limited."[52]

By the fall, the discussion within the Reagan administration had shifted a bit due to changing circumstances, but the search for a permanent detention facility continued. The Cubans who remained at Fort Chaffee (the number was down to 574) could be transferred to a detention facility in Glasgow, Montana, a memo prepared for the president's chief of staff observed. Some of the Haitians had been transferred to a facility in Big Springs, Texas. This had provoked an "infuriated" reaction from the congressional delegation from Texas. Max Friedersdorf, head of congressional relations for the Reagan White House, reported that Texas senator John Tower "is upset (to put it mildly)."[53] Tower complained that "you have tripled the black population of Big Springs, Texas, and not even advised me in advance."[54] The transfer of Haitian detainees to Texas also risked upsetting Democratic representative Charles Stenholm, who was a backer of the president's economic program. As a result, the Haitians were sent instead to Fort Allen, Puerto Rico.[55] To meet other immediate detention requirements, the Reagan administration was considering four possible scenarios: establishing a facility at Fort Drum in Watertown, New York, or at Fort Leonard Wood near Jefferson City, Missouri, or cobbling together a system that would use the combined resources of Westover Air Force Base in Chicopee, Massachusetts; Fort Allen in Puerto Rico; Glasgow Air Force Base in Montana; and "assorted Federal prisons." The recommendation for a long-term solution was "to obtain authorization and budget to build permanent facility (for 10,000) at McAlister, Oklahoma." Citizens in McAlister had "expressed an interest in having a permanent facility, due to favorable economic impacts."[56]

To cultivate local support for the creation of its immigrant detention system, the Reagan administration drew upon many political and financial resources. In November 1981, President Reagan met with Dave Martin, a newly elected Republican member of Congress from New York's 30th District, which was home to Fort Drum. The president's notes for the meeting reiterated the belief that facilities such as Fort Drum were necessary for the administration's "overall effort to stem the flow of illegal aliens—primarily Haitians—to this country and South Florida in particular."[57] Acknowledging that it "will be difficult for you politically" to open up Fort Drum to "5,000 [a maximum of 10,000]" Haitians and other aliens "for a period of 12 to 24 months while we build a permanent facility," the president presented Martin with a quid pro quo. If Martin would pledge his support, the president promised to "build up further defense activity at Fort Drum" and to "assist you in any feasible way in your re-election campaign."[58]

Throughout the search for new detention facilities, the attorney general and other administration officials stressed that the new facilities were most needed to detain Haitians. The attorney general's talking points for a meeting with the president emphasized that "continuing illegal Haitian immigration causes overflow problems in our Florida detention facilities. . . . Justice is seeking additional facilities in the southern part of the country for this purpose. Ultimately, it is desirable to build a permanent detention center."[59] And a memo James Baker prepared for the president acknowledged that the detention system was being created for Haitians. "As part of the administration's immigration policy, a decision was made to detain aliens arriving illegally on our shores and borders," the memo noted. "The continued arrival of Haitians drives our current policy."[60]

It might seem incredible that it was the Reagan administration's response to the influx of Haitian refugees, a group that constituted less than 2 percent of all the illegal entrants to the United States, that reversed twenty-seven years of policy and formally reinstituted the policy of detention. "Why, then, institute such a controversial and costly project for such admittedly limited ends?" ask Norman L. Zucker and Naomi Flink Zucker. One answer is that some government officials considered the presence of undocumented Haitians in the United States to be far from insignificant. At a House Subcommittee Hearing on Immigration, John A. Bushnell, Carter's deputy assistant secretary for inter-American affairs, emphasized the scale of unauthorized migration from Haiti:

> Aside from Mexico, and its common border with the United States, this island of Hispaniola probably has been the source of most illegal immigration to the United States over the course of several decades. Informed estimates place the number of Haitians in the United States at between 300,000 and 400,000, a large proportion illegally.[61]

In addition, the Haitian detention policy might be seen as intended not just for Haitians but for all would-be asylum seekers. According to Zucker and Zucker, the goal of the policy of Haitian detention "was not to reduce the number of illegal entries but rather to reduce the numbers of individuals asking for asylum." Since the Reagan administration was determined "not to expand the asylum apparatus," it would need to find a way "to discourage asylum seekers," a project it initiated by targeting Haitians.[62] As Michael J. Churgin observes, "Haiti would be the test case" in employing detention and interdiction as an experiment in deterrence.[63] Zucker and Zucker observe that at a moment when a growing number of Americans "had come to regard the federal government as utterly ineffectual in stemming the tide of illegal foreign workers," even the most ambitious attempt to halt illegal immigration across the southern border, where most illegal immigration occurred, would be only partially successful. "The Haitian migration, on the other hand, could be stemmed."[64]

In his study of the U.S.-Mexico border, Peter Andreas argues that border policing is "less about achieving the stated instrumental goal of deterring illegal border crossers and more about politically recrafting the image of the border and symbolically reaffirming the state's territorial authority" by projecting "the appearance of a more secure and orderly border."[65] This was as true for Haitians along the border of South Florida as it was for Mexicans and other Latin American migrants along the U.S.-Mexico divide. The detention of asylum seekers proved useful to an administration that was looking for ways to reassert its sovereignty and was thinking far beyond Haiti and its refugees.

Critics of the Reagan administration recognized that Haitians were being singled out for detention. One flyer circulating in New York City in February 1982 informed readers that "thousands of Haitians are confined in concentration camps all over the country and in Puerto Rico" even though they "could be released while their claims for political asylum are being evaluated. Among all national groups only the Haitians have been denied this possibility." The top demand of the protest that was to take place in front of the INS detention center at Brooklyn Navy Yard was "release and political asylum for all Haitian refugees."[66]

In the summer and fall of 1981, the government's interdiction and detention policy drew the attention of national civil rights and religious organizations. In November, the National Association for the Advancement of Colored People (NAACP) sent a letter to President Reagan in which it characterized the administration's "total rejection" of Haitian refugees as a violation of the ruling in the landmark *Civiletti* case and of the Refugee Act of 1980. The letter observed that "the Immigration Service, the Justice Department, and the Executive Office of the President have continued to direct orders and actions which constitute unfair treatment of Haitian refugees." The NAACP claimed that "the Haitians alone have been singled out for a peculiar classification and treatment."[67] On December 1, the NAACP announced "as part of its campaign to free the 2700 Haitian refugees now being held in detention centers" that it was joining with the New York–based Coalition for the Defense of Haitian Refugees to organize a March on Washington to "demand freedom for Haitian refugees by Christmas." In a press release for the march, Rev. Charles Smith, the deputy executive director of the NAACP, called the Haitian interdiction and detention program "an unprecedented policy not applied to other recent refugees, such as the wave of Cubans who were admitted to these shores last year."[68]

The National Council of Churches was another organization that actively opposed the Reagan administration's treatment of Haitian refugees in 1981. The NCC linked the Haitian experience to the government's treatment of refugees from El Salvador, noting that both Salvadorans and Haitians were facing "escalated deportation and exclusion hearings" that threatened to return them to "violence and extreme repression" in their home countries. A resolution approved by the governing board of the NCC called on President Reagan to "halt immediately mass deportations and exclusion proceedings for refugees from El Salvador and Haiti until effective means of guaranteeing constitutional due process are in place and equal protection is provided similar to that accorded the Indochinese, the Cubans, and others who flee persecution."[69] In a letter to President Reagan, an Inter-Religious Council made up of leaders of the NCC, the U.S. Catholic Conference of Bishops, and the Synagogue Council of America, declared that "certainly fundamental ideals of this country have been forgotten when Haitian asylum seekers are incarcerated on a long-term basis in Federal Prisons or on isolated military facilities. This action is unprecedented in our nation's history, and it is clearly discriminatory."[70]

A hearing before the House Subcommittee on Courts, Civil Liberties, and the Administration of Justice also highlighted the unprecedented nature of the Haitian detention program and the troubling precedent it might set. On June 23, 1982, Arthur C. Helton, director of the Political Asylum Project of the Lawyers' Committee for International Human Rights, testified that the "no release detention policy [is being] applied exclusively to Haitians." Helton reminded the committee that "prior to the spring of 1981 INS policy was routinely and regularly to release virtually all aliens seeking admission to the United States including Haitian nationals."[71] But in July 1981,

The detention of Haitians was announced . . . by Attorney General Smith as part of a broader policy that also included the interdiction and forced return of Haitian boats on the high seas by the United States Coast Guard. In explaining the new policy, the Attorney General stated that 'detention of aliens seeking asylum was necessary to discourage people like the Haitians from setting sail in the first place.[72]

This "current policy of detention," Helton added, "can best be understood against a backdrop of prior governmental practices, including the 1978 'Haitian Program' which a Federal Court in Florida found to be 'offensive to every notion of constitutional due process and equal protection.'"[73] Helton added, "We oppose the construction of new facilities for asylum applicants and other aliens. The Haitian program has served only to inflame racial tensions in our society while causing unnecessary suffering."[74]

Despite such warnings, the Reagan administration replicated the Haitian Program. In fact, where Arthur C. Helton had seen a dangerous precedent, some administration officials saw opportunity. As one internal memo recognized, the administration was laying the groundwork for a detention system that could absorb many more groups in the future. "Alien detention requirements are not expected to diminish in the future. Regardless of the Haitian population, further influxes of illegal aliens can be expected and this administration should be prepared to deal with its future detention requirements," notes a report prepared for the president's chief of staff.[75] And prepared it was. One year after the Reagan administration initiated its policy of mandatory detention for all Haitians subject to exclusion, it broadened the policy to mandate imprisonment for all refugees lacking authorization to enter the country. Soon thousands of Salvadorans and Guatemalans who were fleeing Reagan administration-backed violence in Central America would join the Haitians in a growing network of immigrant prisons.

4

Construction of and Resistance to the Detention Regime, 1981–1991

Maxine Petit-Frére had been imprisoned for six months. When the 24-year-old builder from Port-au-Prince had refused to build a house for a member of the Tonton Macoute, members of the paramilitary force accused him of "questioning the government" and tried to kill him. Petit-Frére managed to escape aboard a flimsy boat sailing for the United States. After a seventeen-day journey, he arrived in Florida, where he was arrested, placed in detention, and ultimately transferred to a federal penitentiary in frigid Ray Brook, New York, where he remained in February 1982.

Petit-Frére's tragic odyssey was featured in a February 1, 1982, *Newsweek* article on Haitian detention entitled "Refugees or Prisoners?" The article informed readers that "Maxine Petit-Frére is not alone. There are 2,177 Haitians currently in detention in the United States at seventeen locations from subarctic New York State to sunny Puerto Rico" in conditions that "the Haitians say . . . resemble nothing so much as concentration camps."[1]

Maxine Petit-Frére may have been among the Haitian detainees transferred to one of the various detention camps from the already notorious Krome Avenue Detention Center in Miami. Just over a month earlier, Krome had been the site of a dramatic confrontation between supporters of the imprisoned refugees and their jailers. In a campaign to free the Haitian refugees by Christmas, activists in Miami staged a series of protests outside the gates of Krome. Inside the facility, nearly all of the 730 detainees were engaged in a hunger strike to demand their freedom. When the nearly 700 protesters outside heard rumors that the weakened hunger strikers were being denied medical care, they stormed the gate, clashing with guards and freeing more than 100 prisoners before Krome guards, U.S. Border Patrol officers, and the metro police suppressed the insurrection.[2]

The clash at Krome was only the latest episode in an escalating conflict over detention at Krome. Repeated breakout attempts had freed eighty-six prisoners over the preceding months. The first rebellion among Haitian prisoners at Krome occurred in September 1981, when reports that officials were preparing to transfer more detainees to Fort Allen in Puerto Rico, and to a facility at Glasgow, Montana, sparked a violent conflict in which detainees attacked guards and tore down a fence, allowing nearly 100 prisoners to escape into the surrounding Everglades. In the aftermath of the September incident, immigration officials ordered a riot-trained "react squad" of Border Patrol agents to guard against future rebellions by the increasingly restive population. The "troublemakers" and "malcontents" thought to be leaders of the rebellion were transferred to a federal prison in Otisville, New York, and other facilities far from Miami.[3]

Resistance among Haitian prisoners was spreading to other detention sites as well. Haitians imprisoned at a federal prison in Lexington, Kentucky, carried out a Christmas hunger strike for freedom. Earlier in December, eighty-eight Haitian prisoners at Fort Allen had engaged in an eleven-hour standoff with the facility's guards to prevent the removal of the body of 30-year-old Innocent Miclisse, whose unexplained death they feared officials would either label a suicide or simply cover up. Two weeks later, Haitian detainees at Fort Allen erupted in a full-scale rebellion. And on New Year's Eve, the two dozen Haitians being held in the Leesburg city jail in Central Florida (including Eduard St. Jean, who had been transferred to the facility after leaping out of a taxiing plane set to carry him to Puerto Rico) launched a hunger strike. The string of incidents was significant enough to invite comment by the Reagan administration. Associate Attorney General Rudolph Giuliani warned that such actions "can't and shouldn't affect us" as he pledged to "continue in our resolve to enforce the law."[4]

The increasing violence at Krome and other detention sites and the imprisonment of thousands of Haitians in a far-flung network of jails and prisons was the result of the Reagan administration's new Haitian detention policy. As the administration entered its second year in office, a growing number of people were starting to see the troubling implications of the return of detention. Prison reform expert Michael Kroll observed that "the full and startling effects of a new U.S. immigration policy are slowly emerging." The U.S. government was using "indefinite detention—the long-term imprisonment of aliens who have committed no crime except to seek asylum" as a tool "to discourage further flight to the United States from nearby nations experiencing unrest."[5] Yale law professor Peter Schuck told readers of the *Columbia Law Review* that "the mass, routine incarceration of aliens, sometimes for long periods of time and often under overcrowded and unpleasant conditions, has once again become a fundament of our immigration policy."[6] And a *New York Times* editorial likened the long-term detention of Haitians to "the detention of Japanese-Americans in World War II" and called for the Haitians' release. "After a year of imprisonment, and with no end in sight, conscience calls out for relief," the *Times* editorial declared.[7]

Throughout the 1980s, Haitians and their supporters used a range of tactics in their calls for freedom from detention. The legal challenges Haitians and their advocates brought throughout the decade were the most significant obstacle to the Reagan administration's detention regime, and it was in the courts that the government and the opponents of the detention regime waged the most important battles over the legality and constitutionality of the detention policy. But the contest over detention played out in the realm of politics as well, from the halls of Congress to the streets of Miami and New York and in the prisons, jails, and detention centers across the country, where the detained asylum seekers and undocumented immigrants offered major resistance.

Although the campaign of legal and political challenges and direct resistance succeeded in repeatedly throwing up obstacles to the government's detention program, it failed to reverse the policy. In fact, despite these challenges, in the first ten years after the return of detention, the policy became more entrenched: each challenge led to the development of a more resilient legal, political, and economic rationale for its existence. By the fall of 1991, a decade after Reagan administration officials reinstituted the policy, the detention regime had expanded to an extent that might have impressed even the most ambitious of the policy's early promoters.

The First Decade of Detention

When Ronald Reagan took office in January 1981, hundreds of Cuban and Haitian refugees that had come during the refugee crisis of the previous year were in detention. While many of those eligible for parole under the special entrant status had been released and resettled, most of those who remained in detention did not qualify for the entrant program. Although the influx of Cubans had slowed dramatically by the fall of 1980, the arrival of Haitians continued. In the period October 1, 1980, to May 1, 1981, 5,529 Haitians arrived in the United

States.[8] Several hundred Cuban *marielitos* with criminal records whom the U.S. government would not release and the Cuban government would not allow to return to Cuba were also being held in detention. However, when Reagan took office, the practice of immigration detention was being applied primarily to Haitian asylum seekers. The flow of unauthorized migration from Haiti continued into the spring and summer of 1981.

To staunch the flow of Haitians to U.S. shores and to deter future asylum seekers from trying to reach the United States, President Reagan introduced the dual policies of interdiction and detention. In May 1981, the INS began applying a policy of detention to all Haitian arrivals, which the Reagan administration claimed the right to do under Section 235(b) of the Immigration and Naturalization Act of 1952. The act stated that aliens "who may not appear to the examining immigration officer at the port of arrival to be clearly and beyond a doubt entitled to land shall be detained for further inquiry to be conducted by a special inquiry officer."[9]

Throughout the summer, hundreds of new Haitian arrivals were sent to U.S. immigration detention facilities. Overcrowding was so severe at Krome North, which by July held 1,530 Haitians, that officials began transferring the Haitian prisoners to Bureau of Prison facilities and jails across the country and to Fort Allen in Puerto Rico, which the Reagan administration reopened in August 1981.[10] At this moment, legal scholars Mary Bosworth and Emma Kaufman observe, "in Krome and places like it, the federal government effectively reinvented an immigration imprisonment practice that had died out when Ellis Island closed its doors in 1954."[11]

By the summer of 1982 more than 2,000 Haitians occupied a growing network of detention facilities. The majority of the detainees were being held at Krome North in Miami and at Fort Allen in Puerto Rico. But nearly 700 Haitian detainees were scattered across the country, in federal penitentiaries in Florida, Kentucky, New York, Texas, West Virginia, and Missouri, and in jails and even hospitals and other makeshift centers throughout the nation.[12]

Arthur C. Helton, director of the Political Asylum Project for the Lawyers Committee for Human Rights, offered a portrait of the conditions under which detainees were confined:

Confinement occurs under isolated and depressing conditions. . . . The detainees, most of whom do not speak English, are isolated from family and friends. They are unable to communicate with other aliens, or the authorities, including medical personnel. The physical conditions of confinement vary, depending on the facility, but are generally similar to prison conditions. . . . Boredom is excruciating. Overcrowding is a recurrent problem. In protest of long-term confinement, there are suicides and hunger strikes.[13]

Under these miserable conditions, thirty-one people attempted suicide at Krome in a four-month period from February to June 1982. The most common method of attempted suicide, officials noted, was "attempted hanging," but other common methods were "ingestion of crushed glass," "ingestion of toxic liquid," and "self-laceration."[14] INS spokesperson Duke Austin was dismissive about the significance of the suicide attempts. Of course long-term detention can "put a strain on anybody's mind," Austin allowed, but "they don't have to be detained, they can go back to Haiti."[15]

One year after the initiation of the new Haitian detention program, the imprisoned Haitians and their advocates sued the Reagan administration. The

Figure 4. Separated by detention, Krome, ca. 1981. Photo by Gary Monroe. Used by permission.

plaintiffs argued that the detention policy was illegal, in part because in implementing the new policy, the government had not complied with the Administrative Procedures Act, which required public notification and a period of public comment on the new rule. The plaintiffs also held that since the detention program applied to Haitians alone, it was discriminatory and thus illegal. In order to meet its requirements under the Administrative Procedures Act and to nullify the court's ability to block the government's detention program on the grounds of discrimination, the Reagan administration publicly announced that it was expanding the policy of mandatory detention to include *all* inadmissible aliens. In July 1982, the government issued an interim rule that announced the expanded detention policy: "aliens who appear to be inadmissible, and who have false or no documentation, and/or who arrive at places other than designated ports of entry, will be detained by the [Immigration and Naturalization] Service under Section 235(b) of the [Immigration and Naturalization] Act." Although the new rule continued to allow the exercise of the parole authority for "emergent reasons" or when "strictly in the public interest" (including "serious medical conditions, pregnant women, certain juveniles, aliens with close family relatives in the United States, [and] other unusual situations warranting parole"), the new rule provided the legal basis for a dramatic expansion of the immigration detention system.[16] Over the protests of the United Nations High Commissioner for Refugees, who argued that the rule violated the Refugee Act of 1980 and the United Nations Protocol relating to the Status of Refugees, the INS issued a final rule on October 19, 1982, that formalized the blanket detention policy.[17]

Even before the Reagan administration publicly announced its blanket detention policy, it was planning for the system's expansion. Briefing materials for a March 1982 meeting of top Reagan administration staff laid out the problem as they saw it. The federal prison system was seventeen percent over capacity, due, in large part, to the Haitian detainees and the 400 long-term Cuban prisoners whom it could not return to Cuba, the report noted. The brief added, the "administration is under constant pressure to relieve overcrowding in prisons and to remove Haitians from Miami." INS detention facilities were "filled to capacity," and "longer term detention requirements will continue," particularly since "a very real possibility exists of other major movements of illegal entrants from Central America and the Caribbean into the United States during the next several years." As a result, administration officials were seeking funding for new prisons and a long-term INS detention facility.[18]

In May the Reagan administration submitted a request to Congress for $35 million for two new 1,000-bed detention facilities. The new facilities were to be built and managed by the Bureau of Prisons. The request prompted a House subcommittee hearing on the detention of aliens in Bureau of Prisons facilities.

Robert W. Kastenmeir, a Democrat from Wisconsin who chaired the Subcommittee on Courts, Civil Liberties, and the Administration of Justice of the House Judiciary Committee, opened the hearing by questioning the administration's practice of placing Haitians in federal prisons. "Since last summer when the detention policy was changed, the administration asked the Bureau of Prisons to assume an active role in detaining approximately 600 Haitians" while "another 1,400 are in INS camps," observed Kastenmeir. Even though "none of these Haitians, as far as this subcommittee knows, are considered dangerous, nor do they have criminal backgrounds," they "are being placed in medium security prisons." This action on the part of the government had reversed the "general policy of releasing aliens pending immigration matters," a policy that had been in place "from 1954 until last summer" and "was and still is, a wise policy," Kastenmeir argued.[19]

> I seriously question the need to incarcerate Haitians or any other immigrant group pending resolution of their immigration status, particularly where claims for political asylum are made. . . . The overburdened criminal justice system, it would seem, does not need to have the nonviolent asylum seekers crowding its prisons, nor do taxpayers faced with a failing economy, need to be paying $37 million this year to detain such asylum seekers, nor to pay another $35 million to build new prisons for noncriminal aliens.[20]

To defend its detention program and to justify the funding request for new detention centers, the Reagan administration once again called upon its associate attorney general, Rudolph Giuliani. The new detention centers were "urgently needed if we are to be able to adequately enforce our immigration laws," Giuliani testified. Overcrowding in INS and contract detention facilities "has resulted in less and less use of the INS enforcement branches" and in "relaxed policies of bond or release on personal recognizance. As a result, enforcement of final orders of deportation remains low due to the failure of many aliens to appear for deportation. This situation can no longer be tolerated." The new facilities would allow the administration to respond to expected increases in illegal aliens over the coming years. Giuliani argued that "the Bureau of Prisons is the Attorney General's detention expert . . . experienced in both short-term and long-term detention."[21]

But what about the "healthy skepticism" and "great deal of apprehension" many Americans had about "the political implications of authorizing such detention centers?" Had the administration considered "the prospects for long-term, or short-term . . . detention of people who have not committed a crime in the normal sense of the word?" Kastenmeir asked. "We presently have an underground population of 3.5 to 6 million illegal aliens that actually wreak havoc in certain parts of our country," Giuliani responded, "and it has to stop somewhere and sometime." What's more, the government's treatment of Haitians could be a model for how to solve the immigration problem. The Reagan administration believed that its program of preemptive exclusion and punitive detention was having the deterrent effect it had intended, allowing it to regain territorial control and reassert its sovereignty. Giuliani claimed that "with the institution of a detention program, [and] with the institution of interdiction" for "Haitian aliens," the rate of arrival had dropped to just about zero. "We think we have returned or restored some degree of control to the United States about who comes in, about how many people come in, when they come in, and under what circumstances they should come in."[22]

As members of Congress examined the Reagan administration's proposal, they knew it was important to ascertain how the treatment of immigrant detainees might be shaped by the fact that they would be held in facilities operated by the Bureau of Prisons rather than the INS. "Do you deal with these detainees, who are detained for various reason, any differently than you do a prisoner assigned to your facility?" Chairman Kastenmeir asked Norman A. Carlson, the director of the Federal Bureau of Prisons.

MR. CARLSON. We try to keep them separate from convicted felons, for obvious reasons . . . [but] in terms of the facilities that are provided— the medical care, the food, all the other related activities—there is absolutely no difference. In addition, we try to develop programs to keep them occupied as constructively as we possibly can while they are in detention.

MR. KASTENMEIR. But you do that for prisoners as well, do you not?

MR. CARLSON. That's right.

MR. KASTENMEIR. So the only real difference is that they are separated or segregated from your prison populations in these facilities?

MR. CARLSON. Insofar as possible, that's right

MR. KASTENMEIR. So, in all other respects, they are prisoners just like the other prisoners?

MR. CARLSON. That is correct.[23]

Although administrative detention meant that detainees were not supposed to be subject to the same system as prisoners incarcerated as punishment for crimes, their experience in the prison system was virtually indistinguishable from that of other prisoners.

Ultimately the Reagan administration failed in its bid to open the two proposed Bureau of Prisons detention facilities, but it was able to continue to expand its detention network by other means. By July 1984, the INS-operated facilities held 1,714 detainees, and the Reagan administration was continuing its practice of placing detainees who did not fit into the INS facilities in over 900 state and local jails.[24]

Nearly 60 percent of those in INS facilities in 1984 came from countries with high numbers of asylum requests, suggesting that well into the 1980s long-term detention continued to primarily affect asylum seekers.[25] Bill Frelick, policy analyst for the U.S. Committee for Refugees, notes that long-term detention was the government's response to a historic shift in refugee movements to North America. "Before 1975," Frelick writes, "the United States received about 200 asylum applications per year; in 1985, the number had grown to more than 16,000, and in 1988, more than 50,000 asylum applications were received." But the numbers "only tell part of the story. Refugees coming to North America in the 1980s are more likely than previous refugee influxes to come from the Third World, to be dark-skinned, non-English speaking, and poor . . . often from Central America and the Caribbean." They are more likely to bypass "established channels for 'processing' limited numbers of refugees from overseas."[26] The changing character and volume of refugee movements provides the backdrop for the government's decision to use immigration detention in the United States.

In the 1980s, a growing number of those in detention were refugees from Central America who were fleeing bloody civil wars and the activities of U.S.-backed death squads in El Salvador, Guatemala, and Nicaragua. The INS responded to the influx of Central American refugees by increasingly focusing its detention policy along the U.S.-Mexico border to catch asylum seekers it labeled OTMs (other than Mexicans).[27] As the number of Central American refugees in detention grew, Salvadorans and their advocates joined with Haitians at key stages in the campaign for freedom, asylum, and the end of detention.

The number of INS detention facilities continued to grow for the rest of the decade. By October 1985, INS detention facilities were holding 2,200 to 2,300 prisoners on any given day. By 1986, the number of INS detention facilities had grown from five to seven and the government was holding immigrant detainees in more than 1,000 additional detention facilities, including federal prisons, state and local jails, and privately owned detention centers.[28] The U.S. Committee for Refugees reported that the number of aliens in INS detention as of April had grown to 3,025, and that this group included Afghans, Iranians, and Salvadorans in addition to Haitians and Cubans.[29] The government also created the Alien Border Control Committee, which prepared an emergency detention scenario it called the "South Florida Plan."[30]

In April 1986, the first high-capacity immigration detention center opened in Oakdale, Louisiana, and forty-six detainees were transferred there. The *New York Times* reported on this milestone in the government's expanding detention program, noting that the 300-acre, $17.5 million facility "has the capacity for more aliens than the rest of the facilities combined." It was built to house 1,300 but was capable of holding between 6,000 and 7,000 detainees under emergency conditions. It was "the largest alien detention center in the nation and the first one built to be run jointly by the United States Bureau of Prisons and the Immigration and Naturalization Service."[31]

Opponents of the government's detention program decried the opening of Oakdale as the worst-yet instance of a program that separated detainees from their communities and from much-needed legal assistance. "These people are utterly abandoned, innocent people, ripped off the streets and put into a prison in the middle of Louisiana," argued Rev. Ted Keating, a Roman Catholic priest and staff lawyer with Ecumenical Immigration Services. "This [detention center] will create tremendous social needs. These people are not criminals. It's called a detention center. But it is a United States prison." Immigration officials characterized the purpose of Oakdale differently. "We are overwhelmed with illegal aliens in the United States," argued Leonard E. Rowland, an Oakdale-based immigration official, "and to apprehend and detain them we need additional bed space to be able to house them humanely and properly." As evidence of the humane and proper treatment they planned for Oakdale detainees, prison officials cited their plan to offer recreational activities, prison work (for eleven to thirty-eight cents an hour), and Spanish classes. No English classes would be offered, however, because, the warden's assistant commented, "that only equips them to be better aliens."[32]

The process by which Oakdale, Louisiana, was selected as the location for the high-capacity detention center illuminates another side of the politics surrounding immigration detention. When the Reagan administration made its initial request for two new facilities in 1982, it proposed that they be located in Petersburg, Virginia, and El Reno, Oklahoma. But members of both communities opposed locating the detention centers in their communities. One El Reno resident wrote to Representative Kastenmeir that "we in El Reno are having this federal detention center pushed down our necks."[33] Opposition was stronger and more organized in Prince George County, Virginia, where the Petersburg detention center was to be built. Residents of Prince George County were worried about "increased crime and a continued influx of friends and relatives of illegal aliens being detained" at the center. They were concerned about "a recent Supreme Court decision that mandated the provision of education for the children of illegal aliens . . . who may be attracted here as a result of the center's location," wrote county administrator John G. Kines Jr. to Virginia member of Congress M. Caldwell Butler. Fearful that the presence of illegal aliens in their community might "drain our resources and harm the quality of life," the Prince George County Board of Supervisors unanimously approved a resolution opposing the location of a detention center in their area. Instead, they suggested that the center be built "in an area that is isolated from major population centers, or in areas of heavy alien concentration."[34]

By 1986, the Reagan administration had located a site in Oakdale, Louisiana, that was approximately 200 miles from the two closest population centers, New Orleans and Houston. And unlike residents in Petersburg and El Reno, residents of Oakdale eagerly sought the detention facility, hoping that it would bring jobs and money to a community hurt by a declining lumber industry. To residents of Oakdale, bringing a high-capacity detention center to their community generated "hope in the face of severe economic hardship," claimed the town's mayor, George B. Mowad. As the government's detention program grew, the Oakdale mayor cheerfully forecast that the town was gaining access to "a recession-proof industry."[35]

In 1988, the number of INS facilities increased to eight. These detention centers could house 3,239 under normal conditions and 8,239 in emergency conditions.[36] Reagan's successor, George H. W. Bush expanded the detention network further, particularly in the Lower Rio Grande Valley in South Texas, where, beginning in February 1989, the INS carried out a concentrated campaign to deter Central American refugees from coming to the United States by implementing a policy of mass detention. Following the blueprint created by the Haitian Program of the late 1970s and the Haitian detention program of 1981, the South Texas program mandated detention for all people who applied for political asylum but who were rejected at an initial screening. This was a reversal of a practice the INS had begun one year earlier when the agency had paroled certain asylum applicants and allowed them to travel to other areas of the country. The South Texas detention policy, which the Lawyers Committee for Human Rights attacked as a violation of constitutional and international law, raised the number of aliens in INS custody to 7,500. Timothy J. Dunn observes that this policy resulted in "the detention of thousands of men, women, and children in the valley for months at a time."[37] In 1990, Congress passed the Immigration Act of 1990, which strengthened the government's detention powers. By 1991, there were nine INS detention centers, a response to a new population of Mexicans immigrants who represented a growing proportion of those who were detained.[38]

The growth of the government's detention program from 1981 to 1991 was dramatic. But INS-operated detention centers, jails, and federal prisons were not the only institutions holding immigrant detainees in the 1980s. From 1984 onward, privately owned detention centers made up an increasingly important part of the government's detention network.

A Growth Industry

The first private prisons in the United States were immigration detention facilities. While the government had long employed private services for healthcare and other needs within its prisons and had contracted with private firms to provide guards in its immigration detention facilities, until the mid-1980s, the institutions themselves had not been privately owned and operated. But in 1983, the Reagan administration, desperate for detention space to relieve the overcrowding in INS facilities and federal prisons, offered a contract to the recently founded Corrections Corporation of America (CCA). Because the CCA's Houston detention facility would not be ready until the following year, the company locked up its first immigrant detainees in a motel, which proved to be less than secure when some of the prisoners escaped through the holes designed to contain the air conditioning units. Despite this rather inauspicious start, CCA went on to become the largest private prison company in the country.[39]

Founded in Nashville in 1983 by a group of businessmen headed by Thomas W. Beasley, the former chair of the Tennessee Republican Party, CCA was modeled on the for-profit Hospital Corporation of America. Beasley and his associates had no particular expertise in the field of corrections, but they correctly predicted that it was the right moment to be in the business of incarceration. Prisons could be a business like any other, CCA founder Thomas Beasley claimed: "You just sell it like you were selling cars, or real estate, or hamburgers." CCA also had the backing of powerful political figures in their home state, including Tennessee governor Lamar Alexander, who insisted, "We don't need to be afraid in America of people who want to make a profit."[40] But the CCA's bid to buy the state's entire prison system for $250 million was ultimately unsuccessful, so its first prison was located not in Tennessee, but in Houston, Texas, where it opened an immigration detention center in 1984.[41]

The number of private immigration prisons rose rapidly over the next six years as the growth of private detention facilities mirrored the growth of INS-operated facilities. In 1984, Wackenhut, another firm that would become a major player in the world of privatized prisons, opened an immigration detention facility in Aurora, Colorado. In 1985, the CCA opened another immigration detention center in Laredo, Texas. Eclectic Communications, Inc. opened two private facilities in 1986, one in Los Angeles and another in El Centro, California, that was designed specifically to hold women and children. Other private firms that received government contracts to hold immigrant detainees in the 1980s included GEO Group, Behavioral Systems Southwest, and Management and Training Corporation. At the end of the decade, two more private immigration detention centers were opened in New York City and in Seattle to serve the government's detention needs along the coasts. All in all, seven private immigration detention centers operated throughout the 1980s. By 1988, the private detention centers had the capacity to hold more than 4,000 detainees (or more than 9,000 under emergency conditions). At the end of the decade the average number of immigrant detainees in private facilities on any given day was approximately 500 (one-fourth of the those detained in the United States).[42]

And although the first private prisons in the United States were immigration detention centers, soon other facilities were also privatized. The growth of privatized prisons in the United States generated intense debate. The *New*

York Times reported in February 1985 that "about two dozen major correction facilities are owned or operated by private groups," a number the American Correctional Institute expected to double in the next eighteen months. "Critics question the concept of making a profit on incarceration and ask whether it is compatible with the administration of justice," the article noted. "We're talking about taking away people's liberties, and I have real questions about the propriety of anyone but the state doing that," stated Mark A. Cuniff, executive director of the National Association of Criminal Justice Planners. Critics also had concerns about the treatment of prisoners, particularly immigrant detainees, in private facilities. Immigrant detainees were often forced to work, often for as little as one dollar a day. Private firms won prison contracts on the basis of their claims that they could operate the facilities for much less than the government had done. But critics wondered where the cost savings would come from. Answers to their question soon emerged. In one Houston facility, two immigrant detainees were crowded with fourteen other detainees into a twelve-by-twenty-foot cell for two days. They tried to escape and were shot by a private security guard who had not been trained in the use of firearms. The incident buttressed fears that an emphasis on profits might lead to cutting corners on facilities and staff training.[43]

Not everyone shared these concerns about the spread of private prisons. When private prisons emerged, the federal prison system was well known to be overcrowded, underfunded, and notorious for the poor treatment and poor living conditions it subjected prisoners to. One report that examined the "prison for profit" alternative noted that when private corporations claimed that they could "build institutions faster and cheaper, run them more efficiently, and still make a profit on what they charge the state," many were prepared to give them that chance. "Our basic mission is to provide correctional services to government in an efficient, cost-effective manner," claimed CCA vice-president Travis Snellings. Ted Nissen, president of Behavioral Systems Southwest, stated, "The work done in the public sector in the last thirty years has been a dismal failure." Nissen pledged to keep recidivism rates for the inmates who passed through his institutions well below the national average. Claims that private prisons could remedy the inhumane treatment of prisoners in government-operated institutions by easing overcrowding and improving conditions appealed to supporters of prison reform. And the offer of lucrative government contracts and the ability to exploit prisoner labor appealed to investors and shareholders.[44]

The spread of private immigration prisons and the expansion of the government's immigration detention network must also be seen within the broader context of mass incarceration system in the United States that began to take shape with the launching of the war on crime in the mid-1960s. Elizabeth Hinton has shown that by the 1980s, a bipartisan effort to wage war on crime had led to rising rates of arrest and incarceration during the war on drugs. Rooted in long-held notions of black pathology and criminality, the effort to supervise and control low-income communities of color would eventually produce the modern carceral state. According to Hinton, "relying on the strategies, institutions, and bureaucracy developed at the state and local levels during the War on Crime's first fifteen years, Reagan made the national law enforcement program far more punitive by the end of the 1980s . . . and opened up what had previously been a domestic War on Crime to the military by extending surveillance and patrol to the nation's border." Ultimately, the "vast and ever-expanding network of institutions responsible for maintaining social control in post-Jim Crow America . . . metastasized into the modern carceral state."[45] The same punitive turn that would ultimately throw millions of Americans of color into prisons produced the punitive turn in immigration policy and the immigration detention wing of the carceral state.

In addition to the racialized notions of criminality and the broader punitive turn in American politics and society, the rise of immigration detention and the construction of the broader carceral state overlapped in another important way. Both rested on the idea that the state must protect the rights of those whose claims were legitimate, particularly when they were threatened or undermined by groups who could not claim the same set of rights or state entitlements. As Julilly Kohler-Hausmann observes, Americans who wanted to see a strong response to social disorder "accused the state of protecting the rights of criminals and other outsiders at the expense of 'taxpaying' and 'law-abiding citizens.'" Kohler-Hausmann adds that "the sentiment that the state no longer served the right people was particularly resonant in an era marked by government interventions on behalf of women, people of color, and other traditionally marginalized groups." As these rights-based arguments evolved amid an intensifying war on crime, the corollary that "those who commit crimes forfeited their ability to make claims on the state" added further legitimacy to state efforts to punish those who lacked rights.[46] While this process led authorities to target Americans classified as criminal or dependent (deeply racialized, gendered, and class-based categories that ultimately led the nation's prisons to be filled with poor people of color), it also had a lasting influence on immigration policy and the rise of immigration detention. As immigrants were increasingly characterized as "criminal aliens," and even asylum seekers and refugees were treated as lawbreakers, the government's exclusion and imprisonment of unauthorized migrants could be cast as the state fulfilling its mandate to protect deserving citizens from the undeserving and those lacking in rights.

The federal prison population soared under Reagan. This development was part of a trend that preceded Reagan and that would continue well beyond Reagan's two terms in office. From 1973, when incarceration rates began to rise, to 1990, the combined state and federal prison population rose by 293 percent, surging by 58,700 inmates in a single year, from 1989 to 1990. At the same time, local jail populations were also rising rapidly. By 2001, the number of inmates in U.S. jails and prisons had reached nearly 2 million, up from roughly 500,000 when Reagan took office in 1980.[47]

A large part of this immense increase in incarceration rates stemmed from legislation that criminalized drug possession and its sale and that imposed mandatory minimum sentences on a wide range of drug-related offenses. While the war on drugs was a major reason for the overall rise in incarceration rates in the United States during the 1980s and the years that followed, the government's anti-drug campaign also drove the growth of immigration detention. In 1986, for example, the passage of the Anti-Drug Abuse Act drove up inmate populations in both immigration and non-immigration facilities. The launching of the INS's Alien Criminal Apprehension Program in the same year further contributed to the growth of the government's immigration detention program. Two years later, Congress passed another piece of anti-drug legislation that increased the use of mandatory detention for immigrants and widened the range of deportable offenses. During the 1980s, the marriage of anti-drug and anti-immigrant initiatives was carried forward, journalist Mark Dow observes, by political rhetoric that "brought together two indefensible enemies of the state: the criminal, especially the drug criminal, and the alien."[48]

As the war on drugs expanded, the carceral capacity of the nation neared its limits. To relieve the overcrowding on the nation's prisons, the Reagan administration introduced the Criminal Alien Program, which, Patrisia Macías-Rojas observes, "was designed to purge noncitizens from dangerously overcrowded jails and prisons" by sending them to detention facilities to await deportation. Macías-Rojas sees the introduction and subsequent expansion of the Criminal Alien Program as a pivotal moment that "quietly set off a punitive turn in immigration enforcement that has fundamentally altered detention, deportation, and criminal prosecutions for immigration violations." Macías-Rojas's finding that "the criminal alien mandate stemmed from a desire not to control migration but to free up bed space in the criminal justice system" demonstrates another way that immigration detention was closely related to what Macías-Rojas calls "the hyperincarceration of Black and Latina/o youth."[49]

As a result of the increasing tendency to criminalize immigrants as part of the broader wars on crime and drugs, government officials labeled a growing proportion of the immigration detention population "criminal aliens," a category of detainees that was different from that of asylum seekers and included undocumented immigrants, those authorized to be in the United States, and even legal permanent residents. "Criminal aliens" were confined for drug-related offenses and a wide range of other crimes, some serious and some not so serious.[50] To meet this substantial law enforcement challenge, Congress authorized a huge expansion of the INS, increasing its funding by 185 percent, from $283.1 million in 1978 to $807.8 million in 1988. Congressional appropriation for costs related to detention and deportation grew by 191 percent from 1980 to 1988.[51]

Public policy that relied on incarceration as a method of dealing with the problems of drugs and illegal immigration left public officials scrambling to build jails and prisons to keep up with the exploding prisoner population. Douglas C. McDonald notes that this problem was occurring at the same time that "citizen movements to limit taxation and public indebtedness sharply narrowed public administrators' latitude to build and spend."[52] These citizens' movements often emphasized placing limits on government and favored privatization of public services as the means of achieving reduced governmental power. Private prisons and private immigration detention facilities thus emerged as the solution to the dilemma of increasing demand for law enforcement amid dwindling public resources. As they carried their campaign forward, opponents of immigration detention would have to contend not just with public officials and policymakers who endorsed detention as an immigration enforcement mechanism but also with a private prison lobby that maintained a significant financial stake in the continuation of the detention system.

"A Cruel and Questionable Policy"

Human rights and refugee organizations condemned the government's use of detention to deter asylum seekers as a violation of human rights standards and international and domestic law. And since long-term detention was ordinarily imposed on asylum seekers while they were in exclusion or deportation proceedings, the organizations' critique of the government's detention practices was often expressed as part of a broader concern about the United States' treatment of asylum seekers.

Throughout the 1980s, one of the most prominent critics of the U.S. government's treatment of asylum seekers was the United Nations High Commissioner for Refugees (UNHCR). In the early 1980s, the Office of the UNHCR observed "a growing tendency of states to detain and expel asylum seekers" and, according to UNHCR legal advisor Guy S. Goodwin Gill, to engage in restrictive practices "sometimes in the form of policies or so-called 'humane deterrence' under which refugees and asylum seekers are deliberately detained for indefinite periods." Goodwin-Gill noted that this detention was especially troubling because "next to life itself, liberty of the person and freedom of movement are among the most precious of human rights." Such treatment violated the UN charter and the principles of the Universal Declaration of Human Rights and subsequent human rights treaties, Goodwin-Gill declared, reminding the international community that "states are bound by a complex set of duties with regard to the treatment to be accorded to persons within their territory and jurisdiction." And "the fact that those detained are refugees, asylum seekers, or even ordinary aliens does not expose them to treatment at will by sovereign states," Goodwin-Gill concluded. "The detention of refugees and asylum seekers is never an appropriate solution to their plight."[53]

The U.S. Committee for Refugees echoed the UNHCR's concerns, warning that "a growing restrictiveness toward all aliens has swept refugees and asylum seekers into its net." Many of the Haitians and Salvadorans, two of the largest groups in U.S. detention facilities, met the international standard for refugees, "owing to a well-founded fear of persecution." Yet they were among the groups the U.S. government was least likely to grant asylum. In the period June 1983 to September 1986, the government granted asylum to only 2.6 percent of Salvadoran asylum seekers and 1.8 percent of Haitian asylum seekers. While they awaited their eventual denial of asylum, the U.S. Committee for Refugees argued, Salvadorans and Haitians endured "long-term incarceration," which violated the United Nations Protocol on Refugees, the Refugee Act of 1980, and the due process guarantees of the U.S. Constitution.[54]

The Lawyers Committee for Human Rights concurred with these opinions, calling the U.S. government's use of detention of asylum seekers "a cruel and questionable policy."[55] Arthur C. Helton, director of the Political Asylum Project of the Lawyers Committee for Human Rights, argued that because the government's detention policy was "incompatible with the parole provisions of the Immigration and Nationality Act, the Refugee Act, the fifth amendment to the United States Constitution, and the Protocol relating to the Status of Refugees," the policy must cease. "Only by eliminating the detention policy will the human rights of refugees and other aliens be vindicated."[56]

Despite these strong criticisms from refugee and human rights organizations, the Reagan administration maintained its policies regarding asylum and detention. Gil Loescher and John Scanlan note that despite its advocacy on behalf of asylum seekers, the United Nations High Commissioner for Refugees had "no influence in asylum decision-making in the U.S."[57] The detention regime continued to grow in spite of the public campaigns of its opponents. Reagan administration officials such as INS commissioner Alan Nelson steadfastly defended the government's practices. After fifty-six members of Congress sent a letter to Attorney General Smith in May 1982 that called on the Reagan administration to end its detention of Haitian refugees, Commissioner Nelson responded, calling the government's detention policy "fair and reasonable," "humane," and "critical to the fair and firm enforcement of our immigration law."[58] The president continued to warn the American people that "we've lost control of our borders, and no nation can do that and survive," seeming to justify the harsh treatment of illegal aliens.[59] It was clear that because the U.S. government refused to be moved by political pressure, the most consequential struggles over immigration detention would take place not in the court of public opinion but in the courts of law.

"Hammering at the Gate": The Legal Struggle over Detention

Almost as soon the Reagan administration launched its detention program, detained refugees and their advocates began challenging the policy in the courts. Among the first major legal challenges to the new detention practices, "the most important cases involved Haitians," legal scholars Thomas Alexander Aleinikoff, David A. Martin and Hiroshi Motomura note, "even though other groups such as Salvadorans and Guatemalans, were also affected."[60] Subsequently, key litigation in the struggle over the policy would be brought by other groups.

The litigation that challenged the detention program and the government's treatment of asylum seekers in the early 1980s challenged the foundations of immigration law. Observing the monumental change that was under way, noted immigration law expert Peter H. Schuck observed in 1984 that "sturdy redoubts of classical immigration law," including "a restrictive notion of national community; extraordinary judicial deference; the extraconstitutional status of exclusion . . . [and] broad detention power . . . [are] under siege today." But Schuck believed the outcome of the legal contest between detained asylum seekers and the U.S. government was far from certain.

> Capitulation seems only a matter of time for some of these doctrines, while for others the outcome remains highly uncertain. The forces of change, however, are insistently hammering at the gate, threatening the autonomy and insularity that have long sheltered classical immigration law from developments elsewhere in the legal culture.[61]

The cause of the current moment of immense change was clear, Professor Schuck argued.

> No single development has animated and shaped the current transformation of immigration law more powerfully than the massive influx and subsequent detention of aliens from Cuba, Haiti, El Salvador and other Caribbean Basin countries since 1980. The prolonged incarceration of thousands of aliens, most of them innocent victims of severe economic deprivation, indiscriminate armed conflict, or intense political persecution, has seared the judicial conscience as few events since the civil rights struggles of the 1950s and 1960s have done.[62]

In a long series of legal challenges in the 1980s, the imprisoned asylum seekers and their advocates resolutely pursued freedom, asylum, and an end to the detention program while the U.S. government just as determinedly defended its authority to use detention as a way to deter and control unauthorized migration.

To support its claim that it had the legal authority to detain excludable aliens, the government invoked a Supreme Court ruling in a 1953 case, *Shaughnessy v. United States, ex. rel. Mezei*. Ignatz Mezei, a native of Eastern Europe, had lived in the United States for twenty-five years. After a 21-month trip abroad, Mezei was denied reentry into the United States on undisclosed national security grounds. He remained detained in Ellis Island for sixteen months until American officials announced that they had been unable to locate a nation that would accept him. Indefinite detention at the port of entry appeared to be the man's fate. Mezei turned to the courts to seek his freedom, arguing that as a long-time resident of the United States, he was entitled to certain protections beyond those given to first-time entrants and that his indefinite detention was unlawful. As Hiroshi Motomura observes, Mezei's case raised the following question: "Can the federal government, citing national security, constitutionally exclude a returning lawful immigrant without a hearing, using the same procedure that would apply to a noncitizen seeking first-time admission?" The Supreme Court's answer was yes. It ruled that the attorney general had the authority to detain excludable aliens without a hearing and even without having to reveal the reasons for the detention order. In ruling in favor of the government's authority to indefinitely detain excludable aliens, the Supreme Court upheld the legality of the detention policy in place at the time, albeit in an unusual case. One year later, officials ended the detention program and Mezei was ultimately allowed to enter the United States after four years in detention. But the *Mezei* ruling remained, and Aleinikoff, Martin, and Motomura note that because the detention policy was terminated, the courts had "few opportunities to rethink the result in the case" over the next twenty-eight years.[63]

The courts had their chance to reexamine the government's authority to detain when the Carter administration used detention as a response to the Caribbean refugee crisis of 1980 and when the Reagan administration formally reinstituted the detention policy in 1981. The government's Haitian Program, which used detention as one of its tools to deter asylum seekers, had already been dealt a blow in the 1980 case of *Haitian Refugee Center v. Civiletti*. Other legal challenges brought by asylum seekers and their advocates in 1981 and 1982 would have an even more direct bearing on the government's detention program.

The first major challenges to the detention program were brought by Cuban detainees who, because both the United States and Cuban governments claimed they were criminals, could not be released into the United States and could not be deported to Cuba. While some of the rulings in these cases challenged the constitutionality of immigration detention, others upheld it. In *Rodriguez-Fernandez v. Wilkinson*, a Cuban *marielito* sought freedom from the federal penitentiary he had been detained in for more than six months. The district court ordered the detainee's release and the court of appeals affirmed the ruling, finding that the indefinite detention to which he had been subjected violated international and constitutional law. But other rulings affirmed the constitutionality of detention. For example, the Fourth Circuit's ruling in *Palma v. Verdeyen* agreed with the government that the Immigration and Nationality Act authorized indefinite detention and, citing *Mezei*, denied that the practice violated the Constitution.[64]

Other cases focused on the rights those held in detention were entitled to. *Nunez v. Boldin* centered on abuses of Salvadoran and Guatemalan asylum seekers at Port Isabel prison in Los Fresnos, Texas, and *Orantes-Hernandez v. Smith* dealt with similar abuses at a detention facility in El Centro, California. At Port Isabel, detained Central American refugees were denied access to legal materials and services, then were deceived and coerced into signing statements accepting "voluntary departure." At the detention center in El Centro, California, a Salvadoran woman who had witnessed the rape of her daughter and the execution of her husband was drugged and then forced to sign a form that indicated that she had chosen to waive her right to asylum. In both cases the courts issued injunctions against the abusive INS practices and ordered the INS to restore the legal rights of the detained asylum seekers. Although the ruling in *Nunez v. Boldin* granted protection only to those within the jurisdiction of the Fifth Circuit Court of Appeals, the reach of *Orantes-Hernandez v. Smith* would eventually represent Salvadorans anywhere in the United States. In an April 29, 1988, ruling, U.S. district judge David Kenyon issued a permanent injunction against the INS, rebuking immigration officials for coercing Salvadorans, "a substantial number" of whom "possess a well-founded fear of persecution," into accepting voluntary departure, "even when they had unequivocally expressed a fear of returning to El Salvador." Judge Kenyon also noted the role that INS detention practices played in denying asylum, observing that the "INS knowingly locates its major detention facilities in communities with little or no legal representation available to indigent detainees." Geographically isolated detainees were also "deprived of food and kept incommunicado for extended periods of time." Long-term detention under atrocious conditions, Kenyon argued, was part of a larger program by the U.S. government to deny asylum. Although Kenyon's ruling ordered the government to respect the legal rights of Central American asylum seekers, the abusive practices of the INS continued, including the use of detention to coerce asylum seekers into abandoning their claims.[65]

Haitians continued to lead in the legal struggle against detention and for asylum. In 1982, a group of detained Haitian asylum seekers brought a case that would prove to be the most substantial challenge to the government's detention program to date. Marie Lucie Jean, Lucien Louis, Herold Jacques, and approximately eighty-three other Haitians who originally were represented in the lawsuit had arrived in the United States after the government instituted its new Haitian detention program on May 20, 1981. The detained refugees and the Haitian Refugee Center petitioned the U.S. District Court in the Southern District of Florida for a writ of habeas corpus and an injunction against their final orders of exclusion and against the INS detention policy. They argued that the detention program to which they were subjected was illegal because it was implemented without the procedures required by the Administrative Procedures Act and that it violated the right of the plaintiffs to protection from discrimination under the First and Fifth Amendments of the U.S. Constitution. According to Ira Kurzban, attorney for the Haitian Refugee Center, although the government's detention policy was "characterized as 'neutral,' it was in fact aimed exclusively at Haitians."[66]

In June 1982, in *Louis v. Nelson*, district court judge Eugene Spellman ruled that the government's detention program had violated the procedures set forth by the Administrative Procedures Act and was thus "null and void." Haitians

Figure 5. Regis LaRose and others in the waiting room of the Haitian Refugee Center, 1987. History Miami Museum. Used by permission.

had been subjected to a policy that "makes detention the rule, not the exception," Spellman observed, noting that "the Court cannot think of any administrative action that would have a greater impact on a regulated group of people than a change in policy which results in their indefinite incarceration where, under the previous policy, they would have been free." Ordering an end to the Haitian detention program, the ruling restored the parole policy that had been in place before May 20, 1981. In addition, the court ordered the government to release the 1,800 Haitian detainees represented in the class action lawsuit. The Haitian Refugee Center hailed the Spellman ruling as a "historic legal decision," noting that despite the court's refusal to find the Haitian detention program in violation of the Constitution and despite the judge's rejection of the plaintiff's claim of discrimination, the decision established that "excludable aliens in detention such as Haitians are persons within the meaning of the United States Constitution and are therefore protected by our Constitution."[67]

The Reagan administration responded to the Spellman ruling by meeting the law's statutory requirements so the program could continue. One month after the ruling, the government published its new detention policy, satisfying the requirements of the Administrative Procedures Act and proactively defending against the claim of discrimination that the Haitians and their advocates were pursuing in an appeal. In the government's new policy, detention would no longer be used as a tool to deter Haitians from seeking asylum but henceforth would be applied to all excludable aliens. "The new detention policy is designed to mistreat all equally," argued Arthur Helton of the Lawyers Committee for Human Rights.[68] A U.S. government study interpreted the major policy shift rather more benignly: "INS has remedied the procedural issue and remains committed to a strict detention policy."[69]

Reagan administration officials claimed that Spellman's failure to validate the plaintiff's claim of discrimination exonerated the government from charges of racism and discrimination on the basis of national origin in its treatment of Haitians. "The Judge found in favor of the U.S. government on that point. He found that there was no discrimination, that the policy was being applied fairly to all nationalities," INS commissioner Alan Nelson told a House subcommittee hearing. Edward J. Ennis of the American Civil Liberties Union disagreed, arguing that the government's claims "that Haitians are treated just like other aliens flies in the face of every finding of fact that has been made after careful judicial consideration of the decision." As evidence, he pointed to the New York District Court ruling in *Vigile v. Sava*, another challenge to the government's

Haitian detention program, in which Judge Robert L. Carter ordered the INS to release a group of Haitians detained in New York after finding that the INS district director had been detaining Haitians but releasing non-Haitians. "The conclusion, therefore, is inescapable that [INS district director] Sava denied parole to petitioners because they were black and/or because they were Haitian," declared Judge Carter.[70]

Reagan administration officials may have known that their claims of nondiscrimination put them on shaky ground. The instability of their position became even clearer when the U.S. Court of Appeals for the Eleventh Circuit delivered its ruling in the appeal for *Louis v. Nelson*, which had been designated *Jean v. Nelson*. The appeals court affirmed the district court's finding regarding the government's obligation to comply with the Administrative Procedures Act. However, the appeals court found that Judge Spellman's ruling of insufficient evidence to prove discrimination against the Haitians "clearly erroneous." The government had engaged in "a stark pattern of discrimination" against the detained Haitians in violation of the Constitution, the court declared. This judgement was a landmark decision, wrote Haitian Refugee Center Attorney Ira Kurzban, who claimed that the victory was "the first decision in American legal history where the federal government was found to discriminate on the basis of race or national origin under the Constitution in a non-employment context." In addition, Kurzban wrote, the ruling was "the first decision in American legal history where excludable aliens were found to be protected by the First Amendment and the equal protection guarantees of the Fifth Amendment" and the first "to find that excludable aliens must be informed of their right to seek political asylum in the United States." In ruling that incarcerated aliens were protected by the Fifth Amendment to the Constitution, the court's decision in *Jean v. Nelson* went much further than the ruling in *Rodriguez-Fernandez v. Wilkinson*, the only other decision to assert that detained aliens had constitutional rights. As relief, the Court ordered the INS to parole the Haitians represented in the lawsuit and enjoined the government against any discriminatory application of its detention policy.[71]

But even the landmark victory in *Jean v. Nelson* did not fundamentally alter the government's detention and asylum practices. After that ruling, the government petitioned for a rehearing of the case on the grounds that the court's action encroached on presidential authority regarding immigration. This time the appeals court ruled that the Constitution did not protect the Haitians nor did it entitle aliens to rights with regard to admission to the United States or release from detention. In June 1985, the Supreme Court refused to affirm the constitutional rights of the detained Haitian asylum seekers when it upheld the lower court's ruling ordering the government to stop its discrimination against Haitians, but did so on narrow statutory grounds and remained silent about what rights, if any, detained aliens had under the U.S. Constitution.[72]

Imprisoned asylum seekers continued the legal struggle for freedom, however. In 1984, as Haitian cases continued to wend their way through the courts, a class action habeas corpus suit, *Fernandez-Roque v. Smith*, brought by the more than 1,000 Cuban *marielitos* who were still imprisoned in a federal penitentiary in Atlanta, resulted in what Aleinikoff, Martin, and Motomura call "the most ambitious decision yet, protecting the due process rights of excludable aliens." After hearing the Cubans' case, a U.S. district court ruled that although the attorney general had the authority to detain excludable aliens, the Constitution placed certain limitations on that authority. Because the Cuban plaintiffs had been incarcerated for four years and because the U.S. government could neither send them back to Cuba nor parole them into the United States, it seemed increasingly difficult to justify their ongoing detention on the grounds that doing so was a temporary measure until they were formally excluded from the United States. As a result, the court ruled, "once detention is no longer justifiable simply on the basis of excludability, then a legitimate expectation arises that the detention will end unless some new justification for continuing the detention is established." According to the Constitution, the court added, all persons were "entitled to their liberty absent some legally sufficient reason for detaining them." Excludability could provide a reason for an alien's temporary detention. However, the Court continued, "After this initial period of time . . . the individual's basic entitlement to liberty once again comes to the fore." This liberty interest of the alien detainees required that the government justify its ongoing detention on the grounds that "the detainee, if released, is likely to abscond, to pose a risk to the national security, or to pose a serious and significant threat to persons or property within the United States."[73] By placing limits on indefinite detention, by ruling that the detained aliens enjoyed certain protections under the U.S. Constitution, and by reasserting the basic principles of the pre-1981 parole policy, *Fernandez-Roque* served as a rebuke to the government's use of detention in order to deter unauthorized migration.

In 1985, an even larger class action lawsuit brought on behalf of Salvadoran and Guatemalan asylum seekers posed the greatest challenge to date to the government's asylum policy. The case, *American Baptist Churches v. Thornburgh* (or simply ABC), alleged that the government's treatment of Salvadoran and Guatemalan asylum seekers was discriminatory. The suit sought an injunction against deporting these asylum seekers' and against the government's campaign to disrupt the sanctuary movement that had been built by advocates for the Central American refugees. When the government failed in its efforts to have the case dismissed, it entered into a landmark settlement with the Central American asylum seekers in 1991. The settlement granted the Salvadorans and Guatemalans represented in the case new asylum hearings that were to be fairly adjudicated and the right to work while awaiting their hearings. Finally, as Michael J. Churgin notes, the settlement "also sharply limited INS authority to detain Salvadoran and Guatemalan refugees while their new cases were pending."[74]

The eventual outcome of the landmark ABC lawsuit and cases such as *Jean v. Nelson* and *Fernandez-Roque v. Smith* demonstrated that in some instances the courts could be an avenue through which detained asylum seekers were able to challenge exclusion and gain their freedom. In fact, the more detained asylum seekers and refugees saw litigation as means of challenging their exclusion and detention, the more they used it. Naomi Flink Zucker observed in 1983 that "the Haitian position" of using litigation against the government to fight for due process and civil liberties of aliens, "far from having been weakened by restrictive government measures, seems rather to have animated other groups to take action." Zucker cited the activity of Salvadorans and Ethiopians and accurately predicted that "other refugee groups as well will soon exploit legal or political means to achieve a fairer disposition of their cases."[75] According to Jonathan Simon, this history of legal resistance shows that "immigration imprisonment is in a very real sense a story of rights and liberties as much as it is a story of prejudice and oppression." Inasmuch as immigration detention facilities became the focus of the struggle for detainee rights, Simon argues, the immigration prison might be seen as not just the site of government abuses but also as generative of rights.[76] The courts continued to be a forum in which detained asylum seekers and immigrants would struggle for their freedom.

But the first decade of detention (1981–1991)—including the legal struggles over asylum and the authority to detain—demonstrates how resilient the government's detention program was and how successful it was in fending off fundamental challenges to its detention program. When the courts ruled the government's Haitian Program to be illegal in 1980, the Carter administration attempted to move its detention program beyond the court's reach, and the

Reagan administration subsequently launched its program of interdiction. When the Haitian refugees represented in *Louis v. Nelson* appeared to strike a major blow against the government's authority to detain in 1982, the government rewrote the law and the Supreme Court decided to limit the scope of its ruling to the statutory aspects of detention, leaving aside the more fundamental constitutional issues at the heart of the detention program. And while the government's detention program and asylum policies suffered other defeats throughout the 1980s, detained asylum seekers and their advocates failed to overturn the system or challenge the government's authority to detain excludable and deportable aliens.

As the reinstituted U.S. detention program moved into its second decade, it continued to grow. In 1991, another crisis in the Caribbean would again force tens of thousands of Haitians to seek asylum on American shores, opening a new chapter in the history of immigration and refugee detention.

5

Guantanamo

New Frontiers in Detention, 1991–1994

In January 1993, Haitian refugees detained at the U.S. naval base at Guantanamo Bay launched a hunger strike to protest their indefinite imprisonment. "I might well die, but we can't continue in this fashion," declared Yolande Jean, one of the leaders of the movement. Fifteen days into the strike, military authorities sent in soldiers, who beat the hunger strikers and arrested their leaders. Press coverage of striking Haitian detainees shocked the world and galvanized a movement on their behalf. In the following months, the refugees were joined by prominent leaders, ministers, and college students in solidarity hunger strikes across the United States. Demonstrations and campaigns of civil disobedience spread, demanding that the government release the Haitians from Guantanamo. Celebrities Susan Sarandon and Tim Robbins helped elevate the profile of the movement by calling for the release of the Guantanamo Haitians at the Academy Awards.[1] By the spring of 1994, supporters of democracy in Haiti and of freedom for Haitian refugees had built a national movement and reinvigorated the debate over the U.S. policy of detaining unauthorized migrants and asylum seekers.[2]

The detention of Haitian asylum seekers at the U.S. naval base in Guantanamo Bay, Cuba, which began in 1991, raised questions about the responsibility of the United States to asylum seekers and its obligations under international law. The detention also drew attention to questions about the U.S. government's authority to detain asylum seekers. When a new flood of refugees fled Haiti following that country's coup in September 1991, the U.S. government leaned heavily on its interdiction program to keep Haitians from reaching American shores. But once the refugees were in U.S. custody, officials detained the refugees until they could justify returning them to Haiti.

The government's use of offshore detention facilities, first on board U.S. coast guard cutters and then at the U.S. naval base in Guantanamo Bay, Cuba, must be regarded as a significant expansion of its detention program.

Reversing Revolution in Haiti

On December 16, 1990, Haitian voters went to the polls and overwhelmingly elected Father Jean-Bertrand Aristide, a populist priest and champion of the poor, as president of Haiti. Aristide's landslide victory was more than just an unusual political outcome for Haiti. In many ways, the election of 1990 was the culmination of a popular movement that had emerged in 1985 to topple the nearly 30-year Duvalier dictatorship. In the wake of Jean-Claude Duvalier's departure in February 1986, the movement had continued to grow, fighting against "Duvalierism without Duvalier" and struggling for a revolutionary transformation of Haiti. This popular movement, which included peasants, workers, university students, clergy, and residents of city slums, reached into the neighborhoods, churches, classrooms, fields, and workplaces of the poor and the dispossessed and sought changes that extended well beyond who would be the head of state. When Father Aristide, one of the best-known voices in the popular movement, swept to presidential victory with 67.5 percent of the vote, the strength of the popular movement was undeniable. To many in Haiti and abroad, Aristide's election seemed to be unmistakable evidence of an unfolding popular revolution.[3]

Haiti's poor majority viewed the movement's victory as thrilling and long overdue. But many of Haiti's elite regarded Aristide's victory and the popular movement that had produced it with contempt and fear. Opponents of the movement first tried to remove its head. On September 29, 1991, members of the Haitian military staged a coup d'état that forced President Aristide to leave the country. Next, they attacked the real source of power: the activists and organizations that made up the popular movement. Military and paramilitary forces murdered hundreds in the first days of the coup; numerous sources claimed that the number of dead soon exceeded 1,500. Death squads carried out a campaign of terror, torturing and mutilating their victims. Women, who were the core of the popular movement, were a special target for violence and terror, and rape was often the weapon soldiers and paramilitary forces used against them.[4]

Human rights activists and organizations documented the human rights

Figure 6. A protest march in Miami, 1986. Gary Monroe Photographs, David M. Rubenstein Rare Book & Manuscript Library, Duke University. Used by permission.

catastrophe unfolding in Haiti despite the coup regime's attempts to hide it. A January 1992 Amnesty International report described "grave human rights violations" in Haiti and reported that "hundreds of people have been extra-judicially executed or detained without warrant and tortured. Ira Kurzban, Haitian Refugee Center attorney, cited the report in testimony before Congress the following April: "Many others have been brutally beaten in the streets. Freedom of the press has been severely curtailed and property is being destroyed by members of the military and police forces or by civilians operating in conjunction with them."[5] In another report, Amnesty International observed that "victims of human rights violations have included all sectors of the population, particularly peasants, trade unionists, and popular organizers, students, members of the press and the Catholic Church, and virtually anyone suspected of supporting the return of deposed President Jean-Bertrand Aristide. There is, however, extensive evidence that the security forces have also committed widespread human rights violations for no apparent political reason."[6]

In the face of all this violence, tens of thousands of Haitians fled their country. Some crossed the border to the Dominican Republic and many others left by boat to seek refuge in neighboring countries, including the United States. As fortunate as they were to escape, these Haitian refugees, as those who had come to the United States before they did, faced an uncertain future.

Guantanamo: Embracing Extraterritorial Detention

In the days following the coup in Haiti, the U.S. government joined the Organization of American States in condemning the removal of President Aristide. It supported efforts to isolate the coup government, including imposing an embargo on trade with Haiti and a freeze on U.S. aid and financial transfers to the military junta. Although some would soon question President Bush's commitment to restoring Aristide to office, the U.S. government's initial actions seemed to demonstrate an unequivocal opposition to the coup regime.[7]

The Bush administration's stance toward the thousands of refugees who were soon flowing out of Haiti was less clear. The fact that it had explicitly condemned the regime the refugees were fleeing from made it difficult for the administration to argue that Haitians were economic migrants rather than political refugees and thus were not entitled to asylum. However, U.S. officials were not prepared to open the door to large numbers of Haitian refugees. Because of these two contradictory positions, the Bush administration's Haitian refugee policy remained uncertain in the weeks following the September coup.

The U.S. government blocked the escape of Haitians who fled the country after the coup with U.S. coast guard cutters that already were carrying out the interdiction program established by President Reagan in 1981. The Alien Migrant Interdiction Operation, originally titled the Haitian Migrant Interdiction Operation, functioned as a floating wall between Haiti and the United States, blocking the passage of nearly 25,000 Haitians who attempted to reach U.S. shores in the period 1981 to 1991. Thus, the United States already had an effective tool at its disposal to halt the flow of refugees that began streaming out of Haiti in the wake of the coup. Even though the Inter-American Commission on Human Rights urged the United States to suspend its policy of interdiction of Haitians "because of the danger to their lives," the interdiction program continued. In the first fifty days after the coup, the United States Coast Guard interdicted 2,800 Haitians.[8]

In the weeks following Aristide's removal, the Bush administration was uncertain about what to do with the growing number of Haitians in its custody. Unwilling to grant them entrance to the United States, U.S. officials initially opted to detain them on board coast guard vessels while it tried to persuade Caribbean and Latin American nations to accept them. Conditions for those detained on board the cutters were atrocious. Haitian psychologist Claude Charles, who witnessed these conditions, found "restrained individuals . . . living in very hard daily conditions such as using limited, rough and problematic sanitary accommodations, eating food they were not familiar with back home which is rendering many of them sick, congregating and sleeping on the deck floor over a laid blanket, often exposed to unpleasant circumstances aggravated by lack of decent living space."[9]

Members of the Haitian community and their supporters in the United States were outraged by the State Department's refusal to bring the Haitians to shore. "The first group of interdicted Haitians has been kept at sea by the Coast Guard for over a week while the State Department decides what to do with them. This only puts the Haitian lives at further risk," observed Cheryl Little of the Haitian Refugee Center. Advocates for the refugees rejected the government's claims that full and fair asylum interviews could be conducted on board the coast guard cutters; instead, they insisted, "At the very least, the Haitians should be brought to shore for their interviews," Little argued. "Given what's at stake here (human lives), the Haitians should be given every opportunity to make their case."[10]

By mid-November, as the number of refugees fleeing Haiti multiplied, the government's practice of detaining them at sea became unsustainable. Having failed to persuade any of Haiti's neighbors to accept a substantial number of the thousands of refugees intercepted at sea and unwilling to grant the Haitians temporary protected status or allow them to enter the United States, the Bush administration chose to begin returning the refugees to Haiti. On November 18, 538 of the Haitian refugees were forcibly returned to a Haiti that remained in the violent grip of the coup regime.[11]

Observers throughout the United States reacted with horror. The *Miami Herald* called the Bush administration's interdiction and repatriation of Haitians "illegal," "immoral," and "racist." "It shames this great nation. It must stop," an editorial declared.[12] *The Boston Globe* observed that State Department officials had recently condemned the forced repatriation of Vietnamese refugees seeking asylum in Hong Kong. However, "for Haitians seeking asylum on our shores, the Bush administration apparently has a different standard," an editorial noted. "Even President Bush's protestations against the September coup in Haiti seem transparent and hypocritical now, after the administration's decision to deliver thousands of Haitian men, women, and children into the hands of the brutal government."[13] In congressional hearings held two days after the Bush administration's repatriation of Haitians resumed, New York member of Congress Charles Rangel denounced the return of Haitians "to ruthless, criminal, out-of-control military people that the President has condemned, the United Nations has condemned, the Organization of American States has condemned. . . . Is this America?" Florida member of Congress Larry Smith also called on the Bush administration to abandon its interdiction agreement "made ten years ago with the brutal Duvalier regime." Instead of interdiction and repatriation, Smith argued, the U.S. policy toward the Haitians should be to "allow them in and give them safe haven in a non-prison facility."[14]

But the Bush administration stood by its decision to return the refugees to Haiti. "It is a fair policy," President Bush argued. "It does make a distinction between economic refugees and political refugees. But let me assure you, it is not based on some race or double standard." According to the president and the administration officials, the policies of interdiction and return were designed to protect Haitian lives, not endanger them. "I'm saying that I don't want to have a policy that acts as a magnet to risk these people's lives," the president stated.[15] "Our overriding concern has been to save lives," claimed Deputy Assistant Secretary of State for Inter-American Affairs Robert S. Gelbard. "We have an obligation to prevent an unimpeded flow of Haitians to the United States."

We want to rescue people from vessels that put them at high risk of losing their lives at sea. We want to ensure that those who have a well-founded fear of persecution, and hence a good claim to asylum, are interviewed carefully, identified, and brought to the United States. Above all, we want to avoid any action that would encourage more Haitians to risk their lives by boarding unsafe vessels in the belief that this would ensure them passage to the United States.[16]

The Bush administration's claim that it was primarily concerned with the safety of the Haitians did not persuade many members of the human rights community. Arthur C. Helton, director of the Refugee Project of the Lawyers Committee for Human Rights, for example, observed that despite the Bush administration's characterization of interdiction as a humanitarian mission, "the outrageous and brutal fact is that the United States is returning refugees to a place where they will face persecution. That is as wrong as it gets to be in terms of refugee law."[17]

However, there were many Americans who opposed the admission of thousands of Haitians into the United States and backed the Bush administration's decision. Daniel A. Stein, executive director of the restrictionist Federation for American Immigration Reform, defended the Bush administration against charges of racism and discrimination in its dealings with Haitians and urged the president not to give in to "interest groups and some members of Congress" who wanted to admit the Haitians. This concession would only "produce a massive flood of desperate illegal immigrants, thousands of whom would perish at sea," Stein claimed.[18] Stein and FAIR were not alone in holding these opinions. In fact, there was substantial opposition to admitting large numbers of Haitian refugees, both in the state of Florida and nationwide. A series of polls conducted in the early 1990s showed that a significant majority of Americans supported government efforts to impede the flow of immigration from Haiti and other "third world" nations.[19] Haitians in particular suffered from their association in the public mind with AIDS, stemming from the Centers for Disease Control's flawed declaration years earlier that Haitians constituted one of the four high-risk groups for the disease. In the United States, Paul Farmer notes,

Haiti has long been depicted as a strange and hopelessly diseased country remarkable chiefly for its extreme isolation from the rest of the civilized world. This erroneous depiction fuels the parallel process of "exotification" by which Haiti is rendered weird. According to a journalist writing in 1989 in Vanity Fair, "Haiti is to this hemisphere what black holes are to outer space." Or consider the epithet given Haiti by a U.S. news magazine: "A Bazaar of the bizarre."[20]

In an election year, President Bush must have realized that he could not afford to dismiss the growing political power of immigration restriction and nativism, and he must have calculated that he would pay no political price for closing the door on a people as incomprehensibly different and irredeemably foreign as Haitians.

One day after the U.S. government began returning refugees to Haiti, attorneys for the Haitian Refugee Center filed a complaint in court against the repatriation of the Haitians that sought and received a temporary restraining order against the action. Stymied by the court order, the Bush administration attempted to resolve its Haitian refugee problem another way. Instead of mass detention on board coast guard vessels, the Haitians would be detained at the nearby U.S. naval base at Guantanamo Bay, Cuba. Transfers to Guantanamo began immediately.[21] The establishment of the Haitian refugee camp at Guantanamo Bay, like the establishment of Fort Allen in Puerto Rico and other elaborations of the detention regime before it, was the U.S. government's response to legal resistance by the refugees and their advocates and an attempt by U.S. officials to circumvent the law and their legal obligations to asylum seekers.

The naval base at Guantanamo Bay was the ideal space to implement what some had long called for: an extraterritorial detention facility that could act as a buffer between the United States and nearby nations that were sending unwanted migrants to American shores. Michael Ratner, attorney for the Haitian refugees, has commented that the U.S. government regarded Guantanamo as an attractive location for a new refugee camp because its inaccessibility "would prevent news reporters and others from scrutinizing the treatment of the Haitians." In addition, Ratner notes, "The government could argue that the refugees would have no legal rights on Guantanamo" and thus "could claim that the United States Constitution did not protect foreign nationals outside the country and that refugees could not apply for the protection of political asylum until they set foot in the United States."[22]

Detention facilities at Guantanamo attracted worldwide attention and controversy in the years following the terrorist attacks of September 11, 2001, when the George W. Bush administration began using the naval base in southeastern Cuba to hold "enemy combatants" captured in Afghanistan, Iraq, and elsewhere in the far-reaching and ever-expanding "war on terror." In this post-9/11 moment, Amy Kaplan observed that Guantanamo's extraterritoriality not only placed it beyond the reach of U.S. law and accountability, it also established the site as "one island in a global penal archipelago where the United States indefinitely detains, secretly transports, and tortures uncounted prisoners from around the world." It is the extraterritorial nature of the global network of black sites and prisons that has enabled these practices, which are illegal within the borders of the United States, to continue. But even before Guantanamo became a controversial extraterritorial prison in the war on terror, it was used a decade earlier to detain Haitian refugees, a staging point, as Jana Evans Braziel observes, in an earlier war on refugees.[23]

The expansion of the U.S. government's immigration detention network beyond U.S. boundaries was significant. However, the newness of this policy must not be overemphasized. Cheryl Little of the Haitian Refugee Center saw the transfer of Haitian prisoners from U.S. coast guard cutters to the new detention site at Guantanamo Bay as merely a continuation of the "human shell game" the government had been playing with Haitian refugees since the early 1980s, when it was already shuffling Haitian prisoners between detention centers and prisons scattered across the United States and Puerto Rico.[24] In addition, the rationale behind extraterritorial detention was simply an extension of the government's well-established entry doctrine, which considered aliens caught while trying to enter the United States as having not formally entered the country and therefore not entitled to the same legal rights as those who had formally entered. These "excludable aliens" could be brought to and held at detention facilities in the United States and still be classified as not having officially entered the country. They could be incarcerated alongside "deportable aliens," who, according to the definition of the phrase, had greater legal protection because they had formally entered the United States, albeit illegally. The entry doctrine thus enabled the U.S. government to hold detained people it labeled "excludable aliens" outside the legal boundaries of the United States.

Critics of the U.S. government's treatment of Haitian refugees had long charged that the Haitian interdiction program violated Article 33 of the UN's Convention Relating to the Status of Refugees (1951), which prohibited the return of individuals to a country where they would face persecution. In order to shield the Bush administration from the accusation of noncompliance with the Refugee Convention, Deputy Legal Advisor Alan J. Kreczko of the State Department used the entry doctrine and its extraterritorial rationale. Article 33 was "inapplicable to the Haitian migration interdiction program" because "the article only applies with respect to individuals who have entered U.S. territory," he argued. "Since the interdiction and return program applies only beyond the U.S. territory there is no question of compliance with Article 33 as a legal matter."[25] But refugee law expert Guy S. Goodwin-Gill disagreed. The State Department's position was "an attempt to rewrite the rules," he claimed, since a recent review of international law "confirms acceptance of the rule of non-rejection at the frontier."[26] Arthur C. Helton of the Lawyers Committee for Human Rights supported Goodwin-Gill's position. The government's "entry doctrine" unlawfully stripped Haitians of all constitutional and statutory protections, he argued, because, "interdicted aliens are deprived of redress by their pre-entry situation." Helton anticipated arguments against Haitian imprisonment at Guantanamo:

The arbitrary prolonged incarceration of individual aliens who have committed no crime violates international human rights law. The United States seems to justify the violation by reference to the "entry" doctrine. The time has come, however, to abolish this legal fiction.[27]

However, the U.S. government would not surrender a useful legal tool in its campaign against unauthorized migration so easily. As a result, the Haitian detention camp at Guantanamo became the next site where the battle over extraterritoriality and entry would be waged.

"A World Isolated from the World": Survival and Resistance from Guantanamo to Krome

On April 9, 1992, five months after the U.S. government began to detain Haitian refugees at Guantanamo, Yale University law professor Harold Hongju Koh explained to members of Congress what was occurring at the U.S. naval base in Cuba. This is "a story of broken lives," Koh declared. "Moreover, it is a story of our country, 50 years after the internment of the Japanese Americans, again running an internment camp, which a federal judge has now called 'a world isolated from the world'" in which the Haitian detainees are "treated in a manner worse than the treatment of that would be afforded to a criminal defendant, defenseless against any abuse, exploitation, or neglect to which the officials at Guantanamo may subject them." Koh had the credentials to make his claims credible. He had been co-counsel in *Haitian Centers Council v. McNary*, a case brought jointly by the Allard K. Lowenstein International Human Rights Clinic at Yale University and the Center for Constitutional Rights. *McNary* exposed the government's attempts to use the extraterritorial location of Guantanamo to limit the rights of the detainees. Koh pointed out that the government was conducting asylum screenings of the Haitians at Guantanamo instead of bringing them to the United States because "if they were brought to the United States, they would have procedural safeguards. They would have a lawyer at their own expense. They would have the right to appeal an adverse ruling to an immigration judge. On Guantanamo, they have none of these."[28]

Conflicting accounts of the conditions in which the detainees were being held soon surfaced. A staff report prepared in February 1992 for members of Congress assured lawmakers that "the boat people are well-treated in

Guantanamo. They are housed in five separate tent camps containing 1,000 to 3,000 people each. They are well-fed, receive adequate medical care, publish a newspaper, play soccer, and watch nightly movies." No major "incidents" had occurred since a "disturbance" in mid-December. The report did admit, however, that "one woman was raped by an American serviceman," but it quickly added that "he is now undergoing court martial proceedings." No other details regarding the sexual assault were included.[29] A report by the government's General Accounting Office two months later was somewhat less sanguine. Although investigators found the living conditions at Guantanamo Bay to be "adequate," they observed that "heat and weather conditions preclude the facility's continued use for screening purposes. Haitians are being housed in tents set on an old runway and water is provided through pipes that are laid on the surface. With the onset of hot weather and temperatures well over 100 degrees . . . the tents would become unbearable and the water virtually undrinkable."[30]

Figure 7. Haitian refugees at Camp McCalla, Guantanamo Bay, Cuba, 1991. Photo by Carol Halebian. Used by permission.

Regardless of the material conditions of the Guantanamo camp, as Harold Hongju Koh pointed out, limited rights and lack of freedom meant that the Haitians' detention experience was "prison-like." "Contrary to the notion that Guantanamo is a sanctuary," Haitians at Guantanamo "were denied all right to communicate with the outside world, and [were] summarily punished," Koh reported in testimony to Congress. A group of political activists at the camp managed to overcome the legal isolation of Guantanamo by organizing their compatriots. This group formally asked Professor Koh and the Yale University team to represent them.[31]

However, it took a major campaign just to establish face-to-face meetings between the detainees and their attorneys. Some contact was established with the filing of *Haitian Refugee Center v. Baker*. That lawsuit was filed on November 18, one day after the Bush administration forcibly returned more than 500 refugees to Haiti. The District Court for the Southern District of Florida ordered a temporarily halt to the repatriation process and gave Haitian Refugee Center attorneys access to the Guantanamo Bay detention camp.[32] The attorneys discovered that Haitian asylum seekers were being treated arbitrarily and incorrectly. For example, the officials who were interviewing refugees about their asylum claims had no training and no knowledge of the political conditions in Haiti. Ira Kurzban, general counsel for the Haitian Refugee Center, reported that in its initial visit to Guantanamo, the legal team conducted interviews that revealed that the pre-screening procedures INS officials were using to determine which Haitian could enter the United States to pursue asylum and which would be returned to Haiti "were, either purposely or through indifference, a complete and utter sham—a 'formal' validation of a predetermined result." Kurzban told members of Congress that when lawyers for the detained Haitians tried to point out these problems with the government's screening procedures, the government "took the position that Haitians who were outside of the United States simply had no rights whatsoever. In effect, they asserted that whatever totally arbitrary procedure used and devised by the government was simply not the concern of the courts." In addition, "the INS refused counsel for the plaintiffs any access to their clients" after these discoveries came to light.[33] On appeal, the Eleventh Circuit Court affirmed the government's right to deny the Haitians access to counsel. And then on February 1, 1992, the Supreme Court granted the Justice Department's request for a stay of the injunction against the forcible repatriation of the Haitians and refused to hear the Haitian Refugee Center's appeal. The Bush administration's legal victory in *Haitian Refugee Center v. Baker* allowed it to begin to repatriate the 12,000 refugees in Guantanamo Bay. The government also began to accelerate deportations of Haitians from U.S.-based detention centers.[34]

After the Haitian detainees' legal defeat in *Haitian Refugee Center v. Baker*, Yale University law students and faculty launched another legal challenge on behalf of the refugees at Guantanamo Bay. Filing *Haitian Centers Council v. McNary* on March 17, 1992, gave the Haitians' legal counsel court-ordered access to the refugee camps at Guantanamo. A team of Yale Law students traveled to Guantanamo to investigate and meet with their clients. There attorneys for the Haitian detainees again ran into a wall constructed by a government still seeking to deny the refugees access to legal counsel. Yale law student Sarah Cleveland reported that "the government refused to allow us to enter or view the refugee camps themselves and instead confined our movement to the corner of the base where the airstrip was located, an hour-long ferry ride away from the refugees on the other side of the base."[35]

Nonetheless, the Yale team was able to produce a devastating set of findings regarding detention on Guantanamo: Haitian refugees were "detained wholly incommunicado" with "no access to telephone or to mail," were denied access to international press and to attorneys, were given "no means of communicating with relatives," and were "not allowed to leave Guantanamo to go to any third country, even under their own volition or expense," Cleveland reported. In addition, Cleveland and her partners found that the Haitians were being denied access to medical records or counseling and were "punished and intimidated for asserting their legal rights." Refugees were "detained in an atmosphere of chaos, disinformation and misrepresentation." In fact, some of the Haitians who had already been found to have a "credible fear" of political persecution were being screened again and in many cases repatriated to Haiti. This was the tragic fate of Marie Zette, a young woman who, it had been determined, was eligible to make an asylum claim but who then was mistakenly returned to Haiti. Her fate was disclosed when a new group of refugees arrived at Guantanamo that included relatives of Marie. They reported that Marie had been murdered as soon as she had returned. "In sum, then," Cleveland concluded, "the Haitian clients we visited on Guantanamo are suffering massive injury on several levels. . . . Their liberty is almost completely circumscribed."[36]

Cleveland offered a description of the extraordinary legal isolation that Guantanamo detainees experienced:

Remarkably, none of the severest deprivations which characterize the refugee experience on Guantanamo would be experienced by a Haitian alien in detention in the United States. In contrast to the terror and ignorance that pervades Guantanamo, Haitian detainees at the Krome detention center near Miami are permitted to make and receive telephone calls and to meet privately with family, lawyers, and other visitors. Detainees at Krome are also handed a list of local legal service organizations and telephone numbers when they arrive. These are very simple and fundamental rights. But our brief experience on Guantanamo attests to how much difference the right to communicate—and the right to a lawyer—can make.[37]

Still, it is important to note that while Guantanamo was extraordinary in certain important ways, it was in other important ways simply reflective of the broader U.S.-based system of immigration detention. Quite probably Haitian detainees in the United States would have argued that Cleveland and others were drawing too sharp a distinction between Guantanamo and U.S.-based facilities such as the Krome Avenue Detention Center. For example, for years before the Guantanamo camp refocused attention on Haitian refugee detention, Krome had been the site of numerous incidents of alleged sexual and physical abuse. It had been a place where detainees were consistently deprived of their rights, amounting, according to one report, to "unending cycles of humiliation and abuse." Like the Guantanamo detainees, those detained at Krome were "isolated from family and legal representation, pressured into accepting deportation[,] . . . denied medical care," and experienced retaliation for reporting abuse or for asserting their legal rights. Revelations about the many abuses occurring at the Krome Avenue center in 1991 had led to a major campaign by civil and human rights groups to have the facility closed permanently.[38]

The similarities between the treatment detainees received in the Guantanamo camps and in U.S.-based detention centers extended to detention facilities across the country. A two-year investigation by the Immigrants' Rights Project of the American Civil Liberties Union and the New York Civil Liberties Union into the Varick Street Immigration Detention Center in New York City, the largest INS detention facility in New York, found serious abuses. The investigation disclosed that detainees were "imprisoned in large dormitories without any access to fresh air or sunlight . . . denied meaningful access to legal representation and are subject to arbitrary and punitive segregation." It also found that these conditions were "not unique to Varick Street. INS detention policy in New York is in many ways a microcosm of INS detention policy nationwide."[39] An Americas Watch investigation of human rights abuses along the U.S.-Mexico border also found serious abuses. It found that immigration detainees there were subjected to brutal physical abuse, denied access to legal counsel, and kept incommunicado for long periods of time.[40]

Although forced repatriation was a constant danger for Haitian detainees, nowhere was the threat of repatriation as great as it was at Guantanamo. After filing *McNary*, the detainees' legal advocates received a temporary restraining order and then, on April 6, 1992, a preliminary injunction against the government's repatriation campaign.[41] At this point, 18,095 Haitians had been interdicted since the coup of September 30, 1991. Of that number, 10,149 had been returned to Haiti and 4,301 had been brought to the United States to pursue asylum claims, leaving more than 3,000 in Guantanamo, awaiting transport to the United States or awaiting screening.[42]

But in May another surge of refugees that had been apprehended after they had fled Haiti brought the number of detainees at the Guantanamo camp back up to more than 12,000. The Bush administration responded to the population problem by announcing that it would no longer pick up Haitians and transfer them to Guantanamo. Only those in sinking vessels would be rescued. The rest, if they were "in no imminent danger," would be left to their fate at sea. This shift was the result of the administration's realization that its policy of using Guantanamo as a buffer between Haiti and the United States was unsustainable. The Guantanamo camp and the coast guard cutters that seized the refugees were filled to capacity.

But the new policy also allowed for the possibility that many more Haitians might actually make it to U.S. shores than had arrived safely while the interdiction policy was strictly enforced. From the Bush administration's perspective, this was an unacceptable outcome, so the U.S. government announced yet another change to its Haitian refugee policy. On May 24, 1992, President Bush issued Executive Order 12807, which ordered the United States Coast Guard to return interdicted refugees directly to Haiti without interview or asylum screening. As a result, refugees were returned to the danger they had fled in a country that remained in the grip of a violent and repressive coup regime.

The Bush administration's executive order provoked a firestorm of criticism. Human rights and refugee organizations attacked the action as morally reprehensible, a "gross violation of international law."[43] In testimony to Congress, Rabbi Haskel Lookstein, chair of the New York Coalition for Soviet Jewry, compared the Bush administration's policy on Haitian refugees to the turning away of the 937 Jewish refugees on the *St. Louis* in 1939. "This was one of the most disgraceful things which has happened in American history," Lookstein argued. "It is vitally important that today when history repeats itself with other boat people, we do not repeat the same mistakes."[44] New York member of Congress Stephen Solarz testified that in his nearly two decades in Congress, he could not remember "another foreign policy decision that I consider to be more disgraceful or dishonorable in terms of the fundamental values on which this country was founded."[45]

The Bush administration defended its detention and interdiction policies by claiming its actions were measures "to protect the lives of the Haitians, whose boats are not equipped for the 600-mile sea journey."[46] According to Deputy Assistant Secretary of State Brunson McKinley, the Bush administration had used the Guantanamo base "as a humanitarian sanctuary and location for interviewing Haitian boat people" for as long as it could. But when more than 13,000 Haitians were picked up at sea in the month of May, "we became convinced that the Guantanamo operation and the presence of U.S. Coast Guard cutters had become a magnet, causing more and more Haitians to take to the boats."[47] On the campaign trail, President Bush offered a defense that suggested it was national interest rather than humanitarian impulse that drove the shift: "Yes, the Statue of Liberty still stands, and we still open our arms to people that are politically oppressed," Bush claimed, but, "we cannot and, as long as the laws are on the book, I will not, because I've sworn to uphold the Constitution, open the doors to economic refugees all over the world. We can't do that."[48]

Although the Yale University legal team, led by Harold Hongju Koh and Michael Ratner, sought a restraining order against the new policy of returning refugees directly to Haiti, the District Court for the Eastern District of New York sided with the government. The United States Court of Appeals for the Second Circuit reversed the lower court's decision and ordered the lower court to issue the restraining order. However, on August 1, the U.S. Supreme Court issued a stay. After that, there were no legal obstacles to the Bush administration's direct return policy. Because no more Haitians were brought to Guantanamo and the government systematically worked to empty the camp of its inhabitants, by the end of the summer only several hundred Haitians remained.[49] However, the treatment of this remaining group and the campaign of resistance they and their supporters constructed would once again break new ground in the history of immigration detention in the United States.

"Carceral Quarantine" and the Politics of Refuge

Yolande Jean arrived in Guantanamo on May 14, 1992, just ten days before President Bush issued Executive Order 12807. Jean, a member of the popular movement in Haiti, had been arrested after the overthrow of Aristide and had subsequently been imprisoned and tortured, causing her to lose the child she had been carrying. When she was released from prison, Jean fled Haiti by boat, but the boat was intercepted by the coast guard after two days at sea. The coast guard destroyed the boat, along with all of the refugees' belongings, and took the Haitians to the detention camp at Guantanamo Bay.[50]

Yolande Jean had a strong case for asylum; she and nearly 300 of her compatriots had demonstrated in asylum interviews that they had a credible fear of political persecution. This finding should have resulted in their transfer to the United States to pursue asylum claims. In fact, many of these individuals had been screened again and had even passed the more stringent standard of having a well-founded fear of political persecution. This should have entitled them to asylum in the United States. Unfortunately, another kind of screening had shown these individuals to be HIV-positive, so they were blocked from entering the United States by a provision of the Immigration and Naturalization Act of 1990 that barred the entry of aliens with "communicable diseases of public health significance."[51] By mid-July, the government had transferred most of the Haitian detainees out of Guantanamo and had closed Camp Mc-Calla, the main detention site at Guantanamo that had held thousands of Haitians since November 1991. Yolande Jean and the other refugees that remained were sent to another, more remote location inside the Guantanamo naval base called Camp Bulkeley, "the world's first and only detention camp for refugees with HIV."[52]

The government characterized its detention of HIV-positive Haitians as a "humanitarian mission" that provided care for the refugees in its custody. But A. Naomi Paik has shown that the "carceral quarantine" in which the refugees were held was anything but humane. In Camp Bulkeley, detainees, which included families and children, were housed in communal barracks surrounded by a barbed-wire fence. Because the housing offered little shelter from the elements, detainees tied plastic bags over the windows to shield themselves from the Caribbean wind and rain. In order to provide a degree of privacy in their living quarters, detainees hung sheets to separate their cots from the others in the barracks. The food that Haitians received from the government was literally rotten, sometimes crawling with maggots. The filthy, stinking latrines made the camp dangerously unsanitary. The boredom and sheer monotony of life for the Haitian detainees were made even more unbearable by the fact that they didn't know when or if they would ever be free. Furthermore, the medical care offered to the detainees was utterly inadequate. As patients, the detainees received incomplete information about their health status and were often coerced into receiving treatment and undergoing procedures without their consent. If they resisted or protested, authorities unleashed brutal force, which sometimes was provided by soldiers outfitted in riot gear. As further punitive action, disobedient or rebellious detainees were sent to Camp VII, a segregated disciplinary section of the camp.[53]

Held by the United States but outside U.S. borders, the HIV-positive prisoners were the victims of what A. Naomi Paik calls "layered forms of subjugation—racism, xenophobia, economic and political violence, fears of contagion in general and of HIV/AIDS in particular," all of which rendered them "rightless"—merely "kept in a state between life and death . . . left to waste away from a life-shortening disease."[54] However, the Haitians at Camp Bulkeley, like those before them at Guantanamo's Camp McCalla and in detention centers, prisons, and jails in the United States, found ways to resist and to assert their rights.

Many of the refugees detained at Guantanamo had been political activists in Haiti. Indeed, it was their activism and support for the popular movement and President Aristide that had made them targets of the coup regime and forced them to flee their country. When they found themselves detained against their will by the U.S. government, they drew upon their knowledge and experience of grassroots organizing and mobilization. The Haitian detainees created the Association des Réfugiés Politiques Haïtiens (Association of Haitian Political Refugees) to organize their political activity and to give voice to their demands. In June 1992, they began conducting peaceful protests against their treatment and incarceration at Guantanamo. Authorities at Guantanamo tried to halt the protests by removing twenty individuals who were leaders and placing them in segregation in Camp VII. The remaining refugees reacted with angry protests and broke into Camp VII to free their compatriots. Authorities responded with brutal repression, attacking the protesters with weapons, dogs, and military vehicles, but the detained Haitians fought back. In the resulting clash, the refugees' housing barracks were set ablaze.[55]

The refugees' campaign received political support from allies in the United States. African American organizations like TransAfrica Forum, the NAACP, and the Congressional Black Caucus worked to mobilize their communities on behalf of the Haitians. In New York City, a diverse coalition that included Haitian Women for Haitian Refugees and AIDS activists from ACT UP (AIDS Coalition to Unleash Power) formed the Emergency Coalition to Shut Down Guantanamo. In Washington, D.C., students, civil rights groups, and peace groups pressed lawmakers to admit the Haitian refugees to the United States and to grant them Temporary Protected Status.[56]

As it was an election year, a large part of the political work focused on pressuring the Democratic presidential candidate, Arkansas governor Bill Clinton, to commit to reversing both the Bush administration's direct return policy and its exclusion and detention of the HIV-positive Haitians at Guantanamo Bay. There was good reason for the Haitian detainees and their supporters to think that they had an ally in candidate Clinton. On the campaign trail, Clinton had repeatedly criticized the Bush administration's "cruel" policy of direct return of Haitian refugees. He vowed to end the practice and grant Haitian refugees temporary asylum in the United States if he was elected. Clinton and his running mate, Tennessee senator Al Gore, wrote in their co-authored book, *Putting People First*, that their administration would lift the travel ban on foreign nationals with HIV. Thus, the Haitians detained at Guantanamo looked toward the presidential election of November with a tremendous sense of hope.[57]

The detained refugees were also encouraged by the legal campaign waged on their behalf by the Yale University students and faculty associated with the Allard K. Lowenstein International Human Rights Clinic and the Center for Constitutional Rights. Although the Yale University team had been unable to halt the Bush administration's policy of direct return, their efforts in the summer of 1992 were more successful. In June 1992, the Second Circuit Court of Appeals had barred the U.S. government from repatriating Haitians who had been "screened in" (i.e., successfully passed a screening to show whether they had credible fear of political persecution) without providing them access to attorneys. Co-counsel in the case Michael Ratner observed that the ruling represented "an important victory for the Haitians" because it "established a significant precedent regarding the applicability of the due process clause outside the United States." According to Ratner, this ruling drove the Bush administration to seek a settlement with the refugees and their attorneys, since "it was not willing to let a court decision stand that would permit those aliens access to attorneys. Presumably, it was worried not just about the present case, but about future cases. It wanted Guantanamo available as a refugee-processing center, where the United States Constitution did not apply, and where aliens had no claims to due process."[58]

The government indicated that if the lawyers representing the Haitian detainees would agree to vacate the order and drop the case, it would end the indefinite detention of the detainees and allow them legal counsel while they were processed. The Haitian detainees rejected the deal, however. Even with legal counsel, they wondered why they should allow the Bush administration the chance to return them to Haiti when they could wait until November for the possible election of a candidate that had promised to rescind the HIV ban and grant them temporary asylum.[59]

On November 3, 1992, William Clinton defeated George H. W. Bush to become the forty-second president of the United States. The refugees and their supporters celebrated what they believed was the detainees' imminent release. They were encouraged when Clinton, in his first press conference as president-elect, reiterated his intention to reverse the Bush administration's policy of direct repatriation of refugees to Haiti and guaranteed that they would have asylum hearings, although he stopped short of his earlier pledges to offer temporary asylum to Haitians. Unfortunately for the refugees, on January 14, 1993, Clinton reversed course, announcing that he would not, in fact, be ending his predecessor's policy of direct return for Haitian refugees. Clinton's about-face seems to have been a response to political pressure. According to Joseph Nevins, "in the weeks prior to Clinton's arrival in office, Bush administration officials put forth exaggerated estimates of 200,000–500,000 Haitian refugees who would attempt to flee to the United States upon Clinton's assuming the presidency. And FAIR [the Federation for American Immigration Reform] ran frequent radio announcements in Florida and Georgia warning of an impending huge influx of Haitians."[60] Clinton's reversal on the Haitian question illustrated his willingness to submit to the growing political power of restrictionists and nativists. Six months later, he publicly declared his administration's intention to "make it tougher for illegal aliens to get into our country," and in subsequent years he signed several pieces of legislation that rapidly escalated the criminalization of immigrants and greatly expanded the immigration detention system.[61]

As President Bush had done, Clinton claimed that his administration was concerned that Haitians would risk their lives by attempting to come to the United States if the policy were revoked. To further discourage Haitians from seeking asylum in the United States, the White House ordered twenty-two coast guard cutters and patrol boats to encircle Haiti as a powerful deterrent for would-be refugees. The Clinton administration also subsequently refused to rescind the ban on HIV-positive aliens entering the United States, dashing the hopes of the Haitian detainees at Guantanamo and raising the real possibility that the HIV-positive Haitians and their families might never escape Guantanamo. Attorney Michael Ratner recalls the sense of dismay resulting from Clinton's about-face: "The Haitians had been kept in a barbed-wire camp for over a year, and it appeared more likely than ever that they would remain there indefinitely solely because they were HIV-positive."[62]

Inside Camp Bulkeley, the detainees reacted to Clinton's betrayal with outrage and action. Led by Yolande Jean, the political activist from Haiti who had been in the camp since May 1992 and who had emerged as a leader of detainee resistance, the refugees not only launched a hunger strike but also rejected shelter and medical care. "We called together the committee, and decided to have a hunger strike," Jean remembers. "Children, pregnant women, everyone was lying outside, rain or shine, day and night." After fifteen days of the hunger strike and failure to persuade Jean and the other refugees to call off their action, camp authorities resorted to brutal force.

At four in the morning, as we were lying on the ground, the colonel came with many soldiers. They began to beat us—I still bear a scar from this— and to strike us with nightsticks. . . . True, we threw rocks back at them, but they outnumbered us and they were armed. They then used big tractors to back us against the shelter, and they barred our escape with barbed wire.

In one final effort to destroy detainee resistance, camp administrators placed the leaders of the strike in solitary confinement.[63]

Though it was suppressed, the January hunger strike succeeded in galvanizing the movement to free the Haitians in Guantanamo. "In many ways the hunger strike was the strategic turning point," recalls Michael Ratner. "It brought the press, well-known personalities, and politicians to Guantanamo. It made the HIV camp a public issue. It also made us, the lawyers, pay a lot more attention to our clients." Jesse Jackson and the National Rainbow Coalition led delegations of civil rights leaders and activists to Guantanamo and returned

Figure 8. Painting of demonstration at Camp Bulkeley by Michelet Laurore, Guantanamo Bay, Cuba, 1992. Photo by Carol Halebian. Used by permission.

to the United States to report what they had seen. Civil rights organizations and black clergy organized a series of actions that included days of fasting and hunger strikes in solidarity. In March 1993, college students launched a series of rolling strikes that started at universities and then moved on to churches across the country. Prominent African Americans Randall Robinson and Katherine Dunham engaged in their own well-publicized hunger strikes against the Clinton administration's policies. In reviewing the success of their efforts, Michael Ratner concluded that "by the spring of 1993, we had a substantial campaign operating in the United States."[64] As the campaign for freedom for Haitian refugees gained momentum in the United States, the *Washington Post* observed "a rising tide of activism on Haiti" in which "a growing chorus of ordinary people, celebrities, and lawmakers [were] protesting the US policy of forced repatriation of immigrants from Haiti."[65]

As the resistance continued inside the camp and the solidarity movement grew outside the camp, the Yale legal team directly challenged the U.S. government in court. *Haitian Centers Council v. McNary* contested the legality of the HIV detention camp, claiming that the indefinite detention of the Haitian refugees was illegal on several grounds:

1. The medical care was inadequate.
2. The Haitians were entitled to due process protections prior to any determination that could send them back to Haiti.
3. Continued confinement constituted indefinite detention.
4. Requiring the second well-founded fear determination on Guantanamo was unauthorized by law.
5. The attorney general had abused her parole authority.
6. Barring lawyers from the Haitian Service Organizations from the camp violated the First Amendment.[66]

In March 1993, the trial was held in a federal court in Brooklyn, New York, presided over by Judge Sterling Johnson. Some time after hearing the arguments in the case, Judge Johnson issued an interim order that required the government to provide those detained in Camp Bulkeley adequate medical care or free them. A number of the detainees had already been paroled into the United States to seek medical care, although in some instances they were jailed upon arrival. Finally, on June 8, 1993, Judge Johnson issued his final order, ruling in favor of the plaintiffs. "Although the defendants euphemistically refer to its Guantanamo operation as a 'humanitarian camp,' the facts disclose that it is nothing more than an H.I.V. prison camp presenting potential public health risks to the Haitians held there," wrote Judge Johnson. "The Haitians' plight is a tragedy of immense proportion, and their continued detainment is totally unacceptable to this court." The court ordered the government to close Camp Bulkeley and to release the Haitian refugees to go "anywhere but Haiti." The Haitian refugees of Guantanamo were free.[67]

Guantanamo: An Enduring Solution from Crisis to Crisis

On June 21, 1993, the last detainees of Camp Bulkeley were released and brought to the United States. The notorious HIV prison camp was finally closed. However, the U.S. naval base at Guantanamo Bay remained a potential site for the extraterritorial detention of unauthorized migrants and refugees. In August, the Clinton administration appealed the ruling that had freed the Haitians and closed Camp Bulkeley. In October, the Haitians' legal team and the government reached a settlement: the government agreed to drop its appeal and to reimburse the more than $600,000 the plaintiffs' attorneys had spent in litigating the case, while the Haitians' attorneys agreed to join the government in asking Judge Sterling Johnson to vacate his final order in the case, which he soon did after he had received the request. Because the court's ruling was annulled, the Haitian detainees' legal victory ceased to have any value as a legal precedent, so no legal obstacles blocked the government's use of Guantanamo as a future detention site for Haitians or any other unauthorized migrants the United States might want to hold outside its territorial boundaries.[68]

The proposal to reactivate the camps at Guantanamo resurfaced in the spring of 1994. In May, the Clinton administration had announced that it would be reinstituting asylum hearings for interdicted Haitian refugees instead of continuing the direct return policy without asylum hearings that it had retained from the Bush administration. Questions quickly surfaced about where asylum hearings would be held and where those who had been interdicted would be held while awaiting screening. Clinton administration officials announced that asylum seekers would be taken to the USS *Comfort* and other vessels, would be anchored in Jamaican waters, for screening and that another site in the Turks and Caicos was being set up for processing. In addition, the administration urged Haitians to take advantage of "in-country processing" whereby applicants could apply for asylum while they were still in Haiti, a process critics regarded as unrealistic and even dangerous. Steven Forester, attorney for the Haitian Refugee Center, noted that the approval rate for those that applied for asylum while they were still in Haiti was about 2 percent. Forester objected to the notion that the Clinton administration's change of policy provided those fleeing Haiti with more protection or due process than before. He claimed that the vessel anchored near Kingston should better be called "the USS No Comfort because it is designed . . . to repatriate 95 percent of the people," primarily because those screened aboard the *Comfort* had "no attorneys, no legal assistance whatsoever [and] the highest refugee burden." These asylum interviews were conducted in bad faith, Forester and other critics of the Clinton administration argued, making the government's new posture relating to Haitian refugees nothing more than "a sham."[69]

The dangers of in-country processing and the flaws of offshore asylum screening prompted some of the advocates for Haitian refugees to call for

Guantanamo to be reopened as an interim site for land-based asylum screening. The National Coalition for Haitian Refugees suggested that Guantanamo might be used as one of the "safe haven enclaves" it hoped President Clinton would establish for Haitian refugees in the Caribbean. Steven Forester saw that detained refugees might have more rights at Guantanamo than they had had on board coast guard vessels and attributed the White House's reluctance to reopen Guantanamo to that fact. "Why aren't we using Guantanamo Naval Base, as in 1991–1992?" Forester asked. "Probably to avoid federal court challenge to this sham. When untrained adjudicators on Guantanamo 'screened in' only about 5%, the Haitian Refugee Center sued, causing INS to bring in trained asylum officers and the 'screen in' rate to rise to about 80% for 4 to 6 weeks." The irony of those who had so long fought the detention of Haitians in Guantanamo now calling for the government to reactivate Guantanamo as a site for Haitians to be detained, at least temporarily, must not have been lost on participants in this debate. However, their call to reopen the camps at Guantanamo attests to what they saw as the inadequacy of both in-country and offshore processing and the ongoing grave danger the people of Haiti faced.[70]

In June 1994, a worsening human rights catastrophe in Haiti amid the ongoing coup (which by that point had been ongoing for nearly three years), drove the first of more than 20,000 new refugees from Haiti. At the same time, after the Cuban government authorized voluntary departure from Cuba, the first of 30,000 Cuban *balseros* (raft people) fled their country by boat. This surge in Caribbean refugees toward the United States led the Clinton administration to reopen Guantanamo Bay as a processing center for refugees. The White House characterized the Guantanamo camp as a "safe haven" that it was attempting to establish for refugees throughout the Caribbean. But a sojourn at Guantanamo would not be an effective "safe haven" if it was simply a prelude to a forced return to life-threatening conditions. In the spring and summer of 1994, when both Cubans and Haitians were detained at the reopened Guantanamo camp, the majority of the Cubans ultimately were allowed to enter the United States while most of the Haitians were forced to return to Haiti.[71]

With this new population of detainees, the government anticipated and attempted to neutralize the sort of resistance that had taken root among the earlier group of Haitian detainees., It deployed a psychological approach to the problem, which it named Operation Sea Signal. The psychological objectives for this mission to Guantanamo included ensuring that "informal leaders of migrants understand that they would benefit from a calm and orderly environment while awaiting transfer." The government claimed that its goal was to make sure that the "general migrant population understands that U.S. authorities are genuinely concerned about their problems and that cooperation with the authorities is in the migrants' best interest." Maintaining order seems to have been the top priority in the psychological mission, which aimed to "pacify [the] migrant population through public information while they are processed."[72]

However, as long as Haiti was in the hands of coup leaders who relied upon violence to maintain their power, the United States would be forced to deal with a continual refugee crisis. The Clinton administration recognized as much. As diplomatic efforts to resolve the political crisis in Haiti faltered, the Clinton administration planned a military invasion of the island that sought to restore President Aristide to office. As the Clinton White House prepared for the president's national address in which he intended to announce the military intervention, the refugee issue figured significantly in the administration's justification for taking military action in Haiti. One of the "strong interests in restoring democracy to Haiti," administration talking points maintained, was the problem of "refugee outflow":

> As the atrocities get worse, there is an increased likelihood that we will see a new outpouring of refugees from Haiti to the United States. As the brutality intensifies and the pressures build, it will be increasingly difficult to contain the flow of refugees off U.S. shores.[73]

On September 15, 1994, President Clinton delivered his "Address to the Nation on Haiti." Along with a condemnation of the coup regime and an affirmation of democracy for Haiti, the president informed the American people that "as long as [coup leader General Raoul] Cedras rules, Haitians will continue to seek sanctuary in our Nation." He pointed out the cost of such a situation:

> This year, in less than two months, more than 21,000 Haitians were rescued at sea by our Coast Guard and Navy. Today more than 14,000 refugees are living at our naval base in Guantanamo. The American people have already expended more than $200 million to support them, to maintain the economic embargo. And the prospect of millions and millions more being spent every month for an indefinite period of time loom ahead unless we act.[74]

Days later, U.S. troops entered Haiti. Exactly one month after Clinton's address to the nation, President Aristide returned to Haiti, bringing to an end the bloody coup years and stemming the flow of Haitian refugees, for the time being at least.[75]

Some Haitians and their supporters viewed the restoration of the democratically elected government of Haiti as an undeniable victory for popular democracy and democratic principles. Others regarded Aristide's return as a partial success at best, since the Haitian president returned accompanied by the U.S. military and since Aristide's restoration to the presidency was conditioned upon an acceptance of "market friendly reforms," such as the privatization of state-owned enterprises and the surrender of Haiti's economy to international finance and regulatory agencies.[76] And just as troubling, the U.S. response to Haitian refugees during the coup years created dangerous precedents in dealing with migrants and asylum seekers. The government's practice of enhanced interdiction—the direct return policy that the George H. W. Bush administration initiated, the Clinton administration continued, and the Supreme Court upheld—inaugurated a new, extremely harsh phase in U.S. policy toward refugees. The Clinton administration soon used the practice of interdiction and return in dealing with Chinese refugees it encountered in the Gulf of Mexico.[77] In addition, the government's expansion of its Haitian detention program would have far-reaching consequences. The United States now had an offshore detention camp for unauthorized migrants (and in the aftermath of September 11, 2001, "enemy combatants,"). The U.S. government continued to claim that such migrants had few rights, based on that fact that they were detained outside the boundaries of the United States.

Writing in July 1994, international relations expert Christopher Mitchell cautioned that American authorities were pursuing a policy of "near-summary exclusion" of international migrants and that "U.S. policy toward Haitian boat people may well come to be considered, for better or worse, as exemplary rather than anomalous."[78] Time has indeed shown that its policies toward Haitians constituted the model on which U.S. authorities would base their broadened policy of deterrence and exclusion.

6

Reinforcing the Detention System, 1994–2000

Bernadette, a Haitian national and longtime resident of the United States, spent nineteen months in prison for a criminal offense before she was transferred to the Krome Detention Center to await her deportation to Haiti. While in the South Florida detention facility, she was harassed and assaulted by guards and forced to engage in sexual acts with INS officers at the facility. Bernadette's experience in immigration detention was so bad that it made her long for a return to prison. "I prayed they would ship me back to prison. Krome is disgusting. Far worse than prison," she claimed. "It is pure sexism and the women suffer more than the men."[1]

Reports of the experiences of immigrant detainees in local jails were just as bad. While conducting an extensive investigation into immigration detention in U.S. jails, Human Rights Watch received hundreds of letters from detainees that provided a vivid portrait of the desperation and fear that detention fostered. "Since the day I came to America [September 28, 1997], I have not committed any crime. I have never been in any type of prison system but when I came here they locked me up like I'm some kind of criminal," wrote an Iranian detainee held in Nacogdoches County Jail in Texas.

> They locked me up along with inmates, people that have committed crimes. . . . That's why I fear for my life. . . . The situation here is no good for me, because they don't offer the basic needs in which to live. The food they give us is not enough to live on. When I request something from the officers they either deny me or tell me to write a request form, which they deny afterwards anyways. I don't have an attorney for I cannot afford one. I escaped from my country's army to come to America, but if I go back now to Iran, the consequences will be deadly.[2]

At the Mercer County Detention Center in Trenton, New Jersey, an Egyptian detainee suffered a similar set of indignities:

In June of 1997 my application for immigrant status with the Immigration and Naturalization Service (INS) was rejected. Since then, my presence in the United States became illegal, and that is why I was arrested. . . . After the ruling I was placed in solitary confinement, in a cell with no heat and no hot water. I was not allowed to use the telephone to talk to my lawyer. A Muslim prison employee was prevented from giving me a copy of the Quran. I was not allowed to perform Friday congregational prayers with other Muslim inmates, nor could I go to the gymnasium. To this day, jail management refuses to provide a vegetarian meal. I do not eat meat because of religious convictions. Since my arrest, I have lost 25 pounds.[3]

Although each detention facility and each detainee was different, those in immigration detention in the United States in the late 1990s had these things in common: they were caught up in an ever-widening system that held detainees longer, afforded them fewer rights, and treated them more brutally than ever before.

In the two decades since immigration officials had reinstituted detention as a mechanism of control and deterrence against Haitian refugees, the system had grown enormously. Throughout the 1980s, the U.S. system of mass incarceration increasingly overlapped with its system of immigration control. But in the 1990s, particularly as a result of two pieces of legislation in 1996 that merged criminal and immigration law, the U.S. immigration detention system moved much further down the path to becoming what it is today. Haitian refugees, the detainees involved at the time detention was reinstituted, continued to be incarcerated in U.S. immigration detention. But by the turn of the twenty-first century, the vast detention regime of the United States held refugees and unauthorized migrants from around the world: nearly 200,000 each year and tens of thousands on any given day.

Child Detention and Guantanamo Redux

By the mid-1990s, despite the fact that Haitian refugees were only one group of detainees held in the United States, their presence in America's immigration prisons continued to command disproportionate attention. This situation existed because the Clinton administration was not able to close the chapter on its Haitian refugee controversy, even with the return of President Aristide to Haiti and the restoration of democracy there. After that, the controversy focused on the detention of Haitian children. At the end of February 1995, a group of more than 100 Haitian children detained at the U.S. naval base at Guantanamo Bay, Cuba, sent a letter to President Bill Clinton in which they articulated their position in the controversy.

> President Clinton,
> All the Haitian children in Guantanamo send you their greetings. The purpose of this letter is to ask you what will be done with us.
> We would like to ask you if we are not children too. President Clinton, we would like to ask you why you let the Cuban children in and you leave us here in Guantanamo? Is it because you don't like us? Are we not children too? We would like to ask you if you don't have any children because you seem to be so hard-hearted. . . .
> Are you going to help us? How would you feel if you were placed in a camp like this?
> We would like you to think about your children, think about how you love them—then you will realize how you would feel if they were going through such misery?
> We would like you to send a response for the children please. There are many of them who do have family in the US and there are some who do not have any family at all. Please save them. God will bless you.
> Thank you! Send us a response please.[4]

The Haitian children of Guantanamo were part of the renewed refugee crisis that had led the Clinton administration to reopen the camp at Guantanamo. More than 20,000 Haitians had been interdicted and subsequently transferred to Guantanamo in the spring and summer of 1994. In addition, more than 30,000 Cubans who had fled their country by boat were also transferred to Guantanamo. Soon tens of thousands of Haitians and Cubans were occupying a new detention camp at the U.S. naval base on the southeastern tip of Cuba that had been established for unaccompanied Haitian and Cuban children. Among the Haitians held at the Guantanamo camp were 356 unaccompanied children.[5]

The government ultimately allowed most of the Cubans detained at Guantanamo (including the unaccompanied Cuban children) to enter the United States, while it forcibly returned the majority of the Haitian adults to Haiti. The repatriation of the Haitian adults began in November, shortly after the restoration of the Aristide government. To justify its inclusion of Cubans and its exclusion of Haitians, the U.S. government argued that "Haiti is a democracy again," as opposed to Cuba, which was controlled by a government the United States characterized as a communist dictatorship.[6] This rationale for the return of the Haitians was not persuasive to opponents of the policy such as Cheryl Little, who observed that even before Aristide's restoration "the US Government seems never to have seriously considered allowing these [Haitian] children as a group to enter the US." As Little pointed out, "violence and insecurity continue throughout Haiti, especially in the countryside where 70% of the population receives little or no protection by UN troops." In fact, "Haiti's own government has condemned the involuntary repatriation of all Haitian nationals," including "the forced repatriation of Guantanamo's unaccompanied Haitian children."[7]

For the U.S. government, the best resolution of the refugee problem would be for the Haitians to return to their country voluntarily. To achieve this end, authorities at Guantanamo engaged in what investigators from Florida Rural Legal Services called "a diligent effort to coerce Haitians to return home." After interviews with the detained Haitians at Guantanamo, a fact-finding team found that "the military has regularly gone to the camps with microphones [and loudspeakers] urging Haitians to return because things are safe in Haiti now. Late at night, military personnel have gone into the camps and pointed flashlights at the Haitians[,] urging them to return to Haiti." Worried that the Haitians might be inclined to wait it out in Guantanamo to see if they would eventually be admitted to the United States, "a group of high ranking military officers" told Haitians in the camps at Guantanamo that "the American policy toward them would never change"; they might be detained there for five years or more.[8]

Although there were some unaccompanied minors among the adults in other Haitian camps, the majority of the Haitian children of Guantanamo were kept in Camp 9. There, the hundreds of Haitian children, who ranged in age from two months to seventeen years, lived in tents overseen by Haitian adults designated as "house parents." They received food, clothing, schooling, and recreation facilities provided by the authorities. But the children, many of whose parents had been killed by military or paramilitary forces in Haiti, suffered from severe depression. Some even attempted suicide due to their isolation in the Guantanamo camp and their fear that they would be forced to return to the country they had fled. Abuse also was also a problem for the Haitian children, both in Camp 9 and throughout Guantanamo. In Camp 9, the president of the house parents' group sexually abused a fourteen-year-old girl. One sixteen-year-old girl whose parents had been killed by the Haitian military was raped by three men after she and her fourteen-year-old sister were mistakenly placed in an adult camp when they arrived at Guantanamo. The Haitian children also had to contend with other kinds of abuse from the military authorities of Guantanamo. A camp guard broke one youth's arm. The children suffered from severe disciplinary measures, including being forced to remain on their knees in the blazing sun or being sent to Little Buckley, a children's jail that consisted of "a boxed fence with mesh placed on top." For fighting, one boy was placed in Little Buckley for a day and a half.[9]

By November 1994, their ongoing detention and mistreatment and reports that Cuban children were being admitted to the United States while they remained in Guantanamo led the Haitian children of Camp 9 to hold a demonstration and a hunger strike. Dressed in white, the children of Camp 9 prayed as a form of protest. Those who interviewed the children reported that the strikers "felt they were being treated badly because they were black." The children "felt completely isolated" and wanted to know the truth about what would happen to them. They also were "upset because they were denied access to the press the day before the hunger strike."[10]

The ordeal of the Haitian children of Guantanamo soon drew public attention, engaging members of the same coalition that had fought for Haitian refugees and Haitian democracy for the previous three years. Members of this coalition now shifted their attention to freeing the Haitian youth detained at Guantanamo and called for them to be admitted to the United States. These efforts were led by Fanm Ayisyen Nan Miyami (Haitian Women of Miami). They and their allies formed a coalition of forty professional and grassroots organizations called Justice Coalition for the Haitian Children in Guantanamo. The coalition held a series of protests and rallies calling for the Haitian children at Guantanamo to be freed. The executive director of migration and refugee services for the United States Catholic Conference lent his organization's support to the campaign, writing to the State Department to urge the Clinton administration to resettle the Haitian children in the United States. In addition, the National Organization for Women urged Attorney General Janet Reno to grant humanitarian parole to the Haitian children so they could be brought to the United States. A group of celebrities, including actors Robert Redford, Danny Glover, and Gregory Peck; filmmaker Jonathan Demme; and activist Randall Robinson organized Guantanamo Watch. The group urged Reno to allow the Haitian children of Guantanamo to be reunited with their relatives and sponsors in the United States.[11]

Despite the growing calls for the Clinton administration to release the Haitian youth of Guantanamo and to allow them to enter the United States, on March 8, 1995, the government began forcibly repatriating the children to Haiti. The move prompted a new round of protests by human rights groups and Haitian organizations and their allies. Cheryl Little denounced the government's "forcible repatriation of Guantanamo's most traumatized and vulnerable children" as "a serious humanitarian tragedy." Nonetheless, by the end of April, more than sixty children had been forcibly returned to Haiti.[12]

In early May, as the repatriation of Haitian youth continued, President Clinton announced that nearly all of the remaining Cubans in Guantanamo would be allowed into the United States. At that time, one-third of the more than 300 Haitian children had been repatriated, while only twenty-three had been transferred to the United States. On the morning of May 11, 1995, anger over the U.S. government's actions boiled over. Haitian youth in Camp 9 burned four of the tents and threw stones and oranges at guards. Some launched a new hunger strike.[13]

Approximately 200 Haitian children were in Camp 9 at Guantanamo on May 19, 1995, when the White House announced that none of the Haitian children would remain in Guantanamo past June 30 of that year. Advocates worried that the children would suffer the same fate as the majority of other detainees who had already been forced back to Haiti. But as the June 30 deadline for closing Camp 9 approached, the Clinton administration announced its intention to give most of the remaining 123 children humanitarian parole and allow them to enter the United States, a step that was almost certainly a response to the pressure the campaign to free the Haitian children was applying. Unfortunately, more than half of the Haitian children had already been forcibly returned to Haiti, where they faced an uncertain and often dangerous future. Their repatriation came after enduring a harrowing year of detention at the hands of U.S. military authorities at Guantanamo Bay.

Consummating the Marriage of Immigration Restriction and Mass Incarceration

Although the episode of Haitian child detention in Guantanamo that had attracted so much attention and generated so much controversy was coming to a close by the end of June 1995, the harsh treatment of immigrants and asylum seekers in the United States was not ending. In fact, at that moment, a new nativism that would reshape and greatly expand the U.S. immigration detention regime was rising rapidly.

In the 1990s, opposition to the presence of undocumented immigrants in the United States and support for restricting immigration was on the rise, as signified by California's Proposition 187 in 1994. The proposition denied health care, education, and social services to undocumented immigrants and their families. Daniel Tichenor notes that growing popular support for restricting immigration and for measures such as California's Proposition 187 was the result of many Americans' belief that immigration adversely affected the economy. In the wake of the World Trade Center bombing in 1993, many Americans increasingly associated immigration and terrorism. Nativist sentiment was widespread enough that something of a bipartisan consensus emerged against unauthorized immigration as members of both parties postured as the toughest on illegal aliens. According to Joseph Nevins, federal officials, national politicians, and "a compliant media, helped to construct the perception of a crisis and to stoke public fears" by warning the nation of the security threat that that the "invasion" of illegal immigrants represented.[14]

The Federation for American Immigration Reform also worked to fan the flames of fear and anxiety about immigration. For example, FAIR executive director Dan Stein argued against easing restrictions on Haitian asylum seekers by painting a frightening picture of what would happen when the Third World sent hordes of desperate people to American shores. Dramatic population growth in places such as Haiti, Stein claimed, could produce "a dramatic deterioration in the quality of life, civil disorder, a breakdown in the civil legal structure, an ecology in ruins, an economy in ruins, illiteracy rates as high as 80 percent," all of which were part of "a pattern emerging worldwide" in which country after country would slide into "generalized anarchy and civil war." The result would be unknown numbers of poor and desperate people on America's doorstep, threatening to drive the United States down the very same path. Better to close the nation's doors than to risk this nightmare scenario, Stein said.[15]

At the same time that fear of immigrants was generating growing support for immigration restriction, a political tendency had been gathering momentum since the mid-1980s to get "tough on crime." This impulse continued to drive the parallel growth of mass incarceration and the criminalization of immigration. As Marie Gottschalk explains, "Mass incarceration was fueled in part by stoking public anxieties that crime was out of control. Likewise, support for tougher immigration policies has been whipped up by charges that immigrants are a major source of crime, and that 'border violence is out of control.'" These twin tendencies produced both the "strikingly punitive turn in immigration policy" and the continuing rise of the carceral state.[16]

The intersection of growing nativism and the ostensible anti-crime movement was favorable to a sequence of laws that combined immigration and criminal law, in effect bringing about the criminalization of immigration law and producing what legal scholar Juliet P. Stumpf has called "the crimmigration crisis."[17] The Anti-Drug Abuse Act of 1988 started the process by creating the category of "aggravated felony." The act subjected immigrants convicted of drug-related crimes to deportation and mandated immigration detention for these so-called criminal aliens after their criminal sentence had been served. Most of these criminal aliens were sent to the recently opened immigration prison in Oakdale, Louisiana.[18] Historian Daniel Kanstroom observes that in the following years, "it sometimes seemed as if a tsunami had been unleashed against 'criminal aliens.' A relentless crackdown ensued." The Immigration Act of 1990 grouped additional offenses in the category of "aggravated felony," which further eroded the rights of and protections for convicted immigrants. In 1994, another law created a fast-track procedure for deporting certain aggravated felons, further limited the power of a judge to review and intervene in such cases, and created a tracking program for "criminal aliens." In the same year, congressional Democrats and Republicans united to pass what Heather Ann Thompson calls "the most comprehensive 'tough on crime' bill in American history." The Violent Crime Control and Law Enforcement Act of 1994 fed the growing carceral state by committing $9.7 billion to new prison construction, $1.2 billion to the expansion of border patrol and criminal deportations, and $1.8 billion for the State Alien Criminal Assistance Program. Patrisia Macías-Rojas notes that these policies "further institutionalized the Criminal Alien Program."[19] By 1995, a swelling prison population of more than one million people included a growing number of citizens and non-citizens.[20]

"And then came the 1996 deluge," Kanstroom writes.[21] In 1996, Congress passed the Antiterrorism and Effective Death Penalty Act (AEDPA), which expedited the deportation process for noncitizens convicted of a crime and imposed mandatory detention on those awaiting deportation. Just months after the AEDPA was passed, Congress passed the Illegal Immigration Reform and Immigrant Responsibility Act (IIRIRA), which greatly intensified the assault on "criminal aliens." The law further expanded the list of offenses that were classified as aggravated felonies, expanding the category beyond serious crimes such as murder and rape to include less serious acts such as petty theft and shoplifting, drunk driving, and certain low-level drug-related violations. The statute also required detention for all "criminal aliens" that had been sentenced to at least one year (even if they were never required to do any time) and instructed the attorney general to transfer those who had completed their criminal sentence and were deemed deportable by the new law to immigration detention. In addition, the law applied the new definition of aggravated felony retroactively, so that an immigrant who in the past had pled guilty to or had been convicted of a relatively minor crime that had been reclassified as an aggravated felony was now subject to arrest, mandatory detention, and deportation. In addition, the IIRIRA gave immigration officers at a port of entry the authority to order the summary exclusion of aliens who arrived with false or no documents, it limited the arriving alien's ability to seek further review by a judge, and mandated detention of asylum seekers while their claims were being processed. The law also eliminated judicial review, which had given judges the ability to weigh a host of factors in determining whether an individual should be detained and deported.[22]

Rights groups attacked the 1996 legislation as unfair and unconstitutional. The IIRIRA's elimination of judicial review in particular violated the constitution's guarantee of review by a federal court for something as serious as deportation, they claimed. Congress "cannot bar judicial review altogether when the liberty of an individual is at stake," argued Lucas Guttentag of the ACLU Immigrants' Rights Project. The ACLU and its allies also sought to undo the law's "unfair detention of immigrants" and other provisions.[23] Immigration scholar Tanya Golash-Boza observes that the 1996 laws seemed to be in conflict with the Constitution's Fifth Amendment, which prohibits subjecting a person to punishment for the same offense twice. "It is only by claiming that deportation is not punishment that one could argue that the U.S. government is not violating the U.S. Constitution" when it detains and deports criminal aliens who have already served their time or have otherwise met the requirements of the court, Golash-Boza points out. The 1996 laws also seemed to violate the Sixth Amendment, which provides for the right to counsel. Finally, she notes that the law seemed to violate the Constitution's guarantee of due process, since "there is no way that a person who pled guilty to a crime in 1995 or earlier could have known that crime would be reclassified as an aggravated felony in 1996, and that he or she would face deportation as a result."[24]

But the 1996 laws generated more than just heated legal and political debate. The legislation, which one legal scholar called "some of the toughest measures ever taken against illegal immigration," had immediate consequences for immigrants and refugees in the United States.[25] In the year after the new laws were passed, immigration officials carried out raids and sweeps in communities across the nation, sending a wave of terror through immigrant communities.

Individuals such as Olufolake Olaleye, a Nigerian mother of two, soon found themselves swept up because of the enforcement of the new laws. In 1993, Olaleye had pled guilty to shoplifting fifteen dollars' worth of baby clothes. Although she had in fact purchased the items, she was accused of taking them when she tried to return them without a receipt. She received a small fine, a twelve-month suspended sentence, and then one year of probation. The petty offense did not disqualify Olaleye from eligibility for citizenship when she applied before the 1996 laws were passed. But once IIRIRA became law, Olaleye became an aggravated felon and she faced detention and deportation. The case of 54-year-old Garibaldy Mejia was similar. In 1985, the Dominican-born Mejia had been arrested for possessing a small amount of cocaine. He pled guilty and received a $100 fine and two years' probation. For the next twenty-five years he lived, worked, and raised his family as a legal resident of the United States. But in 2000, when he attempted to reenter the United States after a visit to the Dominican Republic, immigration officials detained him according to the IIRIRA's provisions that made him a criminal alien. Mejia was sent to the detention facility in Oakdale, Louisiana.[26]

The impact of the 1996 laws was felt far and wide. It reached far beyond those the lawmakers claimed to be targeting: the criminal aliens who posed a genuine threat to their communities and the nation. Why would lawmakers support laws that caused such harm? By ostensibly focusing exclusively on the criminal elements of immigrant communities, supporters of the 1996 laws could claim to be against lawbreakers instead of being anti-immigrant. Lawmakers viewed the merging of criminal and immigration law as good politics, Michael Welch argues, because it enabled politicians to "enthusiastically voice their support for legislation targeting illegal immigrants in the same breath with anticrime, antidrug, and anti-welfare rhetoric."[27] Daniel Kanstroom explains it this way:

Figure 9. Krome Detention Center, early 1990s. Photo by Jon Kral. Used by permission.

The post-entry social control deportation system [created by the laws leading up to and culminating in 1996] was a perfect vehicle for politicians to demonstrate toughness on crime at virtually no political cost. Moreover, the turn toward "criminal aliens" offered an easy way to appear to be doing something meaningful about the more intractable, resurgent problem of undocumented immigration. Those individuals, families and communities who bore the brunt of these policies and those who feared their implications and trends went largely unheard.[28]

Together, the 1996 laws led to a massive increase in immigration detention. As David Manuel Hernández notes, "By reinforcing mandatory detention for immigrants facing deportation, removing avenues for judicial relief, and expanding the category of 'aggravated felony' which triggers mandatory detention and deportation proceedings, IIRIRA is responsible for the tripling of immigrant detention in the 1990s." It is no wonder, then, that in 1996, investors saw "a tremendous bull market in corrections."[29] Daniel Wilsher provides figures that illustrate the dramatic growth of immigration detention. In 1995, the detention population was 6,600 a day. By 2001, the number of detained immigrants on a given day had jumped to 20,000, and by 2008 the number was expected to reach 33,400. The number of aliens detained each year had surged from 72,154 in 1994 to 188,547 in 2001.[30]

Lost in the Labyrinth: Despair and Resistance at the End of the Century

In the years after the passage of the draconian immigration- and detention-related legislation of 1996, the worst fears of many immigrant rights advocates were realized. Although the merging of criminal law with immigration enforcement had been developing for some time, the new laws that mandated detention and did away with judicial discretion exacerbated the most restrictive and repressive aspects of the immigration system. A survey of the immigration detention system and reports of those caught in that system at the end of the twentieth century reveal just how formidable—and how cruel—the system had become since its formal reinstitution two decades earlier.

In the 1970s and 1980s, human rights and refugee advocates had decried the government's detention of Haitian asylum seekers, claiming that the practice amounted to an unparalleled violation of the international obligations of the United States to refugees and an unconscionable denial of the detainees' rights. But by the end of the 1990s, detention of asylum seekers was standard practice. In 1998 and 1999, Amnesty International conducted an investigation and published the results in *Lost in the Labyrinth*. Amnesty International found that "thousands of asylum seekers are detained in US detention centers and jails," often indefinitely. Despite the fact that these people "are not criminals," the report observed, "many are confined with criminal prisoners" and treated like criminals, "held in conditions that are sometimes inhuman and degrading," made to endure strip searches, verbal and physical abuse, and being "shackled and chained." They were often "denied access to their families, lawyers, and non-governmental organizations (NGOs) who could help them." Held "in isolation and ignorance of their rights" and frequently transferred from one facility to another, many asylum seekers simply disappeared into the system. Once they were "caught in the labyrinth of the INS detention system, its complexity and almost complete disregard of the needs of refugees create a 'trial by ordeal' from which only the most persistent, courageous, or lucky emerge unscathed."[31]

Twenty years earlier, Haitian refugees and their advocates had also ex-pressed shock and outrage over the government's practice of incarcerating Haitians in a network of state and county jails. But as the twentieth century came to a close, the government's reliance on jails to meets its detention re-quirements had become another standard part of its immigration enforce-ment strategy. In September 1998, Human Rights Watch released a report on immigration detainees in U.S. jails that featured evidence collected in more than 200 interviews and visits to more than a dozen jails in seven states. More than 60 percent of the 15,000 detainees held by the INS were being held in local jails, the report observed. Under the control of local sheriffs and other jail officials, INS detainees (including asylum seekers) who were in adminis-trative detention were "mixed with accused and convicted criminal inmates" and "subjected to physical mistreatment and grossly inadequate conditions of confinement."[32]

Reports of abuse of immigrant detainees in local jails came from all over the country. Detainees in Cell Block 2K in Virginia Beach, Virginia, reported that guards taunted them with racist statements, woke them late at night by drag-ging keys along the bars of their cells, and denied them any chance to leave the overcrowded detention area, except for a 20-minute recreation session once a week.[33] In Union County Jail in New Jersey, nine guards were found to have physically abused the INS detainees in their facility. In Jackson County Jail in Mariana, Florida, detainees reported that they were "subjected to racial and ethnic slurs [and] shackled naked to concrete slabs in spread-eagle positions[,] where they were left for hours, beaten with batons, and shocked with electric riot shields." In Port Manatee Central Jail in Palmetto, Florida, after detainees protested the poor conditions at the jail, sheriff's deputies retaliated against them, beating them, stripping them naked, dragging them through dog and human waste, and leaving them for twenty hours in flooded cells.[34]

The vastly expanded detention requirements of the new laws drove a rapid growth in the system in the last five years of the century. By the year 2000, the detention capacity of the INS had grown to 20,000, up from 7,000 in 1995, and immigration officials were predicting that the system would be able to hold another 4,000 detainees by 2001. This rapidly growing detention system was comprised of four types of facilities: service processing centers owned and op-erated by the INS, privately owned and operated immigration detention facili-ties, county and local jails, and federal prisons. The annual detention budget exceeded $1 billion. But even this vast sum and the greatly expanded detention capacity of the system were not enough to hold all of those the 1996 laws required immigration officials to detain. Fully enforcing the detention provisions of the new laws would require $652 million more, 21,000 additional beds, and 1,500 additional employees, immigration officials claimed.[35]

Child detention became an increasingly significant part of the U.S. immigration detention system in the second half of the 1990s. Just a few years earlier, the detention of the unaccompanied Haitian children of Guantanamo had drawn attention and generated controversy in part because child detention was so unusual. In fact, the INS had been detaining children along the U.S.-Mexico border since the early 1980s, although this practice never achieved the public exposure that the plight of the Haitian children of Guantanamo had.[36] Child detention continued after 1995, ensnaring children from Central and South America but also children from China, Africa, the Indian subcontinent, and elsewhere. Criminal justice scholar Michael Welch observed that the INS apprehended 4,600 undocumented youth in 2000. He claimed that the INS "has 500 youths in its custody each day, but due to limited detention space, the agency ships many of them to juvenile centers and in some instances to adult jails."[37] A Human Rights Watch investigation into the practice of holding unaccompanied children in INS detention found that "at any given time over two hundred children are in long-term custody." The rights organization commented that "children in INS detention are invisible: they have slipped through the cracks."

They are arrested by the INS, detained in highly restrictive settings, and provided with little information about their legal rights and status. Unlike adults detained by the INS, unaccompanied children are not eligible for release after posting bond [and] many of them remain in detention for months on end, bewildered and frightened, denied meaningful access to attorneys and their relatives. Ultimately, most of the children are deported. Because these children speak little or no English and are rarely aware of their rights under U.S. law, and because their relatives in the United States, if they have any, are frequently in the same plight, the children are extremely vulnerable.[38]

Children being held in inappropriate conditions of confinement were exposed to abuse in facilities all over the country. In Los Angeles County, Human Rights Watch found that juvenile INS detainees who had had previous contact with the juvenile justice system were placed in county prisons "and made to wear prison uniforms, although they are being detained for administrative reasons only." They were given no privacy, were barred from keeping personal possessions, and "in some facilities, [were] illegally housed with the general prison population." In Arizona, child detainees were placed in a privately run "shelter-care center," supposedly a positive alternative to the county prisons and other forms of detention. Unfortunately, Human Rights Watch investigators found "conditions in some of the new shelter-care facilities are little better than in the county detention facilities." In the Arizona detention center, children lived in crowded conditions with no privacy and could not leave the grounds. Most troubling, they were denied information about their rights and were unable to make telephone calls to families or attorneys. This effectively denied them access to legal services.[39] At the Berks County Youth Center in Leesport, Pennsylvania, many of the child detainees were treated like criminals; they were strip searched, forced to wear handcuffs while being transported to court, and denied adequate translation and legal services.[40] An investigation by the Women's Commission for Refugee Women and Children into the Liberty County Juvenile Correction Center, a maximum-security facility 90 minutes outside Houston, discovered children wearing prison uniforms and being forced to remain in their cells twenty-three hours a day. When members of the commission visited the facility in June 1998, they found over eighty incarcerated children, most of whom had no criminal conviction or record of running away from the minimum-security shelter facilities, the only conditions that were supposed to warrant placing immigrant children in facilities such as the Liberty County Juvenile Correction Center.[41]

After a two-year assessment of detention conditions for women and children, the Women's Commission for Refugee Women and Children determined that each of the approximately thirty detention facilities it had observed were "prisons or the equivalent" in which "women and children [were] particularly at risk of abuse and neglect." Wendy Young of the women's commission provided some particularly disturbing examples of the sort of abuse detained women faced in her testimony to the Senate Subcommittee on Immigration. In Wicomico County Prison in Maryland, a pregnant Haitian woman was placed in solitary confinement for several days while her pleas to see a doctor were ignored. When the woman started hemorrhaging, she was finally transported to a hospital in handcuffs and shackles. She ultimately suffered a miscarriage. At the Kern County Detention Center in Bakersfield, California, a young Chinese woman was shoved against a wall and then placed in solitary confinement for using too much toilet paper after her repeated requests for a sanitary napkin went unheeded. And in York County Prison in Pennsylvania, a distraught Ugandan Muslim woman was stripped naked by guards in riot gear and placed in restraints, injected with sedatives, and then left for three days.[42]

Because many of the detention facilities that held women and children had been established relatively recently, they had fairly brief histories of detainee mistreatment. In contrast, the Krome Detention Center, where immigration detention had been reborn in 1980, had a long and sordid history of detainee abuse. By the turn of the century a much broader cross-section of the world's migrants had been exposed to the brutal conditions at Krome. By 2000, the facility held asylum seekers from nations around the world, including "Algeria, Angola, eastern Europe, Yugoslavia, Nicaragua, Guatemala, Colombia, Sierra Leone, Somalia, Sudan, Ecuador, Afghanistan, China and others."[43]

At the end of the 1990s, Krome remained riddled with problems of all sorts. A report by the Florida Immigrant Advocacy Center, directed by Cheryl Little, formerly of the Haitian Refugee Center, observed the myriad hardships that detainees at Krome had to endure:

Lack of access to counsel, overcrowding, long stays of detention, irrational and arbitrary parole, the placement of "criminal aliens" in with the non-criminal population, transfers to county jails, unhygienic living conditions, harassment and physical abuse by guards, misuse of segregation and isolation, the absence of a grievance procedure, lack of proper medical care, the lack of access to basic necessities and reading material, lack of access to the press and human rights groups, and the singling out of Nigerians and other Africans for special abuse.[44]

The Krome detention center remained a particularly dangerous place for women and children detainees. At the end of the decade, Krome was even more dangerous because of severe overcrowding. The treatment of detained women and children had become so intolerable that a group of detention officers took it upon themselves to intervene. In a letter to their superior, they outlined the troubling situation:

1) Criminal Aliens and Male Detainees share the same restroom with minors.

2) Women and children eat their meals on the floors, because they don't have any seats or tables to sit on.

3) There is [*sic*] only six beds for thirty-nine women to sleep or sit on.
4) Ventilation is poor for thirty-nine women and children to be housed in one room.
5) Women and children don't have any recreation at all.
6) The noise level is extremely high making it very difficult to interview and process Detainees.[45]

Sexual abuse of detained women was a serious problem at Krome. The Women's Commission for Refugee Women and Children summarized it findings:

> The reports of sexual misconduct are repugnant in their detail, ranging from rape to molestation to trading sex for favors. Women report that often officers use the women's lack of immigration status as an inducement to participate in sexual activities. They report that the officers make false promises that they could release a woman from detention if she participated in sexual acts. In other cases, detainees say that deportation officers have threatened them with deportation or transfer to a county prison if they resisted a guard's sexual advances or if they complained of a guard's treatment.[46]

After a new sexual abuse scandal at Krome became public in May 2000, many of the women detainees were transferred out of the facility. But they were just as vulnerable at other facilities. Days after they were transferred from Krome to a Miami-Dade County jail, transferred women reported that one male inmate had exposed himself to them and another had followed one of the women into a room and attacked her.[47]

As desperate as things were in the last years of the 1990s for those in detention, detainees continued to resist. In some locations, they even seemed to intensify their resistance. As in the past, one of the major tools of resistance was the hunger strike, a method of protest that prisoners with little power and few resources could use. In the early 1990s, well over 100 detainees had participated in a hunger strike at the Krome Detention Center each year. In the late 1990s, detainees continued their use of hunger strikes. In July 1998, for example, detainees in the El Centro Service Processing Center in the Imperial Valley of California launched a hunger strike. In the same year, detainees engaged in hunger strikes in Louisiana, New Hampshire, and elsewhere to protest mistreatment and poor conditions. In the summer of 1999, detainees at a facility in Queens operated by the Wackenhut Corporation engaged in a hunger strike.[48]

Sometimes the detainees' resistance moved from protest to outright rebel-

Figure 10. Haitian women at Krome Detention Center, early 1990s. Photo by Jon Kral. Used by permission.

lion. One of the most dramatic of such episodes occurred in the spring of 1995 in Elizabeth, New Jersey, at a detention facility operated by the Esmor Corporation. Angry over atrocious living conditions and physical abuse and harassment by the center's guards, the 300 detainees rioted, seizing the facility for six hours and holding two guards hostage. Others just sought to liberate themselves, as the two detainees who had escaped from Krome had done in January 1999.[49]

Detainees also organized within the facilities and collectively notified facility administrators of their problems. For example, in January 1996, 157 detainees at Krome sent a detailed list of grievances to the detention center director asking for immediate remediation. Other detainees appealed to human rights organizations for help and transmitted information about the otherwise invisible abuses occurring inside detention facilities. Immigrant and refugee rights advocates pressed for the removal of the harshest elements of the 1996 laws and worked to reinstitute programs that would ameliorate the worst abuses of the system, such as the Asylum Pre-Screening Officer Program, which allowed for the release of asylum seekers who did not pose a flight risk and were found to have a credible asylum claim.[50]

. . .

Each of the key elements of the Haitian detention experience of the 1970s through the 1990s was manifest in the fully matured detention system. For example, the government used detention in a punitive way in the hope of deterring Haitians and other asylum seekers. The policy of detaining asylum seekers, which had been regarded as unusual and extraordinarily harsh when the government applied this practice to Haitian refugees in the late 1970s and early 1980s, had become a legal requirement by the late 1990s. The incarceration of immigrant detainees in jails and prisons alongside prisoners serving criminal sentences had become an accepted and standard part of immigration control. In addition, the kind of physical and sexual abuse Haitian detainees suffered in places such as Krome and Guantanamo had become widespread. The merging of criminal and immigration law in the 1990s also had precedent in the treatment of Haitians. From the time Haitians had arrived in the 1970s, many had regarded them as potential criminals and the U.S. government had treated their asylum claims as criminal acts for which they needed to suffer detention and exclusion.

Conclusion

On December 3, 2001, a boat containing 187 Haitians arrived in Miami. The United States Coast Guard transferred the Haitians to INS custody. The INS determined that all but two had a credible fear of persecution. Having passed their credible fear interview, they should have been free, since asylum seekers who met this standard were eligible for release pending the final adjudication of their asylum claim. But these Haitians remained in detention.

Marie Jocelyn Ocean was among the Haitians who were placed in detention. "We thought the Americans would treat us with dignity and that they would protect us after what we had suffered," she stated.

> So I was shocked at how they treated us. Instead of finding freedom, we were thrown in jail. We were treated worse than nothing, we were treated as criminals. There was almost no one to help us when we were in detention. . . . It became clear to us that the only reason we were in jail indefinitely is because we were Haitian.[1]

The sense of Marie Jocelyn Ocean and the other detainees that they were being singled out for being Haitian was correct. The Haitians who arrived in December 2001 and those who arrived after that were subject to a Haitian-only detention policy. According to Cheryl Little, executive director of the Florida Immigrant Advocacy Center, in December 2001, "INS headquarters issued a directive to Miami INS not to release any Haitian asylum seekers in expedited removal without explicit INS approval."[2] Although immigration officials initially claimed that the policy was intended to save Haitian lives endangered by the risky voyage to the United States, Wendy Young of the Women's Commission for Refugee Women and Children reported that INS officials "admitted in the context of a federal lawsuit that the decision not to parole Haitian asylum seekers who arrived on the December boat was an attempt to deter a mass exodus from Haiti to the United States.[3]

In addition to mandatory detention without parole, the new guidelines for responding to the arrival of Haitian asylum seekers included fast-tracked asylum adjudications and a disregard for due process. According to Wendy Young, "in addition to being subjected to prolonged detention, the Haitian asylum seekers . . . [were] subjected to accelerated scheduling and processing of their removal proceedings" and "very quick calendaring of their cases" that forced most detainees "to appear before a judge without representation." Judges then "conducted cursory hearings," resulting in the denial of asylum for "the overwhelming majority of the claimants."[4] The INS was following the same playbook it had used when it implemented the Haitian Program of 1978.

The United Nations High Commissioner for Refugees and the Lawyers Committee for Human Rights attacked the government's treatment of Haitians as a violation of the internationally recognized rights of asylum seekers. The Miami-Dade Chapter of the NAACP, writing on behalf of more than sixty civil rights and human rights organizations, urged the George W. Bush administration to end its discrimination against Haitian asylum seekers.[5] But instead of submitting to public pressure to reverse the government's Haitian detention policy, immigration officials sought to shield themselves from criticism by expanding the detention policy to all "boat people." In an astonishing parallel to the government's creation of the blanket detention policy twenty years earlier, the Haitian detention policy of 2001 once again mutated into a blanket detention policy. As Amnesty International reported,

On November 13, 2002, after refusing to parole from detention Haitian passengers from another boat that ran aground on the coast of Florida on October 29, and in response to more criticism about the disparity in treatment of Haitian boat people, the INS announced that all boat people—with the exception of Cubans—would be subject to mandatory detention upon arrival or placed into expedited removal proceedings.[6]

Although the George W. Bush administration's treatment of Haitian asylum seekers sounds all too familiar, what was different this time around was the context in which its actions occurred. The recent terrorist attack of September 11, 2001, allowed U.S. officials to cite national security as the primary justification for the mass exclusion of Haitian refugees. According to Amnesty International, after some Haitian children and other asylum seekers successfully petitioned for release from detention, Attorney General John Ashcroft personally moved to block further Haitians from obtaining their freedom. The attorney general instructed immigration judges "to refuse to release undocumented asy-lum seekers if the government argues that 'significant national security interests are implicated.'" Ashcroft further specified "that all Haitians constitute such a group since releasing Haitian asylum-seekers might encourage other Haitians to come to the U.S., which could injure national security by straining the re-sources of the Coast Guard." Therefore, he ordered, "Haitians must be kept in detention irrespective of whether they personally pose any threat."[7]

Fears within immigrant and refugee communities that national security claims might be invoked as a pretext for mass detention and exclusion in the wake of 9/11 seemed to be well founded. And once again, it was painfully clear to Haitians that they were being singled out for extraordinarily harsh treat-ment, albeit with a different justification.

The 9/11 Effect and the Global Spread of Immigration Detention

The terrorist attacks of September 11, 2001, opened a new chapter in the ongo-ing debate about the role of detention in immigration enforcement, particularly because many Americans responded to the tragedy by associating immigrants with terrorists. How legitimate was this association? If aliens were regarded as potential terrorists, how might that shape immigration policy? The different perspectives in this debate were on full display at a May 2003 congressional hearing entitled "War on Terrorism: Immigration Enforcement since Sep-tember 11, 2001." The subcommittee chair, Indiana member of Congress John Hostettler, observed that "no one would argue that all aliens are terrorists, but no one can deny that all of the terrorist hijackers who committed the most egre-gious attack on our country in its history were aliens."[8] Michael Dougherty, di-rector of operations for the Bureau of Immigration and Customs Enforcement of the Department of Homeland Security, a new agency that had absorbed the INS, claimed that the association of aliens with terrorists justified the govern-ment's steps after 9/11. Bush administration initiatives included Operation Lib-erty Shield which "aimed at identifying and collecting information regarding individuals who might pose a threat to the safety and security of the American people," the National Security Entry-Exit Registration System, which registered and monitored "persons from certain countries of concern," and the Absconder Apprehension Initiative, which "tracks, apprehends, and removes aliens who have violated U.S. immigration laws."[9]

At the hearing, Laura Murphy of the American Civil Liberties Union presented a very different perspective on the Bush administration's response to the terrorist attacks. Murphy derided the administration's programs as a "plethora of ad hoc and disjointed immigration policies" that "have the net effect of equating immigration with terrorism, especially as far as Arabs, Muslims, and South Asian immigrants are concerned." Murphy also attacked the "massive preventive detention campaign" the Bush administration implemented in the aftermath of the attacks, arguing that the detention effort "resulted in the secret detention and deportation of close to 1,000 immigrants," virtually all of who had "no connection to terrorism."[10]

In the immediate aftermath of the events of September 11, 2001, it was sometimes difficult to decipher exactly what the government was doing and how many people were affected by its decision. But subsequent investigations and reports make it possible to see the full extent of the government's post-9/11 detention effort. More than 700 foreign nationals were detained from September 11, 2001, until August 2002. David Cole notes that "of these, not a single one was charged with any terrorist crime, and virtually all were cleared of any connection to terrorism by the FBI." The government seized the opportunity in the aftermath of the attack to expand its detention authority, lengthening the amount of time the law allowed for the detention of individuals not charged with a crime. This led to more long-term detention, including that of thirty-five individuals who were held for one to three months without charge.[11]

Despite the fact that in 2001, the Supreme Court ruled in *Zadvydas v. Davis* that indefinite detention of aliens was illegal and ordered that aliens could be detained only "for a period necessary to secure their removal," the government continued to cite national security when it defended an expansive detention authority after September 11, 2001. David Cole, a fierce critic of the Bush administration, observes that immigration law served "a useful pretext" for "extremely broad discretion" of the attorney general. In fact, immigration law became "the centerpiece of the preventive detention campaign" of the George W. Bush administration. "At every opportunity since September 11," Cole argues, "[Attorney General John] Ashcroft has turned immigration law from an administrative mechanism for controlling entry and exit of foreign nationals into an excuse for holding suspicious persons without meeting the constitutional requirements that ordinarily apply to preventive detention."[12] While immigration detention had become a tool used to deter and punish unauthorized migrants and asylum seekers throughout the 1970s, 1980s, and 1990s, in the post-9/11 period it also became tool of the expanding national security state.

The result was a detention and deportation system that grew rapidly in the twenty-first century. By the end of the first decade of the new century, daily detention rates were averaging 33,000, up from 20,000 in 2001.[13] And while national security claims continued to provide broad justification for intensified immigration enforcement, the pre-9/11 policy of using detention to deter unwanted migrants remained the driving force for this expansion. In 2005, for example, the Bush administration introduced Operation Streamline, which expanded criminal prosecution for unauthorized border crossers, first in Texas and then increasingly throughout the southwestern United States. Julie A. Dowling and Jonathan Xavier Inda observe that in formally shifting toward this more punitive response to unauthorized migration, the Department of Homeland Security's premise was "that routing immigrants through the federal criminal justice system and into prison, rather than simply removing them, serves to increase deterrence."[14]

This campaign to punish unauthorized migrants with detention and deportation continued into the Obama presidency. In 2009, Congress acted to ensure that the massive increase in immigration detention would not be rolled back by passing a law that required the Department of Homeland Security to maintain a "bed quota" of at least 33,400 in immigration detention facilities. The Obama administration continued to feed the detention system, placing record numbers of immigrants behind bars in service of its unprecedented mass deportation campaign that peaked at the record-breaking level of more than 400,000 deportations in 2012.[15]

As the United States expanded its detention regime in the first decade of the twenty-first century, the world followed its lead. When the United States launched its Haitian detention policy in the 1970s, and then formally reinstituted its detention program in 1981, "immigration detention was seen as a special state muscle to be exercised only in exceptional times," Amy Nethery and Stephanie J. Silverman observe. Although it was "used by few states" before the turn of the century, "today nearly every state around the world has adopted immigration detention policy and practice in some form." For example, during the years since 2003, when the detention system in the United States has grown by 75 percent to the current point, where it holds more than 400,000 prisoners annually, immigration detention has been adopted across the European Union. The number of detainees in EU member states exceeded 570,000 in 2011. By 2014, the United Kingdom had grown its detention capacity to approximately 29,000 and Australia was detaining approximately 8,400 annually. Immigration detention policies have become more oppressive in the Netherlands, France, Finland, Turkey, South Africa, Israel, Canada, and elsewhere. Nethery and Silverman note that in contrast to 2000, when immigration detention was a rarely used practice internationally, it "has grown and developed to reach its now ubiquitous status."[16]

The practice of extraterritorial detention that seeks to contain unwanted migrants before they even reach their destination country has also increased. This effort often involves wealthy states funding detention programs in poorer neighboring countries so that the poorer countries will act as a barrier between migrants and would-be asylum seekers and the land and resources of the wealthier countries. The European Union has funded detention centers in Ukraine and in many other states along its border; Australia funds detention programs in Nauru, Papua New Guinea, and Indonesia; and the United States finances detention facilities in Mexico and Guatemala.[17]

Extraterritorial detention also enables states to skirt international obligations and laws. Nethery and Silverman observe that since many of the poorer states that now host the extraterritorial detention programs are not signatories of the Refugee Convention of 1951, which requires states to protect those fleeing persecution, "the effect is that asylum seekers can become trapped in immigration detention with limited access to protection mechanisms." Lucy Fiske concurs, arguing that the practice of extraterritorial detention interrupts refugee journeys by "holding them outside the potentially protective embrace of western liberal democratic states' legal systems."[18]

The United States is more than merely a participant in the global practice of extraterritorial detention. It is responsible for originating this practice. Just as it did with the practice of punitive detention as deterrence, the United States pioneered and modeled the practice of extraterritorial detention. More than two decades before it became a common practice for states to interdict and detain migrants before they could reach their destination, the U.S. government introduced its Haitian interdiction policy. Furthermore, the detention camp at Guantanamo Bay, Cuba, provided the model on which the now-widespread practice of extraterritorial detention is based. According to Azadeh Dastyari, the detention of refugees and asylum seekers at the U.S. naval base in Cuba provided the blueprint for Australia's Pacific Solution, whereby it detains asylum seekers on Nauru and Papua New Guinea's Manus Island before they can reach Australian shores.[19]

The transfer of immigration detention practices from wealthy nations to poor nations on the margins of the global economy is but one manifestation of a much larger neoliberal transformation. By the second decade of the twenty-first century, global inequality had reached record levels. The richest 1 percent of the world's population had accumulated more wealth than the entire rest of the world combined.[20] This extreme inequality is the culmination of decades of corporate globalization that was driven by neoliberal policies that prioritized privatization and increased capital mobility. The increasing imbalance of wealth and the economic shifts that accompany corporate globalization also drove displaced people from the global periphery to the centers of capital, setting in motion a new phase of global migration.

In response, wealthy nations fortified their borders. They realized that if they wanted to preserve the highly unequal distribution of wealth and resources, they needed to restrict migrant mobility. As Aristide Zolberg explains, greater mobility for migrants from poor regions would "result in an equalization of conditions and hence produce a vast redistribution of income to the benefit of the populations of the poorer countries." In effect, Zolberg argues, "borders serve to prevent labor from commanding the same price everywhere, and also prevent people from poorer countries from gaining access to the bundles of 'public goods' dispensed by the more affluent states, which now constitute an important part of their populations' income."[21]

The idea that migrants could trigger a redistribution of wealth and resources from the wealthy to the poor and the challenge to state sovereignty that large-scale migration poses has led to the proliferation of new border walls in every corner of the world (and even *within* nations, in the form of gated communities). Peter Andreas observes that the embrace of border walls and enforcement "has been most pronounced along the geographic fault lines that divide rich and poor countries, particularly the southern border of the United States and the eastern and southern external borders of the European Union."[22] Constructing border walls, criminalizing immigration and immigrants, removing unauthorized migrants through campaigns of mass deportation, and holding immigrants, refugees, and asylum seekers in detention (within or outside national boundaries) are mutually reinforcing practices that serve the same function of preserving global inequality. As Jenna M. Loyd, Matt Mitchelson, and Andrew Burridge observe, both "walls and cages are fundamental to managing the wealth, social inequalities, and opposition to the harms created by capitalism and the present round of neocolonial dispossession."[23] Any collective effort to reckon with the global rise of immigration detention must acknowledge that state polices that punish unauthorized migrants are as much about wealth and inequality as they are expressions of nativism or the desire to assert state sovereignty.

At the Intersection of State Sovereignty and Universal Human Rights

Concerns about the integrity of state sovereignty in the face of unauthorized migration are another factor that drives the construction of border walls and detention regimes. States routinely cite claims regarding sovereignty when they engage in these practices and are called upon to justify their use of immigration detention and other restrictive and punitive measures. State sovereignty has become the principle weapon states use to attack those they classify as outsiders and the shield they use to protect themselves from legal and political challenges to their detention regimes and other questionable practices.

Refugees, asylum seekers, and other migrants seeking freedom and security far from home have sought to protect themselves by citing the obligation of states to respect international agreements and universal principles of human rights. But when they do so, they routinely run into the problem of citizenship and the bigger problem of state sovereignty and territoriality that undergirds it. How, in light of international standards of human rights, can states justify the arbitrary treatment and immense violence they unleash upon them? these people ask. It is the right of sovereign states to draw distinctions between citizens and noncitizens and to protect their borders, they are told. Thus, "the unauthorized immigrant's body constitutes a violation of sovereignty and the very site of border enforcement through detention or expulsion," argue Alexander C. Diener and Joshua Hagen.[24] The "deportation and detention of unwanted foreigners make clear what sovereignty is about," argues Galina Cornelisse, "both with regard to its aspect of monopolist violence and with regard to its claim to determine the 'inside' from the 'outside.' Ultimately the indiscriminate detention of unwanted foreigners, under conditions that seem to flagrantly violate some of the very values that supposedly underpin liberal Western democracies, makes painfully clear that the modern discourse of human rights has not been able to live up to its universal aspiration."[25] The problem of immigration detention thus lies at the intersection of state sovereignty and universal human rights.

In fact, long before the modern detention and deportation regimes developed and even before the modern state system on which they rely took shape, the U.S. government had discovered it could claim sovereignty as a basis for policies that treated foreigners differently from citizens. In the late nineteenth century, the Supreme Court declared that the government's plenary power, which derived from its status as a sovereign state, allowed it to deport aliens and treat those subject to immigration control as outside of the reach of the constitution. According to Daniel Kanstroom, the establishment of the plenary power doctrine became a cornerstone in the "citizenship-as-membership" model that left noncitizens vulnerable to deportation and detention, practices that the Supreme Court has repeatedly affirmed as legal and legitimate actions that sovereign states are entitled to take.[26]

Despite the fact that states have long relied on claims of sovereignty to justify their exclusion and differential treatment of noncitizens, the increasing force and violence that states are now mobilizing to exclude, contain, and expel unauthorized migrants and other noncitizens demands renewed scrutiny of the appropriate relationship between state sovereignty and universal human rights. The global rise of immigration detention highlights the urgency of this task. "Immigration detention is at once the inevitable outcome of contemporary territoriality, and the ultimate illustration of the immunization of territorial sovereignty against conventional forces of legal correction," observes Galina Cornelisse. "Indeed, the untamed existence of a practice as violent as immigration detention is only possible because international human rights are incapable of fully addressing the human interests that are affected whenever the national state bases the exercise of power on its territorial sovereignty."[27] With these concerns in mind, Rachel Ida Buff argues that "the current moment compels a creative reconsideration of the limits of citizenship."[28] Without new ways to defend people whom states characterize as foreigners or aliens, those who cross borders will continue to be subject to escalating levels of state violence.

Detention and Freedom: An Unwritten Future

Despite the immense growth of detention regimes in the United States and around the world in recent years, the sustainability of immigration detention is by no means assured. This uncertainty is the result of a growing movement to end immigration detention and an increasing awareness of detention's place in the larger system of racialized mass incarceration. As in the past, those who are detained and imprisoned are playing a leading role in reenergizing the opposition movement through the actions they have taken from inside detention facilities and solidarity campaigns by supporters on the outside have helped bring attention to the detainees' actions and to the system itself. In the spring and summer of 2014, for example, prisoners at the Northwest Detention Center in Tacoma, Washington, a facility owned and operated by the private prison company GEO Group, launched a hunger strike over poor conditions at the facility and the rapid pace of deportations. The Tacoma action was inspired by an increasingly mobilized community that had held a demonstration outside the facility in February and by a similar action by detainees at another facility months earlier in Arizona.[29]

In 2015, seventy mothers who were being held in the Karnes County Residential Center in Texas, another facility operated by GEO Group, launched a hunger strike over their prolonged detention. The women and children in the Karnes County facility and hundreds of others at the South Texas Family Residential Center in Dilley, Texas, were part of a large wave of nearly 70,000 people who were seeking asylum in the United States after fleeing El Salvador, Guatemala, and Honduras. But like the Haitian and Central American asylum seekers who arrived in United States in the 1980s, they were detained and faced deportation. In May 2015, opponents of the government's detention practices marched from San Antonio to Dilley and held a large demonstration outside the Dilley detention center, calling on the government to "close Dilley" and "end immigrant family detention once and for all."[30] Action against immigration detention continued in August 2016, when twenty-two mothers who were enduring prolonged detention at the Berks County Residential Center in Pennsylvania engaged in a hunger strike. And the abhorrent treatment of transgender and LGBT detainees was the focus of activist demonstrations and hunger strikes in southern California in 2015 and 2016 that were motivated in part by a Human Rights Watch report on abuse of transgender women in immigration detention in the United States.[31]

The leading organization in the national movement against immigration detention is Detention Watch Network, which was founded in 1997 by religious and immigrant rights organizations. In addition to initiating and leading campaigns against immigration detention in the United States, Detention Watch Network partners with human and civil rights organizations to expose abuses in the detention system. It also maintains resources and a communication network for activists, advocates, and scholars working on the problem of immigration detention. As "the only national network that focuses exclusively on immigration detention," Detention Watch Network brings together "diverse constituencies to advance the civil and human rights of those impacted by the immigration detention system."[32] Detention Watch Network has counterparts in other countries around the world, signaling how the global problem of immigration detention is increasingly being met by an international movement to end it.[33]

The actions of detainees and their supporters have also helped amplify the findings of the human rights organizations that work to expose the abuses of the immigration detention system. In addition, the joint action and exposure campaigns by detainees and the human rights community have brought increasing media attention to the issue of immigration detention. This, in turn, has brought additional scrutiny to the government's detention practices and the circumstances and conditions in which detainees are held.[34]

As a result of this activism, in the spring of 2015 it seemed that opposition to immigration detention in the United States might be reaching a tipping point. In addition to the increasing frequency of hunger strikes of detainees and solidarity actions by their supporters, a growing number of prominent individuals and institutions had begun to vocally oppose the government's use of immigration detention. In May, a *New York Times* editorial called on the U.S. government to end immigration detention, calling it a system that "breed[s] cruelty and harm, and squanders taxpayer money." The editorial stated that immigration detention "denies its victims due process of law, punishing them far beyond the scale of any offense. It shatters families and traumatizes children. As a system of mass incarceration—particularly of women and children fleeing persecution in Central America—it is immoral." The *Seattle Times* articulated its opposition to immigration detention four days later. In addition, the United States Conference of Catholic Bishops, in partnership with the Center for Migration Studies, issued a scathing critique of the U.S. immigrant detention system in a detailed report on how to transform the system. In Congress, lawmakers introduced a bill called Accountability in Immigration Detention Act of 2015, which aimed to impose stricter oversight over the immigration detention system and its standards. One hundred thirty-six lawmakers signed a letter that called on the Obama administration to halt the detention of Central American asylum seekers and to end its practice of child and family detention.[35]

At this critical juncture, the U.S. immigration detention system seemed ripe for reform. Thus, when President Obama moved to close privately run federal prisons, activists were hopeful that the administration might take similar steps for immigration detention facilities and pressed the Department of Justice to take this first step toward doing away with the current system.[36]

But with the election of Donald J. Trump months later, the hope of doing away with immigration detention evaporated. It quickly became clear that the new administration's heightened emphasis on the arrest and deportation of undocumented immigrants (and its prioritization of "law and order" initiatives) would lead to a much greater use of immigration detention as an enforcement mechanism. Just days after taking office, the president signed an executive order instructing ICE agents to increase the number of immigration arrests and deportations. Nationwide sweeps of immigrant communities followed. The Trump administration also began expanding its detention capacity so it would be able to absorb the swelling numbers of immigrants in custody and announced plans to open new detention facilities. In response to this rapid change of fortune for the detention and prison industry, stock prices in private prison companies surged.[37]

Nonetheless, opponents of the U.S. immigration detention system continue their campaign of resistance. As they do, they might examine the history of immigration detention of Haitian refugees, who have been struggling against the government's use of detention for more than four decades. Their history of struggle offers guidance and inspiration to those involved in the movement to end immigration detention today. "America's incarcerated people have never stopped struggling against this country's worst and most punitive practices," writes Heather Ann Thompson, noting that the Attica prison uprising of 1971 and the many other acts of prisoner resistance and rebellion in the United States show that "even the most marginalized citizens will never stop fighting to be treated as human beings." The history of immigration detention reminds us that migrants, refugees, and other groups the state refuses to recognize as citizens share an "irrepressible demand for justice."[38] Over three decades ago, the office of the United Nations High Commissioner for Refugees called upon the world to recognize that "next to life itself, liberty of the person and freedom of movement are among the most precious of human rights."[39] These words still reverberate. For those who believe that states must not detain and punish those who cross borders without permission, they remain a call to action.

Notes

Introduction

1. "Immigration Detention 101," *Detention Watch Network*, accessed March 8, 2017, https://www.detentionwatchnetwork.org/issues/detention-101; "Immigrants' Right and Detention," *American Civil Liberties Union*, accessed March 8, 2017, https://www.aclu.org/issues/immigrants-rights/immigrants-rights-and-detention; Tom K. Wong, *Rights, Deportation, and Detention in the Age of Immigration Control* (Stanford, Calif.: Stanford University Press, 2015), 119–123; Torrie Hester, "Deportability and the Carceral State," *The Journal of American History* 102, no. 1 (2015): 141.

2. Daniel Wilsher, *Immigration Detention: Law, History, Politics* (Cambridge: Cambridge University Press, 2012), 18–29; Erika Lee, *The Making of Asian America: A History* (New York: Simon and Schuster, 2015), 96–100; Peter H. Schuck, "The Transformation of Immigration Law," *Columbia Law Review* 84, no. 1 (1984): 29; Timothy J. Dunn, *The Militarization of the U.S.-Mexican Border, 1978–1992: Low-Intensity Conflict Doctrine Comes Home* (Austin: Center for Mexican American Studies, University of Texas at Austin, 1996), 217n51. Justice Clark quoted in Margaret Regan, *Detained and Deported: Stories of Immigrant Families under Fire* (Boston: Beacon Press, 2016), xviii.

3. Peter Gatrell, *The Making of the Modern Refugee* (Oxford: Oxford University Press, 2015); Lucy Fiske, *Human Rights, Refugee Protest and Immigration Detention* (London: Palgrave Macmillan, 2016), 2, 10, 214–215; Jonathan Xavier Inda and Julie A. Dowling, "Introduction: Governing Migrant Illegality," in *Governing Immigration through Crime: A Reader*, edited by Julie A. Dowling and Jonathan Xavier Inda (Stanford, Calif.: Stanford University Press, 2013), 3; Rachel Ida Buff, ed., *Immigrant Rights in the Shadows of Citizenship* (New York: New York University Press, 2008), 2, 10–18.

4. Lucy Fiske, for example, documents protests, marches, hunger strikes, riots, and other acts of resistance by immigrant detainees around the world in the first fifteen years of the twenty-first century. See Fiske, *Human Rights, Refugee Protest and Immigration Detention.*

5. Patrick Ettinger, *Imaginary Lines: Border Enforcement and the Origins of Undocumented Immigration, 1882–1930* (Austin: University of Texas Press, 2010), 7–8. Rachel St. John also finds that state power was "never absolute"; she argues that what emerged on the U.S.-Mexico border was a form of "negotiated sovereignty." See Rachel St. John, *Line in the Sand: A History of the Western U.S.-Mexico Border* (Princeton, N.J.: Princeton University Press, 2012), 2, 7–9.

6. The Africana Cultures and Policy Studies Institute: Zachery Williams, Robert Samuel

Smith, Seneca Vaught, Babacar M'Baye, "A History of Black Immigration into the United States through the Lens of the African American Civil and Human Rights Struggle," in *Immigrant Rights in the Shadows of Citizenship*, edited by Rachel Ida Buff (New York: New York University Press, 2008), 161–165; Millery Polyné, *From Douglass to Duvalier: U.S. African Americans, Haiti, and Pan Americanism, 1870–1964* (Gainesville: University Press of Florida, 2010).

7. Mary Ellen Curtin, "'Please Hear Our Cries': The Hidden History of Black Prisoners in America," in *The Punitive Turn: New Approaches to Race and Incarceration*, edited by Deborah E. McDowell, Claudrena N. Harold, and Juan Battle (Charlottesville: University of Virginia Press, 2013), 34–37; Heather Ann Thompson, "From Researching the Past to Reimagining the Future: Locating Carceral Crisis and the Key to Its End, in the Long Twentieth Century," in *The Punitive Turn: New Approaches to Race and Incarceration*, edited by Deborah E. McDowell, Claudrena N. Harold, and Juan Battle (Charlottesville: University of Virginia Press, 2013), 49–51, 55–58.

8. This, too, builds upon and reinforces the findings of historians who have documented the critical role of legal resistance in prisoners' campaign. Heather Ann Thompson, for example, argues "when prisoners could be heard in courts of law, they could dramatically change their circumstances. Once again, the path toward improving penal conditions and, ultimately, to ending the most recent national carceral crisis was paved by determined legal activism. Notably, even as the country grew more conservative in the 1980s and 1990s, inmates continued to look to the legal system to restore their human and civil rights." Thompson, "From Researching the Past to Reimagining the Future," 65.

9. Christina Elefteriades Haines and Anil Kalhan, "Detention of Asylum Seekers En Masse: Immigration Detention in the United States," in *Immigration Detention: The Migration of a Policy and Its Human Impact*, edited by Amy Nethery and Stephanie J. Silverman (New York: Routledge, 2015), 69, 71.

10. David Manuel Hernández, "Pursuant to Deportation: Latinos and Immigrant Detention," in *Governing Immigration through Crime: A Reader*, edited by Julie A. Dowling and Jonathan Xavier Inda (Stanford, Calif.: Stanford University Press, 2013), 203–205; César Cuauhtémoc García Hernández, "Immigration Detention as Punishment," *UCLA Law Review* 61 (2014): 1346–1415.

11. Galina Cornelisse, *Immigration Detention and Human Rights: Rethinking Territorial Sovereignty* (Leiden: Martinus Nijhoff Publishers, 2010), 24. Although in Europe, the common employment of punitive detention might be a relatively recent development, in the United States, the punitive character and purpose of immigration detention has long been established. Kelly Lytle Hernández traces the punitive origins of immigration detention back as far back as the 1930s, when Mexican migrants "convicted of felony reentry" were "sentenced to time served since the moment of arrest." According to Hernández, judges thus "reinterpreted immigrant detention as a period of criminal punishment," transforming "the meaning of immigrant detention" into detention as punishment for crime. Kelly Lytle Hernández, *City of Inmates: Conquest, Rebellion, and the Rise of Human Caging in Los Angeles, 1771–1965* (Chapel Hill: University of North Carolina Press, 2017), 144–146.

12. Stephanie J. Silverman and Amy Nethery, "Understanding Immigration Detention and Its Human Impact," in *Immigration Detention: The Migration of a Policy and Its Human Impact*, edited by Amy Nethery and Stephanie J. Silverman (New York: Routledge, 2015), 5.

13. See, for example, Mary Bosworth, *Inside Immigration Detention* (Oxford: Oxford Uni-

versity Press, 2014); Cornelisse, *Immigration Detention and Human Rights*; Patrisia Macías-Rojas, *From Deportation to Prison: The Politics of Immigration Enforcement in Post–Civil Rights America* (New York: New York University Press, 2016); Mark Dow, *American Gulag: Inside U.S. Immigration Prisons* (Berkeley: University of California Press, 2005); Tanya Golash-Boza, *Immigration Nation: Raids, Detentions, and Deportations in Post-9/11 America* (Boulder, Colo.: Paradigm Publishers, 2012); Hernández, "Pursuant to Deportation"; Robert S. Kahn, *Other People's Blood: U.S. Immigration Prisons in the Reagan Decade* (Boulder, Colo.: Westview Press, 1996); Wilsher, *Immigration Detention*; Michael Welch, *Detained: Immigration Laws and the Expanding I.N.S. Jail Complex* (Philadelphia: Temple University Press, 2002).

14. Dierdre Conlon and Nancy Hiemstra, *Intimate Economies of Immigration Detention: Critical Perspectives* (New York: Routledge, Taylor and Francis Group, 2017); Fiske, *Human Rights, Refugee Protest and Immigration Detention*; Maria Joao Guia, Robert Koulish, and Valsamis Mitsilegas, *Immigration Detention, Risk and Human Rights* (Cham, Switzerland: Springer International Publishing, 2016); Wesley Kendall, *From Gulag to Guantanamo: Political, Social, and Economic Evolutions of Mass Incarceration* (New York: Rowman & Littlefield International, 2016); Amy Nethery and Stephanie J. Silverman, *Immigration Detention: The Migration of a Policy and Its Human Impact* (London: Routledge, 2017); Wong, *Rights, Deportation, and Detention in the Age of Immigration Control*.

15. A notable exception is the work of Jana K. Lipman, which argues that Haitians must be repositioned "at the center of contemporary US immigration and detention policy." Jana K. Lipman, "'The Fish Trusts the Water, and It Is in the Water That It Is Cooked': The Caribbean Origins of the Krome Detention Center," *Radical History Review* 115 (2013): 115–141. Other scholars who have searched this history and to some extent recognized the centrality of Haitians in the origins and early development of the detention system include María Cristina García, *The Refugee Challenge in Post–Cold War America* (Oxford: Oxford University Press, 2017); Mary Bosworth and Emma Kaufman, "Foreigners in a Carceral Age: Immigration and Imprisonment in the United States," *Stanford Law and Policy Review* 22, no. 1 (2011): 429–454; A. Naomi Paik, *Rightlessness: Testimony and Redress in U.S. Prison Camps since World War II* (Chapel Hill: The University of North Carolina Press, 2016); Dunn, *The Militarization of the U.S.-Mexican Border, 1978–1992*; Alex Stepick, "Haitian Boat People: A Study in the Conflicting Forces Shaping U.S. Immigration Policy," *Law and Contemporary Problems* 45, no. 2 (1982): 163–196; Jonathan Simon, "Refugees in a Carceral Age: The Rebirth of Immigration Prison in the United States," *Public Culture* 10, no. 2 (1998): 577–607; Norman L. Zucker and Naomi Flink Zucker, *The Guarded Gate: The Reality of American Refugee Policy* (San Diego: Harcourt Brace Jovanovich, 1987). As this book was going to press, another book that seems likely to explore some of these questions was scheduled for publication: Jenna M. Loyd and Alison Mountz, *Boats, Borders, and Bases: Race, the Cold War, and the Rise of Migration Detention in the United States* (Berkeley: University of California Press, 2018). Scholarship that has contributed to our historical understanding of immigration detention in the United States but has not necessarily fully acknowledged the central role of Haitians in this history includes Hernández, "Pursuant to Deportation"; Hester, "Deportability and the Carceral State"; Daniel Kanstroom, *Deportation Nation: Outsiders in American History* (Cambridge, Mass.: Harvard University Press, 2007); Wilsher, *Immigration Detention*; Hernández, *City of Inmates*; Marie Gottschalk, *Caught: The Prison State and the Lockdown of American Politics* (Princeton, N.J.: Princeton University Press, 2016); and Macías-Rojas, *From Deportation to Prison*.

16. Heather Ann Thompson, "Why Mass Incarceration Matters: Rethinking Crisis, Decline, and Transformation in Postwar American History," *Journal of American History* 97, no. 3 (2010): 706.

17. Kelly Lytle Hernández, Khalil Gibran Muhammad, and Heather Ann Thompson, "Introduction: Constructing the Carceral State," *Journal of American History* 102, no. 1(2015): 18–19.

18. Heather Ann Thompson, "From Researching the Past to Reimagining the Future," 45.

19. The Africana Cultures and Policy Studies Institute: Zachery Williams, Robert Samuel Smith, Seneca Vaught, Babacar M'Baye, "A History of Black Immigration into the United States through the Lens of the African American Civil and Human Rights Struggle," 159–162.

20. Mae M. Ngai, *Impossible Subjects: Illegal Aliens and the Making of Modern America* (Princeton, N.J.: Princeton University Press, 2004), 8.

21. Kunal M. Parker, *Making Foreigners: Immigration and Citizenship Law in America, 1600–2000* (Cambridge: Cambridge University Press, 2015), 3–12, 217–219.

22. Nathalie Peutz and Nicholas De Genova, "Introduction," in *The Deportation Regime: Sovereignty, Space and the Freedom of Movement*, edited by Nicholas De Genova and Nathalie Peutz (Durham, N.C.: Duke University Press, 2010), 15.

23. Hester, "Deportability and the Carceral State," 142.

24. Hernández, "Pursuant to Deportation," 207, 211.

25. Kelly Lytle Hernández, *Migra! A History of the U.S. Border Patrol* (Berkeley: University of California Press, 2010), 233.

26. Hernández, *City of Inmates*, 2.

Chapter 1. Making a Path for the Return
of Immigrant Detention, 1973–1980

1. Affidavit of Jean-Paul George, April 30, 1976, box 4, folder 2, Haitian Refugee Collection, Schomburg Center for Research in Black Culture, The New York Public Library (hereafter cited as Haitian Refugee Collection).

2. Affidavit of Emanuel François, January 10, 1976, box 4, folder 2, Haitian Refugee Collection.

3. Cheryl Little, "United States Haitian Policy: A History of Discrimination," *New York Law School Journal of Human Rights* 10, part 2 (1993): 270.

4. Church World Service, "Haitian Refugees Need Asylum: A Briefing Paper," April 9, 1980, 245, in U.S. Congress, Senate, Committee on the Judiciary, *Caribbean Refugee Crisis: Cubans and Haitians, Hearing before the Committee on the Judiciary, United States Senate, Ninety-Sixth Congress, Second Session, May 12, 1980* (Washington, D.C.: U.S. Government Printing Office, 1980), 245.

5. Carl Lindskoog, "Refugees and Resistance: International Activism for Grassroots Democracy and Human Rights in New York, Miami, and Haiti, 1957 to 1994" (PhD diss., City University of New York, 2013), 67.

6. Christopher Mitchell, "U.S. Policy toward Haitian Boat People, 1972–93," *Annals of the American Academy of Political and Social Science* 534 (July 1994): 70.

7. Michel-Rolph Trouillot, *Haiti, State against Nation: The Origins and Legacy of Duvalierism* (New York: Monthly Review Press, 1990); Alex Stepick, "Structural Determinants of

the Haitian Refugee Movement: Different Interpretations," Occasional Papers Series, Dialogues #4, Latin American and Caribbean Center, Florida International University, 1981, 6–7, http://digitalcommons.fiu.edu/laccopsd/60/; Lindskoog, "Refugees and Resistance," 13–14.

8. Josh DeWind and David H. Kinley, *Aiding Migration: The Impact of International Development Assistance on Haiti* (Boulder, Colo.: Westview Press, 1988), 57; Alex Dupuy, *Haiti in the New World Order: The Limits of the Democratic Revolution* (Boulder, Colo.: Westview Press, 1997), 24–27, 33; Trouillot, *Haiti: State against Nation*, 212–213; Paul Farmer, *The Uses of Haiti* (Monroe, Maine: Common Courage Press, 2006), 100–101; Lindskoog, "Refugees and Resistance," 69–74.

9. Michelle Bogre, "Haitian Refugees: (Haiti's) Missing Persons," *Migration Today* 7, no. 4 (1979): 9.

10. Carol C. Laise to W. Sterling Cary, July 24, 1974, box 32, folder 1, Haitian Refugee Collection.

11. Ghoshal and Crowley put the figure of approved Haitian asylum cases at 55 out of 9,000 for the period 1972 to 1979. See Animesh Ghoshal and Thomas M. Crowley, "Refugees and Immigrants: A Human Rights Dilemma," *Human Rights Quarterly* 5, no. 3 (1983): 337. Michel Laguerre puts the number of asylum cases approved at 25 out of more than 50,000 asylum seekers for the period 1972 to 1980: Michel S. Laguerre, *Diasporic Citizenship: Haitian Americans in Transnational America* (New York: St. Martin's Press, 1998), 82.

12. Stepick, "Haitian Boat People: A Study in the Conflicting Forces Shaping U.S. Immigration Policy," *Law and Contemporary Problems* 45, no. 2 (1982): 165; Stepick, "Structural Determinants of the Haitian Refugee Movement," 17, 20–21; Naomi Flink Zucker, "The Haitians versus the United States: The Courts as Last Resort," *Annals of the American Academy of Political and Social Science* 467 (May 1983): 153.

13. Thomas Aleinikoff and David Martin, *Immigration: Process and Policy* (St. Paul, Minn.: West Publishing Co., 1985), 60–61; "The Indefinite Detention of Excluded Aliens: Statutory and Constitutional Justifications and Limitations," *Michigan Law Review* 82, no. 1 (1983): 74n49.

14. Christopher Mitchell, "The Political Costs of State Power: U.S. Border Control in South Florida," in *The Wall around the West: State Borders and Immigration Controls in North America and Europe*, edited by Peter Andreas and Timothy Snyder (Lanham, Md.: Rowman and Littlefield, 2000), 85.

15. Alex Stepick, "The Refugees Nobody Wants: Haitians in Miami," in *Miami Now! Immigration, Ethnicity, and Social Change*, edited by Guillermo J. Grenier and Alex Stepick III (Gainesville: University Press of Florida, 1992), 58–60.

16. Mitchell, "U.S. Policy toward Haitian Boat People, 1972–93," 70.

17. James Silk, *Despite a Generous Spirit: Denying Asylum in the United States* (Washington, D.C.: U.S. Committee for Refugees, 1986), 15.

18. Quoted in Zucker, "The Haitians versus the United States," 154.

19. Gilburt Loescher and John Scanlan, "Human Rights, U.S. Foreign Policy, and Haitian Refugees," *Journal of Interamerican Studies and World Affairs* 26, no. 3 (1983): 332–333.

20. Lindskoog, "Refugees and Resistance," 15–27.

21. Ibid., 89–90; For more on the background of the involvement of the National Council of Churches in the movement for Haitian refugees, see Carl Lindskoog, "Defending the

Haitian Boat People: Origins and Development of a Movement," in *International Conference on Caribbean Studies Selected Proceedings*, edited by Héctor R. Romero (Edinburgh: Tex.: University of Texas-Pan American Press, 2007), 185–199.

22. "Resolution in Support of Haitian Refugees," National Council of Churches of Christ in the U.S.A., February 28, 1974, box 21, folder 17, Haitian Refugee Collection.

23. "Statement of Purposes," Rescue Committee for Haitian Refugees, n.d., box 28, folder 8, Haitian Refugee Collection.

24. "Emergency! Save the Haitian Refugees!" February 14, 1974, box 21, folder 6, Haitian Refugee Collection.

25. "Support Haitian Boat People," Haitian Refugee Center, n.d., box 23, folder 3, Haitian Refugee Collection.

26. Ibid.

27. "Haitians Demand Asylum," *Amsterdam News*, March 30, 1974, box 21, folder 2, Haitian Refugee Collection; "Emergency Demonstration to Save Haitian Refugees!" March 23, 1974, box 21, folder 2, Haitian Refugee Collection; "Come to the Rally on April 8th—Help Free Your Haitian Brother," n.d., box 23, folder 3, Haitian Refugee Collection.

28. Biographical and historical information on Ira Gollobin is available in "Haitian Refugee Collection, 1972–2004: Biographical/Historical Information," accessed October 3, 2017, http://archives.nypl.org/scm/20934. For information on the establishment and activities of the Haitian left in New York City leading up to the mid-1970s, see Lindskoog, "Refugees and Resistance," 38–51.

29. Eddy Two Rivers and Kenneth Little Fish to Paul Lehman, April 6, 1974, box 32, folder 1, Haitian Refugee Collection.

30. L. F. Chapman Jr. to Bella S. Abzug, June 27, 1974, box 32, folder 1, Haitian Refugee Collection.

31. "U.S. Govt. Continues Persecution of Haitian Refugees," March 15, 1975, box 28, folder 5, Haitian Refugee Collection.

32. Members of Congress to Joshua Eilberg, August 2, 1976, box 22, folder 14, Haitian Refugee Collection.

33. The Haitian Refugees at Immokalee to the District Supervisor of the Immigration Service, March 4, 1977, box 32, folder 1, Haitian Refugee Collection.

34. Press Release: Jailed Haitian Refugees Protest Cruel Treatment and Indignities," March 28, 1977, box 28, folder 5, Haitian Refugee Collection.

35. Letter from the Haitian Prisoners in El Paso Camp, February 10, 1977, box 4, folder 15, Haitian Refugee Collection.

36. Tom Butler, "Haitian Detainee Fails in Attempted Hanging," *El Paso Times*, February 9, 1977, 1B, box 4, folder 15, Haitian Refugee Collection.

37. [Ira Gollobin,] Memorandum on Status of Legal Proceedings on Behalf of Haitian Refugees in Miami, March 29, 1976, box 33, folder 10, Haitian Refugee Collection.

38. Judge James Lawrence King, order in *Marie Sannon vs. The United States*, May 17, 1976, box 3, folder 10, Haitian Refugee Collection.

39. Loescher and Scanlan, "Human Rights, U.S. Foreign Policy, and Haitian Refugees," 335; Zucker, "The Haitians versus the United States," 154–155.

40. Press release, Department of Justice, November 8, 1977, box 34, folder 7, Haitian Refugee Collection.

41. Press release, National Urban League, June 22, 1978, box 28, folder 2, Haitian Refugee Collection.

42. Document on Haitians Seeking Asylum, February 2, 1978, box 22, folder 4, Haitian Refugee Collection; Loescher and Scanlan, "Human Rights, U.S. Foreign Policy and Haitian Refugees," 338.

43. Joyce A. White to U.S. Secretary of State, October 11, 1979, box 11, folder 6, Haitian Refugee Collection.

44. Loescher and Scanlan, "Human Rights, U.S. Foreign Policy, and Haitian Refugees," 338–339; Zucker, "The Haitians versus the United States," 155–157.

45. The fact that local immigration and public officials were highly influential in determining this policy change provides more evidence to support the conclusions in a growing body of literature that immigration and border policy is often determined by local officials and influenced by local conditions. See, for example, Patrick Ettinger, *Imaginary Lines: Border Enforcement and the Origins of Undocumented Immigration, 1882–1930* (Austin: University of Texas Press, 2010); and Rachel St. John, *Line in the Sand: A History of the Western U.S.-Mexico Border* (Princeton, N.J.: Princeton University Press, 2012).

46. Quoted in Stepick, "Haitian Boat People," 183.

47. Ibid., 183–185; Loescher and Scanlan, "Human Rights, U.S. Foreign Policy, and Haitian Refugees," 338–339; Zucker, "The Haitians versus the United States," 155–157.

48. "Action to be Taken by Operating Divisions Regarding Undocumented Haitian Aliens," August 4, 1978, box 11, folder 5, Haitian Refugee Collection.

49. "Haitian Program," memorandum from Richard H. Gullage, n.d., box 11, folder 5, Haitian Refugee Collection.

50. Zucker, "The Haitians versus the United States," 155–156; Stepick, "Haitian Boat People," 183–184; Loescher and Scanlan, "Human Rights, U.S. Foreign Policy, and Haitian Refugees," 338–339.

51. "Demonstration," August 3, 1978, box 21, folder 6, Haitian Refugee Collection.

52. Rescue Committee for Haitian Refugees, Press Release: Priest Discovers 8-Year-Old Child of Jailed for Two Weeks by Immigration Authorities," December 4, 1978, box 28, folder 6, Haitian Refugee Collection.

53. Rescue Committee for Haitian Refugees, Press Release: Seventy Jailed Refugees on Hunger Strike, February 13, 1979, box 28, folder 6, Haitian Refugee Collection.

54. Ibid.

55. Stepick, "Haitian Boat People," 185–186; Loescher and Scanlan, "Human Rights, U.S. Foreign Policy, and Haitian Refugees," 339–340.

56. Deposition of Patrick Lemoine in *Haitian Refugee Center v. Civiletti,* October 5, 1979, box 9, folder 7, Haitian Refugee Collection; Patrick Lemoine, "One Man's Tale of Terror from Haiti's Gulag," *Sunday Newsday,* May 20, 1979, 5, 11, box 36, folder 6, Haitian Refugee Collection.

57. Final order granting relief in *Haitian Refugee Center v. Civiletti,* July 2, 1980, box 13, folder 6, Haitian Refugee Collection.

58. Ibid.

59. Ward Sinclair, "U.S. Formulated a Haitian Refugee 'Solution' 2 Years Ago," *Washington Post,* April 20, 1980, 224, in *Caribbean Refugee Crisis: Cubans and Haitians,* 224.

60. Zucker, "The Haitians vs. the United States," 157–158; Norman L. Zucker and Naomi

Flink Zucker, *The Guarded Gate: The Reality of American Refugee Policy* (San Diego: Harcourt Brace Jovanovich, 1987), 198–199.

61. Shirley Chisholm, "U.S. Policy and Black Refugees," *Issue: A Journal of Opinion* 12, nos. 1–2 (1982): 23–24.

Chapter 2. The Refugee Crisis of 1980: Forging the Detention Tool

1. U.S. Immigration and Naturalization Service, "Federal Correction Institute, Miami Florida, U.S. Immigration and Naturalization Service," March 5, 1980, reel 3, *Immigration during the Carter Administration: Records of the Cuban-Haitian Task Force* (Bethesda, Md.: LexisNexis, 2009) (hereafter *Records of the Cuban-Haitian Task Force*).

2. Southeastern Federal Regional Council, "Haitian Processing Center, Federal Correction Institute, Miami Florida, established by the Southeastern Regional Federal Council on March 7, 1980," reel 3, *Records of the Cuban-Haitian Task Force*.

3. María Cristina García, *Havana USA: Cuban Exiles and Cuban Americans in South Florida, 1959–1994* (Berkeley: University of California Press, 1996), 46, 60–61. For a thorough review of the origins and consequences of the Mariel boatlift, see 46–80.

4. Gilburt Loescher and John Scanlan, "Human Rights, U.S. Foreign Policy, and Haitian Refugees," *Journal of Interamerican Studies and World Affairs* 26, no. 3 (1983): 340–341.

5. Norman L. Zucker and Naomi Flink Zucker, *The Guarded Gate: The Reality of American Refugee Policy* (San Diego: Harcourt Brace Jovanovich, 1987), 61. Carter administration officials put the number closer to 900,000; see "Overview of the United States Government's Policy and Programs Regarding Recent Cuban/Haitian Arrivals into the United States," reel 3, *Records of the Cuban-Haitian Task Force*.

6. María Cristina García, *The Refugee Challenge in Post–Cold War America* (New York: Oxford University Press, 2017), 4–5.

7. Loescher and Scanlan, "Human Rights, U.S. Foreign Policy, and Haitian Refugees, 341–342; Zucker and Zucker, *The Guarded Gate*, 50–58.

8. "Cuban-Haitian Fact Sheet," September 1, 1980, reel 3, *Records of the Cuban-Haitian Task Force*; Jana K. Lipman, "'The Fish Trusts the Water, and It Is in the Water That It Is Cooked': The Caribbean Origins of the Krome Detention Center," *Radical History Review* 115 (2013): 120.

9. García, *Havana USA*, 62–63.

10. "Haitians," reel 18, *Records of the Cuban-Haitian Task Force*.

11. Syl Ligsukis to Phyllis Dichter, "Comments on Draft Memo of 8/1/80: 'Cuban Haitian Arrivals After June 19," August 5, 1980, reel 12, *Records of the Cuban-Haitian Task Force*.

12. Alex Stepick, "Haitian Boat People: A Study in the Conflicting Forces Shaping U.S. Immigration Policy," *Law and Contemporary Problems* 45, no. 2 (1982): 187; Zucker and Zucker, *The Guarded Gate*, 67.

13. Stepick, "Haitian Boat People," 187–188; Loescher and Scanlan, "Human Rights, US Foreign Policy, and Haitian Refugees," 343.

14. Statement of Edward M. Kennedy, committee chair, in U.S. Congress, Senate, Committee on the Judiciary, *Caribbean Refugee Crisis: Cubans and Haitians: Hearing Before the Committee on the Judiciary, United States Senate, Ninety-Sixty Congress, Second Session, May*

12, 1980 (Washington, D.C.: U.S. Government Printing Office, 1980), 1–2. (Hereafter *Caribbean Refugee Crisis.*)

15. Statement of Archbishop Edward A. McCarthy, in *Caribbean Refugee Crisis*, 9.

16. Statement of Monsignor Bryan Walsh, director of Catholic Charities for the Archdiocese of Miami, in *Caribbean Refugee Crisis*, 22.

17. Exchange between Edward M. Kennedy and Victor Palmieri, U.S. Coordinator for Refugee Affairs, in *Caribbean Refugee Crisis*, 28–29.

18. Statement of Michael H. Posner, executive director of the Lawyers Committee for Human Rights, in *Caribbean Refugee Crisis*, 194–195.

19. Statement of Member of Congress Walter Fauntroy, in *Caribbean Refugee Crisis*, 53–54.

20. David M. Reimers, *Unwelcome Strangers: American Identity and the Turn against Immigration* (New York: Columbia University Press, 1998), 28–29.

21. Joseph Nevins, *Operation Gatekeeper and Beyond: The War on "Illegals" and the Remaking of the U.S.-Mexico Boundary* (New York: Routledge, 2010), 13.

22. Max J. Castro, "The Politics of Language in Miami," in *Miami Now! Immigration, Ethnicity, and Social Change*, edited by Guillermo J. Grenier and Alex Stepick III (Gainesville: University Press of Florida, 1992), 119–123, 128.

23. García, *Havana USA*, 66–67.

24. "Statement by Victor H. Palmieri, United States Coordinator for Refugee Affairs," June 20, 1980, reel 3, *Records of the Cuban-Haitian Task Force.*

25. Lipman, "'The Fish Trusts the Water, and It Is in the Water That It Is Cooked,'" 123.

26. Loescher and Scanlan, "Human Rights, US Foreign Policy, and Haitian Refugees," 344.

27. "Statement by Victor H. Palmieri, United States Coordinator for Refugee Affairs," June 20, 1980, reel 3, *Records of the Cuban-Haitian Task Force;*

28. Roger C. Adams to Christian R. Holmes, "Action Plan for Haitian Entrant Program," August 12, 1980, reel 12, *Records of the Cuban-Haitian Task Force.*

29. Ibid.

30. Roger C. Adams to Phyllis Dichter, "Legal Status of Haitian Entrants," August 11, 1980, reel 12, *Records of the Cuban-Haitian Task Force.*

31. Haitian Coordinating Committee for Refugees to Victor H. Palmieri, September 9, 1980, reel 26, *Records of the Cuban-Haitian Task Force.*

32. Lipman, "'The Fish Trusts the Water, and It Is in the Water That It Is Cooked,'" 121.

33. Phyllis Dichter to Syl Ligsukis, "Policy Issues for the Haitian Entrant Program," August 5, 1980, reel 12, *Records of the Cuban-Haitian Task Force.*

34. For more on the background of Krome before it became a refugee camp, see Lipman, "'The Fish Trusts the Water, and It Is in the Water That It Is Cooked,'" 115–126.

35. Ibid., 123.

36. Larry Mahoney, "Inside Krome," *Miami Herald, Tropic Magazine*, January 10, 1982, Haiti 1982, folder Jan. and Feb., Alex and Carol Stepick Collection, Florida International University (hereafter Alex and Carol Stepick Collection).

37. Kurzban quoted in Christian R. Holmes to David Crosland, "Haitian INS Processing and Procedures," ca. August 28, 1980, reel 26, *Records of the Cuban-Haitian Task Force.*

38. Haitian Coordinating Committee for Refugees to Victor H. Palmieri, September 9, 1980.

39. Kurzban quoted in Holmes to Crosland, "Haitian INS Processing and Procedures."

40. Mahoney, "Inside Krome."

41. "Patricia Roberts Harris," *Discover Diplomacy*, accessed March 18, 2017, http://diplomacy.state.gov/discoverdiplomacy/explorer/peoplehistorical/170238.htm.

42. Patricia Roberts Harris to Victor H. Palmieri, August 9, 1980, reel 12, *Records of the Cuban-Haitian Task Force*; Patricia Roberts Harris to Eugene Eidenberg, August 19, 1980, reel 3, *Records of the Cuban-Haitian Task Force*.

43. Syl Ligsukis, "Note to Chris Holmes and Jim Smith," September 8, 1980, reel 4, *Records of the Cuban-Haitian Task Force*.

44. Eugene Eidenberg to Patricia Roberts Harris, August 20, 1980, reel 4, *Records of the Cuban-Haitian Task Force*; Paul Schmidt to Nathan J. Stark, August 28, 1980, reel 4, *Records of the Cuban-Haitian Task Force*.

45. Phyllis Dichter to Christian R. Holmes, "Plan for Immediate Improvements to Krome South," August 15, 1980, reel 12, *Records of the Cuban-Haitian Task Force*.

46. Christian R. Holmes to Eugene Eidenberg, "Care and Resettlement of Haitians," August 19, 1980, reel 12, *Records of the Cuban-Haitian Task Force*.

47. Lipman, "'The Fish Trusts the Water and It Is in the Water That It Is Cooked,'" 125–126.

48. Manny Suarez and Harry Turner, "US to Use Fort Allen to Use Cuban, Haitian Refugees," *San Juan Star*, September 29, 1980, folder Haiti 1980; "Chaffee Ready for Regrouping of Refugees for Winter," *San Juan Star*, folder Haiti 1980, Alex and Carol Stepick Collection.

49. Harry Turner, "Carter Aide Blames 'Leak' for Delay in Warning CRB," *San Juan Star*, October 2, 1980, folder Haiti 1980, Alex and Carol Stepick Collection

50. "Arkansas Officials Protest Refugee Camp Status," *San Juan Star*, September 26, 1980, folder Haiti 1980, Alex and Carol Stepick Collection; Lipman, "'The Fish Trusts the Water, and It Is in the Water That It Is Cooked,'" 127.

51. Manny Suarez, "P.R. Denies 'Economic Plans' for New Refugees," *San Juan Star*, September 20, 1980; Manny Suarez, "CRB Threatens Suit on Refugees if Standards Not Met," *San Juan Star*, September 26, 1980; Harry Turner, "Number of Exiles Due at Fort Allen Remains up in Air," *San Juan Star*, September 30, 1980; Maggie Bobb, "Feelings Mixed over Influx of Refugees at Fort Allen," *San Juan Star*, September 25, 1980. All in folder Haiti 1980, Alex and Carol Stepick Collection.

52. Lipman, "'The Fish Trusts the Water, and It Is in the Water That It Is Cooked,'" 128.

53. Manny Suarez, "End of Sealift Doesn't Alter Fort Allen Relocation Plan," *San Juan Star*, September 27, 1980; "Feelings Mixed over Influx of Refugees at Fort Allen," *San Juan Star*, September 25, 1980; Harold J. Liden, "EQB Orders Construction of Refugee Center Cease," *San Juan Star*, October 2, 1980. All in folder Haiti 1980, Alex and Carol Stepick Collection. See also Lipman, "'The Fish Trusts the Water, and It Is in the Water That It Is Cooked,'" 128.

54. Congressional Black Caucus members to Jimmy Carter, October 16, 1980, reel 26, *Records of the Cuban-Haitian Task Force*.

55. Amnesty International statement on Fort Allen, reel 26, *Records of the Cuban-Haitian Task Force*.

56. Congressional Black Caucus quoted in Lipman, "'The Fish Trusts the Water, and It Is in the Water That It Is Cooked,'" 127.

57. Thomas Dorney, "2 Suits Filed to Stop Influx of Cubans, Haitians," *San Juan Star*, September 30, 1980; Manny Suarez, "Island Files Suit to Bar Opening Refugee Camp," *San Juan Star*, October 1, 1980, both in folder Haiti 1980, Alex and Carol Stepick Collection See also Lipman, "'The Fish Trusts the Water, and It Is in the Water That It Is Cooked,'" 128.

58. Lipman, "'The Fish Trusts the Water, and It Is in the Water That It Is Cooked,'" 129–130.

59. "Haitian Arrivals by Month, 1980–1981," n.d., reel 4, *Records of the Cuban-Haitian Task Force*; Loescher and Scanlan, "Human Rights, U.S. Foreign Policy, and Haitian Refugees," 344.

60. "Contingency Planning for a Possible Future Influx of Cubans and/or Haitians," n.d., reel 4, *Records of the Cuban-Haitian Task Force.*

Chapter 3. Immigration Detention Reborn, 1981–1982

1. "Haitian Refugee Project: Appeal to the People of the United States," April 2, 1982, box 23, folder 3, Haitian Refugee Collection.

2. "Haitian Refugee Update," March 17, 1982, box 22, folder 7, Haitian Refugee Collection.

3. Statement by Senator Allen Simpson, chair of the Subcommittee on Immigration and Refugee Policy, in U.S. Congress, Senate, Committee on the Judiciary, Subcommittee on Immigration and Refugee Policy, *United States as a Country of Mass First Asylum: Hearing before the Subcommittee on Immigration and Refugee Policy, United States Senate, 97th Congress, 1st Session, July 31, 1981* (Washington, D.C.: U.S. Government Printing Office, 1982), 1. (Hereafter *United States as a Country of Mass First Asylum.*)

4. Statement by Thomas O. Enders, assistant secretary of state for inter-American affairs, in *United States as a Country of Mass First Asylum*, 5.

5. Statement by Doris Meisner, acting commissioner of the Immigration and Naturalization Service, in *United States as a Country of Mass First Asylum*, 12–13.

6. Statement by Kentucky senator Walter Huddleston, in *United States as a Country of Mass First Asylum*, 81.

7. Statement by Illinois representative Robert McGlory, in *United States as a Country of Mass First Asylum*, 107.

8. Statement by Florida senator Lawton Chiles, in *United States as a Country of Mass First Asylum*, 44–48.

9. Statement by Florida senator Paula Hawkins, in *United States as a Country of Mass First Asylum*, 37.

10. Refugee Act of 1980, Public Law 96-212, March 17, 1980, https://www.gpo.gov/fdsys/pkg/STATUTE-94/pdf/STATUTE-94-Pg102.pdf.

11. Peter H. Schuck, "The Transformation of Immigration Law," *Columbia Law Review* 84, no. 1 (1984): 39–40.

12. Michael J. Churgin, "Mass Exoduses: The Response of the United States," *International Migration Review* 30, no. 1 (1996): 310. >

13. Naomi Flink Zucker, "The Haitians versus the United States: The Courts as Last Resort." *Annals of the American Academy of Political and Social Science* 467 (May 1983): 153.

14. Gil Loescher and John A. Scanlan, *Calculated Kindness: Refugees and America's Half-Open Door, 1945–Present* (New York: The Free Press, 1986), 186–187.

15. Mae M. Ngai, *Impossible Subjects: Illegal Aliens and the Making of Modern America* (Princeton, N.J.: Princeton University Press, 2004), 11.

16. Maxine S. Seller, "Historical Perspectives on American Immigration Policy: Case Studies and Current Implications," *Law and Contemporary Problems* 45, no. 2 (1982): 158.

17. Julilly Kohler-Hausman, *Getting Tough: Welfare and Imprisonment in 1970s America* (Princeton, N.J.: Princeton University Press, 2017), 21–22.

18. Statement by Thomas O. Enders.

19. Ibid.

20. Immigration Task Force, "Issue Paper," quoted in Zucker, "The Haitians versus the United States," 159. For a further explanation of this process, see Richard F. Hahn, "Constitutional Limits on the Power to Exclude Aliens," *Columbia Law Review* 82, no. 5 (1982): 959–960nn17–19.

21. James Baker to Ronald Reagan, March 13, 1981, folder Haitian Refugees (5 of 6), box 1, Michael J. Luttig Files, Ronald Reagan Library.

22. Ibid.

23. Justice Department to Attorney General, n.d., folder Haitian Refugees (5 of 6), box 1, Michael J. Luttig Files, Ronald Reagan Library.

24. Assistant Attorney General Theodore B. Olson, memo to the Attorney General, August 1, 1981, ID # 033441, Subject File: Immigration, box 2, folder 1, Ronald Reagan Library.

25. Fred Fielding to Richard Darman, September 22, 1981, ID # 033441, Subject File: Immigration, box 2, folder 1, Ronald Reagan Library.

26. Olson to the Attorney General, August 1, 1981.

27. Kate Moore to Frank Hodsoll, August 4, 1981, ID # 033441, Subject File: Immigration, box 2, folder 1, Ronald Reagan Library.

28. "'High Seas Interdiction of Illegal Aliens' by the President of the United States of America, a Proclamation," September 29, 1981, Immigration IM ID # 033441, Subject File: Immigration, box 2, folder 1, Ronald Reagan Library.

29. Ibid.

30. "Coast Guard Migrant Interdictions at Sea, Fiscal Year 1982–2003," Folder Interdiction Stats '82-'93, Women's Refugee Commission Records, David M. Rubenstein Rare Book & Manuscript Library, Duke University. (Hereafter Women's Refugee Commission Records.)

31. Statement by New York member of Congress Shirley Chisholm, in *United States as a Country of Mass First Asylum*, 113, 115.

32. James Silk, *Despite a Generous Spirit: Denying Asylum in the United States* (Washington, D.C.: U.S. Committee for Refugees, 1986), 25.

33. Walter E. Fauntroy to Ronald Reagan, August 13, 1981, ID # 036134, Subject File: Immigration, box 3, Ronald Reagan Library.

34. David Crosland to Walter Fauntroy, ID # 036134, Subject File: Immigration, box 3, Ronald Reagan Library.

35. Silk, *Despite a Generous Spirit*, 24.

36. Christopher Mitchell, "U.S. Policy toward Haitian Boat People, 1972–93," *Annals of the American Academy of Political and Social Science* 534, no. 1 (1994): 73.

37. Associated Press, "Demonstrations Will Not Change Policy, Official Says," December 31, 1981.

38. Mitchell, "U.S. Policy toward Haitian Boat People, 1972–93," 74.

39. Loescher and Scanlan, *Calculated Kindness*, 193.

40. Silk, *Despite a Generous Spirit*, 18; Loescher and Scanlan, *Calculated Kindness*, 192–193; Loescher and Scanlan, "Human Rights, U.S. Foreign Policy, and Haitian Refugees," 345.

41. Timothy J. Dunn, *The Militarization of the U.S.-Mexico Border, 1978–1992: Low-Intensity Conflict Doctrine Comes Home* (Austin: Center for Mexican American Studies, University of Texas, 1996), 46.

42. Associated Press, "Demonstrations Will Not Change Policy, Official Says."

43. William French Smith to Allen Nelson, June 11, 1982, ID # 094873, Subject File: Immigration, box 9, Cubans and Haitians folder, Ronald Reagan Library.

44. Ibid.

45. Mike Horowitz to Ed Harper, Glenn Schleede, and Annelise Anderson, September 16, 1981, ID # 033441, Subject File: Immigration, box 2, Ronald Reagan Library.

46. Ibid.

47. H. P. Goldfield to Fred F. Fielding, October 20, 1981, ID # 033441, Subject File: Immigration, box 2, Reagan Presidential Library.

48. Memo from William French Smith to Ronald Reagan, July 16, 1981, ID # 018148, Subject File: Immigration, box 1, Ronald Reagan Library.

49. Thomas R. Maddux, "Ronald Reagan and the Task Force on Immigration, 1981," *Pacific Historical Review* 74, no. 2 (2005): 214.

50. Smith to Reagan, July 16, 1981.

51. On the detention of Salvadorans and Guatemalans at Port Isabel, see Robert S. Kahn, *Other People's Blood: U.S. Immigration Prisons in the Reagan Decade* (Boulder, Colo.: Westview Press, 1996).

52. Smith to Reagan, July 16, 1981.

53. Frank Hodsoll to Jim Baker, October 6, 1981, folder Cuban-Haitian, box 1, Kate L. Moore Files, Ronald Reagan Library.

54. Friedersdorf quoted in Maddux, "Ronald Reagan and the Task Force on Immigration, 1981," 214–215

55. Frank Hodsoll to Jim Baker, October 6, 1981, folder Cuban-Haitian, box 1, Kate L. Moore Files, Ronald Reagan Library.

56. Kate Moore and Kathy Collins to James Baker and Edwin Meese, November 3, 1981, folder Cuban-Haitian, box 1, Kate L. Moore Files, Ronald Reagan Library.

57. "Suggested Talking Points for Meeting Congressman Dave Martin (R-NY)," November 10, 1981, folder Cuban-Haitian, box 1, Kate L. Moore Files, Ronald Reagan Library.

58. Ibid.

59. Frank Hodsoll to Jim Baker, October 6, 1981.

60. Kate Moore and Kathy Collins to James Baker and Edwin Meese, November 3, 1981.

61. Statement by John A. Bushnell, Subcommittee on Immigration of the House Judiciary Committee, June 17, 1980, reel 12, *Immigration during the Carter Administration: Records of the Cuban-Haitian Task Force* (Bethesda, Md.: LexisNexis, 2009).

62. Norman L. Zucker and Naomi Flink Zucker, *The Guarded Gate: The Reality of American Refugee Policy* (San Diego: Harcourt Brace Jovanovich, 1987), 163.

63. Churgin, "Mass Exoduses," 321.

64. Zucker and Zucker, *The Guarded Gate*, 181.

65. Peter Andreas, *Border Games: Policing the U.S.-Mexico Divide* (Ithaca, N.Y.: Cornell University Press, 2009), 85.

66. "Release the Haitian Refugees," February 27, 1982, box 1, folder 26, Haiti/Dechoukaj Collection, Schomburg Center for Research in Black Culture, The New York Public Library. (Hereafter Haiti/Dechoukaj Collection.)

67. NAACP to Ronald Reagan, November 25, 1981, box 24, folder 3, Haitian Refugee Collection.

68. Press release, "NAACP and Haitian Coalition Demand Freedom for Haitian Refugees by Christmas," December 1, 1981, box 24, folder 3, Haitian Refugee Collection.

69. National Council of Churches, "Resolution on Refugees from El Salvador and Haiti," adopted May 14, 1981, box 22, folder 7, Haitian Refugee Collection.

70. NCC/Inter-Religious Council to President Ronald Reagan, October 30, 1981, box 22, folder 7, Haitian Refugee Collection.

71. Statement of Arthur C. Helton, Lawyers' Committee for International Human Rights, in *The United States as a Country of Mass First Asylum*, 12.

72. Ibid., 9.

73. Ibid., 7.

74. Ibid., 17.

75. "Termination of Ft. Chaffee Operations," n.d., file Cubans and Haitians, box 10, James W. Cicconi Files, Ronald Reagan Library.

Chapter 4. Construction of and Resistance to the Detention Regime, 1981–1991

1. "Refugees or Prisoners?" *Newsweek*, February 1, 1982, in U.S. Congress, House Committee on the Judiciary, Subcommittee on Courts, Civil Liberties, and the Administration of Justice, *Detention of Aliens in Bureau of Prisons Facilities, Hearing before the Subcommittee on Courts, Civil Liberties, and the Administration of Justice of the Committee on the Judiciary, 97th Congress, Second Session on Detention of Aliens in Bureau of Prisons Facilities, June 23, 1982* (Washington, D.C.: U.S. Government Printing Office, 1983), 370. (Hereafter *Detention of Aliens in Bureau of Prisons Facilities*.)

2. Brenda Eady, "Haitians, Guards Scuffle at Krome," *Miami Herald*, n.d.; Joan Fleischman, "Chronology of Troubles at the Krome Center," *Miami Herald*, December 29, 1981; Brenda Eady, "Immigration Adds 77 Agents to Camp Security Force," *Miami Herald*, December 30, 1981; Glenda Wright-McQueen and Kathy McCarthy, "The Clash at Krome," *Miami News*, December 28, 1981. All in box 3, folder Haiti 1981 II, Alex and Carol Stepick Collection, Florida International University. (Hereafter Alex and Carol Stepick Collection.)

3. "Krome: A Way Station for Human Misery," *Miami Herald*, September 4, 1981; "Escapees, 'Troublemakers,' to Be Sent to New York," *Miami Herald*, September 4, 1981; Brenda Eady, "U.S. Moving Haitian 'Malcontents,'" *Miami Herald*, October 3, 1981; Anders Gyllenhaal, "Haitian Refugees Demand Freedom from Krome Center by Christmas," *Miami Herald*, December 22, 1981; Rick Thames, "Haitians at Krome Staging Hunger Strike," *Miami News*, December 25, 1981; "Haitians at 2 Detention Sites Refusing to Eat and to Talk," *New York Times*, December 25, 1981; Mary Voboril, "Haitians Vow to Fast Until They Are Free," *Miami Herald*, December 25, 1981. All in box 3, folder Haiti 1981 II, Alex and Carol Stepick Collection.

4. "Haitian Camp Visit Put Off," *Miami Herald*, December 7, 1981; Guillermo Martinez, "'All I Can Do Is Pray,' Jailed Haitian Laments," *Miami Herald*, December 21, 1981; Jo Thomas, "At Fort Allen, Boredom Is a Disease," *Miami News*, December 22, 1981; Associated Press, "Angry at Barbed-Wire Christmas, Haitian Refugees Riot at Fort Allen," *Miami News*, December 21, 1981; "Haitians at 2 Detention Sites Refusing to Eat and to Talk"; Associated Press, "Justice

Official: Protest Can't End Detention of Haitian Boat People," *Miami News*, January 1, 1982. All in box 3, folder, Haiti 1981 II, Alex and Carol Stepick Collection.

5. Michael Kroll, "'Indefinite Detention' Now the Policy for Illegal Aliens," *Los Angeles Daily Journal*, July 29, 1982.

6. Peter H. Schuck, "The Transformation of Immigration Law," *Columbia Law Review* 84, no. 1 (1984): 29.

7. "Release the Haitians," *New York Times*, April 19, 1982, in *Detention of Aliens in Bureau of Prisons Facilities*, 376.

8. "CHTF Director's Briefing Materials for the Senate Appropriations Committee Hearings Held during the Week of March 2, 1981," 14, reel 40, *Immigration during the Carter Administration: Records of the Cuban-Haitian Task Force* (Bethesda, Md.: LexisNexis, 2009).

9. U.S. General Accounting Office, *Detention Policies Affecting Haitian Nationals: Report* (Washington D.C.: U.S. General Accounting Office, 1983), 1, 15; Department of Justice, Immigration and Naturalization Service, "Detention and Parole of Inadmissible Aliens; Interim Rule with Requests for Comments," *Federal Register* 47, no. 132 (July 9, 1982), in *Detention of Aliens in Bureau of Prisons Facilities*, 205.

10. U.S. General Accounting Office, *Detention Policies Affecting Haitian Nationals*, 15, 18.

11. Mary Bosworth and Emma Kaufman, "Foreigners in a Carceral Age: Immigration and Imprisonment in the United States." *Stanford Law and Policy Review* 22, no. 1 (2011): 432.

12. Immigration and Naturalization Service, "Haitians in Detention Facilities," April 30, 1982, in *Detention of Aliens in Bureau of Prisons Facilities*, 187.

13. Arthur C. Helton, "The Legality of Detaining Refugees in the United States," *New York University Review of Law and Social Change* 353 (1986): 364.

14. "Summary of Suicide Attempts, Krome Processing Center," in *Detention of Aliens in Bureau of Prisons*, 387.

15. Kroll, "'Indefinite Detention' Now the Policy for Illegal Aliens."

16. Department of Justice, Immigration and Naturalization Service, "Detention and Parole of Inadmissible Aliens; Interim Rule with Request for Comments," Federal Register, vol. 47, no. 132, July 9, 1982 in *Detention of Aliens in Bureau of Prisons Facilities*, 205.

17. U.S. General Accounting Office, *Detention Policies Affecting Haitian Nationals*, 12; Helton, "The Legality of Detaining Refugees in the United States," 359–360.

18. Edward C. Schmults to James A. Baker and staff, March 10, 1982, box 10, file Cubans and Haitians, James W. Cicconi Files, Ronald Reagan Presidential Library.

19. *Detention of Aliens in Bureau of Prisons Facilities*, 1–2.

20. Ibid.

21. Ibid., 3–6.

22. Ibid., 17–20.

23. Ibid., 22.

24. Helton, "The Legality of Detaining Refugees in the United States," 363, 365; Timothy J. Dunn, *The Militarization of the U.S.-Mexico Border, 1978–1992: Low-Intensity Conflict Doctrine Comes Home* (Austin: Center for Mexican American Studies, University of Texas, 1996), 49.

25. Helton, "The Legality of Detaining Refugees in the United States," 363, 365.

26. Bill Frelick, *The Back of the Hand: Bias and Restrictionism towards Central American Asylum Seekers in North America* (Washington, D.C.: U.S. Committee for Refugees, 1988), 1–2.

27. María Cristina García, *Seeking Refuge: Central American Migration to Mexico, the United States, and Canada* (Berkeley: University of California Press, 2006), 91.

28. Helton, "The Legality of Detaining Refugees in the United States," 363.

29. James Silk, *Despite a Generous Spirit: Denying Asylum in the United States* (Washington, D.C.: U.S. Committee for Refugees, 1986), 20.

30. Dunn, *The Militarization of the U.S.-Mexico Border*, 54–56.

31. Frances Frank Marcus, "Prison for Aliens Opens in Louisiana," *New York Times*, April 9, 1986.

32. Ibid.

33. Jack Walsh to Robert W. Kastenmeir, June 24, 1982, in *Detention of Aliens in Bureau of Prisons Facilities*, 367.

34. John G. Kines Jr. to M. Caldwell Butler, June 28, 1982, in *Detention of Aliens in Bureau of Prisons Facilities*, 211–214.

35. Mowat quoted in Bureau of Prisons and the U.S. Parole Commission, *Oversight Hearing before the Subcommittee on Courts, Civil Liberties, and the Administration of Justice of the Committee on the Judiciary, House of Representatives, 99th Congress, First Session on Bureau of Prisons and the U.S. Parole Commission, March 28, 1985* (Washington, D.C.: U.S. Government Printing Office, 1985), accessed January 14, 2017, https://archive.org/stream/bureauofprison-suoounit/bureauofprisonsuoounit_djvu.txt.

36. Dunn, *The Militarization of the U.S.-Mexico Border*, 47–48.

37. "Preface," in Asim Varma and Craig M. Tateronis, *The Detention of Asylum Seekers in the United States: A Cruel and Questionable Policy: A Briefing Paper* (New York: Lawyers Committee for Human Rights, 1989), 3, 25–26, 41–42; Dunn, *The Militarization of the U.S. Mexico Border*, 91–93; García, *Seeking Refuge*, 110.

38. Bosworth and Kaufman, "Foreigners in a Carceral Age," 442; Dunn, *The Militarization of the U.S.-Mexico Border*, 71–72.

39. Douglas C. McDonald, "Private Penal Institutions," *Crime and Justice* 16 (1992): 381; Mark Dow, *American Gulag: Inside U.S. Immigration Prisons* (Berkeley: University of California Press, 2005), 97; Dunn, *The Militarization of the U.S.-Mexico Border*, 40.

40. Eric Schlosser, "The Prison Industrial Complex," *The Atlantic*, December 1998, accessed November 12, 2016, https://www.theatlantic.com/magazine/archive/1998/12/the-prison-industrial-complex/304669/.

41. Philip Mattera, Mafruza Khan, and Stephen Nathan, *Corrections Corporation of America: A Critical Look at Its First 20 Years* (n.p.: Grassroots Leadership, 2003), accessed October 19, 2016, http://grassrootsleadership.org/sites/default/files/uploads/CCAAnniversaryReport.pdf; Dow, *American Gulag*, 97.

42. McDonald, "Private Penal Institutions," 382; Aviva Chomsky, *Undocumented: How Immigration Became Illegal* (Boston: Beacon Press, 2014), 108–109; Dunn, *The Militarization of the U.S.-Mexico Border*, 49.

43. Martin Tolchin, "As Privately Owned Prisons Increase, So Do Their Critics," *New York Times*, February 11, 1985, A1; Dunn, *The Militarization of the U.S.-Mexico Border*, 49.

44. Snellings and Nissen quoted in Kevin Krajick, "Prisons for Profit: The Private Alternative," *State Legislatures*, April 1983, 9–14 (1984); Tolchin, "As Privately Owned Prisons Increase, So Do Their Critics," A1.

45. Elizabeth Hinton, *From the War on Poverty to the War on Crime: The Making of Mass*

Incarceration in America (Cambridge, Mass.: Harvard University Press, 2016), 4, 11, 14–15, 19. For a thorough explanation of the process by which race and criminality became associated in the American mind, see Khalil Gibran Muhammad, *The Condemnation of Blackness: Race, Crime, and the Making of Modern Urban America* (Cambridge, Mass.: Harvard University Press, 2010).

46. Julilly Kohler-Hausmann, *Getting Tough: Welfare and Imprisonment in 1970s America* (Princeton, N.J.: Princeton University Press, 2017), 16, 253–255.

47. McDonald, "Private Penal Institutions," 392; Dow, *American Gulag*, 163.

48. Torrie Hester, "Deportability and the Carceral State," *Journal of American History* 102, no. 2 (2015): 149; Daniel Wilsher, *Immigration Detention: Law, History, Politics* (Cambridge: Cambridge University Press, 2012), 69; Dow, *American Gulag*, 163–164.

49. Patrisia Macías-Rojas, *From Deportation to Prison: The Politics of Immigration Enforcement in Post–Civil Rights America*. (New York: New York University Press, 2016), 8–9, 59, 75.

50. Dunn, *The Militarization of the U.S.-Mexico Border*, 73–76.

51. Ibid., 35, 181.

52. McDonald, "Private Penal Institutions," 392.

53. Guy S. Goodwin-Gill, "International Law and the Detention of Refugees and Asylum Seekers," *International Migration Review* 20, no. 2 (1986): 193–195, 197–198, 211, 217.

54. Silk, *Despite a Generous Spirit*, 2–3, 9–10, 21.

55. Varma and Tateronis, *The Detention of Asylum Seekers in the United States*.

56. Helton, "The Legality of Detaining Refugees in the United States," 369, 381.

57. Gilburt Loescher and John Scanlan, *Calculated Kindness: Refugees and America's Half-Open Door 1945–Present* (New York: Free Press, 1986), 196.

58. Allen C. Nelson to Robert W. Kastenmeir, June 25, 1982, in *Detention of Aliens in Bureau of Prisons Facilities*, 202–204.

59. Reagan quoted in Robert S. Kahn, *Other People's Blood: U.S. Immigration Prisons in the Reagan Decade* (Boulder, Colo.: Westview Press, 1996), 24n4.

60. Thomas Alexander Aleinikoff, David A. Martin, and Hiroshi Motomura, *Immigration: Process and Policy*, 3rd ed. (St. Paul, Minn.: West Publishing Co., 1998), 447.

61. Schuck, "The Transformation of Immigration Law," 34.

62. Ibid., 68.

63. Hiroshi Motomura, *Americans in Waiting: The Lost Story of Immigration and Citizenship in the United States* (New York: Oxford University Press, 2006), 101–102; Schuck, "The Transformation of Immigration Law," 29; Helton, "The Legality of Detaining Refugees in the United States," 354–355; Aleinikoff, Martin, and Motomura, *Immigration: Process and Policy*, 445–446.

64. Aleinikoff, Martin and Motomura, *Immigration: Process and Policy*, 447–448; Arthur C. Helton, "The Mandate of U.S. Courts to Protect Aliens under International Human Rights Law," *Yale Law Journal* 100, no. 8 (1991): 2337.

65. Frelick, *The Back of the Hand*, 19–21; Kahn, *Other People's Blood*, 17–19; García, *Seeking Refuge*, 108–109.

66. Jeffrey C. Gilbert and Steven Kass, "*Jean v. Nelson*: A Stark Pattern of Discrimination," *University of Miami Law Review* 36 (1982): 1007–1010; Jonathan Simon, "Refugees in a Carceral Age: The Rebirth of Immigration Prison in the United States," *Public Culture* 10, no. 3

(1998): 586–587; Ira J. Kurzban, "'Long and Perilous Journey': The Nelson Decision," *Human Rights* 11, no. 2 (1983): 41.

67. Gilbert and Kass, *"Jean v. Nelson,"* 1012–1013; Silk, *Despite a Generous Spirit*, 18–19; *Detention of Aliens in Bureau of Prisons Facilities*, 67; Press Release, Haitian Refugee Center, June 18, 1982, box 22, folder 21, Haitian Refugee Collection, Schomburg Center for Research in Black Culture, The New York Public Library.

68. Helton quoted in Silk, *Despite a Generous Spirit*, 19.

69. U.S. General Accounting Office, *Detention Policies Affecting Haitian Nationals*, 12.

70. *Detention of Aliens in Bureau of Prisons Facilities*, 30, 39, 61–62; Richard F. Hahn, "Constitutional Limits on the Power to Exclude Aliens," *Columbia Law Review* 82, no. 5 (1982): 960n20.

71. Gilbert and Kass, *"Jean v. Nelson,"* 1024–1025, 1028–1029; Kurzban, "'Long and Perilous Journey,'" 41–43.

72. Gilbert and Kass, *"Jean v. Nelson,"* 1014; Mary Jane Lapointe, "Discrimination in Asylum Law: The Implications of Jean v. Nelson," *Indiana Law Journal* 62, no. 1 (1986): 127–128; Aleinikoff, Martin, and Motomura, *Immigration: Process and Policy*, 461.

73. Aleinikoff, Martin, and Motomura, *Immigration: Process and Policy*, 450.

74. "American Baptist Churches v. Thornburgh (ABC)," *U.S. Citizenship and Immigration Services*, accessed July 27, 2016, https://www.uscis.gov/laws/legal-settlement-notices/american-baptist-churches-v-thornburgh-abc-settlement-agreement; Kahn, *Other People's Blood*, 24; García, *Seeking Refuge*, 111–112; Michael J. Churgin, "Mass Exoduses: The Response of the United States," *International Migration Review* 30, no. 1 (1996): 321.

75. Zucker, "The Haitians versus the United States," 160.

76. Simon, "Refugees in a Carceral Age," 599–600.

Chapter 5. Guantanamo: New Frontiers in Detention, 1991–1994

1. Azadeh Dastyari, *United States Migrant Interdiction and the Detention of Refugees in Guantánamo Bay* (Cambridge: Cambridge University Press, 2015), 31.

2. Paul Farmer, *The Uses of Haiti* (Monroe, Maine: Common Courage Press, 2006), 233; Carl Lindskoog, "Refugees and Resistance: International Activism for Grassroots Democracy and Human Rights in New York, Miami, and Haiti, 1957 to 1994" (PhD diss., City University of New York, 2013), 355–358; A. Naomi Paik, *Rightlessness: Testimony and Redress in U.S. Prison Camps since World War II* (Chapel Hill: University of North Carolina Press, 2016), 135; Michael Ratner, "How We Closed the Guantanamo HIV Camp: The Intersection of Politics and Litigation," *Harvard Human Rights Journal* 11 (1998): 251–261.

3. Lindskoog, "Refugees and Resistance," 192–299.

4. Ibid., 299–303; Beverly Bell, *Walking on Fire: Haitian Women's Stories of Survival and Resistance* (Ithaca, N.Y.: Cornell University Press, 2001), 13; Farmer, *The Uses of Haiti*, 153–155; Christopher Mitchell, "U.S. Policy toward Haitian Boat People, 1972–93," *Annals of the American Academy of Political and Social Science* 534, no. 1 (1994): 74.

5. Ira J. Kurzban quoted in U.S. States Congress, House, Committee on Government Operations, Legislation and National Security Subcommittee, *U.S. Human Rights Policy toward Haiti, Hearing before the Legislation and National Security Subcommittee of the Committee on Government Operations, House of Representatives, 102nd Congress, Second Session, April 9,*

1992 (Washington, D.C.: U.S. Government Printing Office, 1993), 91. (Hereafter *U.S. Human Rights Policy toward Haiti.*)

6. Urgent Action: Haitian Asylum Seekers, May 27, 1992, Amnesty International USA, box 5, folder Haitian Refugees, Alex and Carol Stepick Collection, Florida International University, Miami. (Hereafter Stepick Collection.)

7. Statement by Principal Deputy Assistant Secretary of State for Inter-American Affairs Robert S. Gelbard, in U.S. Congress, House, Committee on the Judiciary, *Cuban and Haitian Immigration, Hearing before the Subcommittee on International Law, Immigration, and Refugees of the Committee on the Judiciary, 102nd Congress, 1st Session, November 20, 1991* (Washington, D.C.: U.S. Government Printing Office, 1992), 58–59. (Hereafter *Cuban and Haitian Immigration.*)

8. Edith Márquez Rodríguez to James A. Baker, October 4, 1991, box 18, folder Immigration Haitians, 1990–1991, Americans for Immigrant Justice Records, David M. Rubenstein Rare Book & Manuscript Library, Duke University (hereafter Americans for Immigrant Justice Records); *Cuban and Haitian Immigration*, 48, 58.

9. Statement by Claude Charles, in *U.S. Human Rights Policy toward Haiti*, 83.

10. Cheryl Little to Kerry, November 7, 1991, "Detention Guantanamo; Guantanamo 1991–1992" folder, Americans for Immigrant Justice Records.

11. Statement by Principal Deputy Assistant Secretary of State for Inter-American Affairs Robert S. Gelbard; Summary Chronology of Haitian Refugees on Guantanamo, in *U.S. Human Rights Policy toward Haiti*, 93.

12. "Stop Haitian Interdiction!" *Miami Herald*, November 20, 1991, in *Cuban and Haitian Immigration*, 41.

13. "A Haitians-Stay-Home Policy," *Boston Globe*, November 22, 1991, folder Immigration Haitians, 1990–1991, Americans for Immigrant Justice Records.

14. *Cuban and Haitian Immigration*, 21, 38.

15. Bush quoted in Al Kamen, "Bush Defends Policy on Return of Haitians," *Washington Post*, November 21, 1991, folder Immigration Haitians, 1990–1991, Americans for Immigrant Justice Records.

16. Gelbard statement in *Cuban and Haitian Immigration*, 57–58.

17. Statement of Arthur C. Helton, in *Cuban and Haitian Immigration*, 115.

18. Statement of Daniel A. Stein, in *Cuban and Haitian Immigration*, 184–185.

19. Christopher Mitchell, "The Political Costs of State Power: U.S. Border Control in South Florida," in *The Wall around the West: State Borders and Immigration Controls in North America and Europe*, edited by Peter Andreas and Timothy Snyder (Lanham, Md.: Rowman and Littlefield, 2000), 89–91; David M. Reimers, *Unwelcome Strangers: American Identity and the Turn against Immigration* (New York: Columbia University Press, 1998), 30.

20. Paul Farmer, *AIDS and Accusation: Haiti and the Geography of Blame* (Berkeley: University of California Press, 2006), 4.

21. *Cuban and Haitian Immigration*, 58–59, 93–96; Brandt Goldstein, Rodger Citron, and Molly Beutz Land, *A Documentary Companion to Storming the Court* (Austin, Tex.: Wolters Kluwer Law & Business, 2009), 4–5.

22. Ratner, "How We Closed the Guantanamo HIV Camp," 191–192.

23. Amy Kaplan, "Where Is Guantánamo?" *American Quarterly* 57, no. 3 (2005): 831–832, 839–841; Jana Evans Braziel, "Haiti, Guantanamo, and the 'One Indispensable Nation': US

Imperialism, 'Apparent States,' and the Postcolonial Problematics of Sovereignty," *Cultural Critique* 64 (2006): 130, 139.

24. *Cuban and Haitian Immigration*, 143.

25. Statement of Alan J. Kreczko, in U.S. Congress, House, Committee on the Judiciary, Subcommittee on International Law, Immigration, and Refugees, *Haitian Detention and Interdiction: Hearing before the Subcommittee on Immigration, Refugees, and International Law of the Committee on the Judiciary, 101st Congress, 1st Session, June 8, 1989* (Washington, D.C.: U.S. Government Printing Office, 1989), 33.

26. Statement of Guy S. Goodwin-Gill, in ibid., 167–168.

27. Statement of Arthur C. Helton, in ibid., 158.

28. Statement of Harold Hongju Koh, in *U.S. Human Rights Policy toward Haiti*, 97–98.

29. U.S. Congress, Senate, Committee on the Judiciary, Subcommittee on Immigration and Refugee Affairs, *Haitian Democracy and Refugees: Problems and Prospects: Staff Report* (Washington, D.C.: U.S. Government Printing Office, 1992), 11.

30. Statement of Harold J. Johnson, in *U.S. Human Rights Policy toward Haiti*, 20–21.

31. Statement of Harold Hongju Koh, in U.S. Congress, House, Committee on Foreign Affairs. Subcommittee on Western Hemisphere Affairs and Subcommittee on International Operations, *U.S. Policy toward Haitian Refugees: Joint Hearing and Markup before the Subcommittees on Western Hemisphere Affairs and International Operations of the Committee on Foreign Affairs, House of Representatives, One Hundred Second Congress, Second Session, on H.R. 5360, June 11 and 17, 1992* (Washington, D.C.: United States Government Printing Office, 1992), 71.

32. Goldstein, Citron, and Land, *A Documentary Companion to Storming the Court*, 5.

33. Statement of Ira Kurzban, in *U.S. Human Rights Policy toward Haiti*, 75–81.

34. Lizette Alvarez, "INS Again Deporting Haitians Now in US Detention Centers," *Miami Herald*, February 14, 1992, A5.

35. Goldstein, Citron, and Land, *A Documentary Companion to Storming the Court*, 6; *U.S. Human Rights Policy toward Haiti*, 173.

36. Statement of Harold H. Koh, in *U.S. Human Rights Policy toward Haiti*, 100–101; statement of Sarah H. Cleveland, in ibid., 174–179.

37. Statement of Sarah Cleveland, in *U.S. Human Rights Policy toward Haiti*, 180.

38. "Summary of Documentation of Abuses at Krome North Service Processing Center," n.d., box 4, folder Abuses at Krome 1989 (1 of 2); "Index to Documentation of Abuse at Krome North Service Processing Center," n.d., box 4, folder Abuses at Krome 1989 (1 of 2); Ardy Friedberg and Mike Billington, "Abuse Charges Spur Call for Krome Investigation," *Sun-Sentinel*, April 5, 1990, box 15, folder Abuse/ILEMP/Krome 1990; Jeanne DeQuine, "Critics Call for Closure of Immigration Center," *USA Today*, June 14, 1991, box 4, folder Abuse/ILEMP/Krome 1990; Mayor Xavier Suarez to Senator Mack, June 7, 1991, box 15, folder Detention General; Detention Abuses 1987–1991 (1 of 3). All in American for Immigrant Justice Records.

39. American Civil Liberties Union, *Justice Detained: Conditions at the Varick Street Immigration Detention Center* (New York: American Civil Liberties Union, 1993).

40. Human Rights Watch, *Brutality Unchecked: Human Rights Abuses along the U.S. Border with Mexico* (New York: Human Rights Watch, 1992).

41. Goldstein, Citron, and Land, *A Documentary Companion to Storming the Court*, 6.

42. Statement of Harold J. Johnson, in in *U.S. Policy toward Haitian Refugees*, 7–8.

43. Lindskoog, "Refugees and Resistance," 332–333.

44. Testimony of Rabbi Haskel Lookstein, in *U.S. Policy toward Haitian Refugees*, 87–88.

45. Testimony of Representative Stephen Solarz, in ibid., 5.

46. "White House Statement on Haitian Migrants," May 24, 1992, *The American Presidency Project*, accessed December 20, 2017, http://www.presidency.ucsb.edu/ws/index.php?pid=21000&st=&st1=.

47. Statement of Brunson McKinley, in *U.S. Policy toward Haitian Refugees*, 40.

48. "Remarks and a Question-and-Answer Session with the Mount Paran Christian School Community in Marietta," May 27, 1992, *The American Presidency Project*, accessed December 20, 2017, http://www.presidency.ucsb.edu/ws/index.php?pid=21006.

49. Goldstein, Citron, and Land, *A Documentary Companion to Storming the Court*, 7.

50. For the story of Yolande Jean, see Farmer, *The Uses of Haiti*, 223–243.

51. Daniel J. Whelan, "Permanent Exile: The U.S. Exclusion of HIV-Positive Haitian Refugees—Public Health, Politics, and International Law," *Swords and Ploughshares* 2, no. 2 (1993): 8. A 1987 law had added HIV to the list of "dangerous contagious diseases" that barred HIV-positive aliens from entering the United States. That language was changed to "communicable diseases" in the 1990 law, which gave the Department of Health and Human Services the authority to determine whether or not to classify HIV as one of the diseases to which the law applied. See Ratner, "How We Closed the Guantanamo HIV Camp,"195–197.

52. Ratner, "How We Closed the Guantanamo HIV Camp," 187. See also Paik, *Rightlessness*, 87; Whelan, "Permanent Exile," 10; and Goldstein, Citron, and Land, *A Documentary Companion to Storming the Court*, 7.

53. Paik, *Rightlessness*, 105–113; Farmer, *The Uses of Haiti*, 228–231; Lindskoog, "Refugees and Resistance," 338–339.

54. Paik, *Rightlessness*, 88.

55. Lindskoog, "Refugees and Resistance," 339; Paik, *Rightlessness*, 122–126; Farmer, *The Uses of Haiti*, 231.

56. Lindskoog, "Refugees and Resistance," 340–341; Ratner, "How We Closed the Guantanamo HIV Camp," 212; "National March and Rally: Democracy for Haiti," flyer, June 27, 1992, folder Washington Office on Haiti May Overview 1992, Washington Office on Latin America Records, David M. Rubenstein Rare Book & Manuscript Library, Duke University. (Hereafter Washington Office on Latin America Records.)

57. Lindskoog, "Refugees and Resistance," 335; Ratner, "How We Closed the Guantanamo HIV Camp," 200–201.

58. Ratner, "How We Closed the Guantanamo HIV Camp," 199–200.

59. Ibid.; Goldstein, Citron, and Land, *A Documentary Companion to Storming the Court*, 7.

60. Joseph Nevins, *Operation Gatekeeper and Beyond: The War on "Illegals" and the Remaking of the U.S.-Mexico Boundary* (New York: Routledge, 2010), 109.

61. Peter Andreas, *Border Games: Policing the U.S.-Mexico Divide* (Ithaca, N.Y.: Cornell University Press), 89; Marie Gottschalk, *Caught: The Prison State and the Lockdown of American Politics* (Princeton, N.J.: Princeton University Press, 2016), 220.

62. Lindskoog, "Refugees and Resistance," 342–345; Goldstein, Citron, and Land, *A Documentary Companion to Storming the Court*, 7; Ratner, "How We Closed the Guantanamo HIV Camp," 202, 206.

63. Yolande Jean quoted in Farmer, *The Uses of Haiti*, 233; Paik, *Rightlessness*, 135–145; Lindskoog, "Refugees and Resistance," 343–345.

64. Ratner, "How We Closed the Guantanamo HIV Camp," 208, 215.

65. "Student Hunger Strike for Haitians in Guantanamo," Box 178, folder Haiti Aristide, Washington Office on Latin America Records; Lindskoog, "Refugees and Resistance," 56–358; Memo from the National Immigration Forum, April 29, 1994, folder Randall Robinson Hunger Strike '94, Americans for Immigrant Justice Records; Ratner, "How We Closed the Guantanamo HIV Camp," 208, 215.

66. Ratner, "How We Closed the Guantanamo HIV Camp," 202–203.

67. Mary B. W. Tabor, "Judge Orders Release of Haitians," New York Times, June 9, 1993, accessed February 20, 2017, http://www.nytimes.com/1993/06/09/nyregion/judge-orders-the-release-of-haitians.html; Goldstein, Citron, and Land, A Documentary Companion to Storming the Court, 9; Ratner, "How We Closed the Guantanamo HIV Camp," 203.

68. Goldstein, Citron, and Land, A Documentary Companion to Storming the Court, 9–10; Paik, Rightlessness, 149.

69. U.S. Congress, House, Committee on the Judiciary, Subcommittee on International Law, Immigration, and Refugees, Haitian Asylum Seekers: Hearing before the Subcommittee on International Law, Immigration, and Refugees of the Committee on the Judiciary, House of Representatives, 103rd Congress, 2nd session, on H.R. 3663, H.R. 4114, and H.R. 4264, June 15, 1994 (Washington, D.C.: U.S. Government Printing Office, 1994), 106, 157–164, 173–185. (Hereafter Haitian Asylum Seekers.)

70. Ibid., 164, 269–277.

71. "Terror Prevails in Haiti: Human Rights Violations and Failed Diplomacy," Human Rights Watch/Americas 6, no. 5 (1994), in Haitian Asylum Seekers, 409–454; Michael J. Churgin, "Mass Exoduses: The Response of the United States," International Migration Review 30, no. 1 (1996): 332; Jana K. Lipman, Guantanamo: A Working-Class History between Empire and Revolution (Berkeley: University of California Press, 2009), 206–207; Cheryl Little, Not in Their Best Interest: A Report on the US Government's Forcible Repatriation of Guantánamo's Unaccompanied Haitian Children (Miami: Florida Rural Legal Services, 1995), 1; Mitchell, "The Political Costs of State Power," 90–91; Paik, Rightlessness, 149–150.

72. "Operation Uphold Democracy, Haiti," series 6, folder 8, United States Army, Psychological Operation Company (Fort Bragg) Publications, Rare Books Collection, University of North Carolina, Chapel Hill.

73. Anthony Lake and Mark Gearan, memorandum for the president, Points for Interview with Wire Services, n.d., PRS-Presidential Records [Haiti and Lake] 9407362 [OA/ID 480], William J. Clinton Presidential Library, Little Rock, Arkansas.

74. William J. Clinton, "Address to the Nation on Haiti," September 15, 1994, The American Presidency Project, accessed January 25, 2017, http://www.presidency.ucsb.edu/ws/?pid=49093; White House Statement on Haitian Migrants," May 24, 1992, Public Papers of President George Bush. Accessed December 3, 2016, http://bushlibrary.tamu.edu/research/public_papers.php?submit=Search&search=haiti.

75. Lindskoog, "Refugees and Resistance," 369–373.

76. Dupuy, Haiti in the New World Order, 150–151. See also Lindskoog, "Refugees and Resistance, 370–374. Refugees continued to flee Haiti for the United States, albeit in fewer numbers, after Aristide's restoration as president. This produced a schism among Haitians in the United States: some continued to claim that Haitian refugees were entitled to the protection of those fleeing persecution while others argued that those fleeing an Aristide-controlled

Haiti were primarily economic refugees. See Carolle Charles, "Political Refugees or Economic Immigrants? A New 'Old Debate' within the Haitian Immigrant Communities but with Contestations and Divisions," *Journal of American Ethnic History* 25, nos. 2–3 (2006): 190–208.

77. Harold Hongju Koh, "The 'Haiti Paradigm' in United States Human Rights Policy," *Yale Law Journal* 103, no. 2391 (1994): 2202–2205.

78. Mitchell, "U.S. Policy toward Haitian Boat People," 80.

Chapter 6. Reinforcing the Detention System, 1994–2000

1. Bernadette quoted in Women's Commission for Refugee Women and Children, *Behind Locked Doors: Abuse of Refugee Women at the Krome Detention Center* (New York: Women's Commission for Refugee Women and Children, 2000), 10–11, accessed January 7, 2017, https://www.womensrefugeecommission.org/images/zdocs/krome.pdf.

2. *Locked Away: Immigration Detainees in Jails in the United States*, special issue, *Human Rights Watch* 10, no. 1 (1998), accessed January 5, 2017, https://www.hrw.org/legacy/reports98/us-immig/.

3. Ibid.

4. Haitian Children at Guantanamo to President Clinton, February 29, 1995, in Cheryl Little, *Not in Their Best Interest: A Report on the U.S. Government's Forcible Repatriation of Guantanamo's Unaccompanied Haitian Children* (Miami: Florida Rural Legal Services, 1995), iv.

5. Little, *Not in Their Best Interest*, 1.

6. Kate Jastram, "The Kids before Khadr: Haitian Refugee Children on Guantanamo," *Santa Clara Journal of International Law* 11, no. 1 (2012): 90–91.

7. Little, *Not in Their Best Interest*, 1.

8. Sharon Ginter for Cheryl Little, memo to Helena and Brian, December 9, 1994, box 1, folder GTMO Affidavits 1994, Americans for Immigrant Justice Records.

9. Ibid.; Mireya Navarro, "Many Haitian Children View Camps' Limbo as Permanent," *New York Times*, May 1, 1995, in Little, *Not in Their Best Interest*, 88–90; Fabiola Santiago, "Haitian Kids Tell of Harsh Camp Life," *Miami Herald*, February 28, 1995, in Little, *Not in Their Best Interest*, 101–102.

10. Affidavit of Pierre-Onel Antoine, December 7, 1994, box 1, folder GTMO Affidavits 1994; Sharon Ginter for Cheryl Little, memo to Helena and Brian, December 9, 1994.

11. Little, *Not in Their Best Interest*, 30–35, 37; Patricia Ireland to Janet Reno, November 12, 1994, box 2, folder Letters: Congressional, etc. Nov. 1994–July 1995, Americans for Immigrant Justice Records; "Rally to Protest Detention of Haitian Children of Guantanamo," press release, January 5, 1995, box 1, folder GTMO Children, Americans for Immigrant Justice Records; press release by the Justice Coalition for the Haitian Children in Guantanamo, February 11, 1995, box 1, folder GTMO Children, Americans for Immigrant Justice Records.

12. Little, *Not in Their Best Interest*, 1–2, 6, 26–27.

13. Liz Balmaseda, "Rhetoric Aside, U.S. Abandons Haitian Kids," *Miami Herald*, May 20, 1995, series 5, box 4, folder Haiti 1995, Alex and Carol Stepick Collection, Florida International University, Miami; "Haitian Youth Riot at Base," *Daily News*, May 11, 1995, series 8, box 169, folder 1241, Taylor Branch Papers #5047, Southern Historical Collection, Louis Round Wilson Library, University of North Carolina at Chapel Hill.

14. Daniel J. Tichener, *Dividing Lines: The Politics of Immigration Control in America* (Princeton, N.J.: Princeton University Press, 2009), 274–278; Aviva Chomsky, *Undocumented: How Immigration Became Illegal* (Boston: Beacon Press, 2014), 192–195; Maire Gottschalk, *Caught: The Prison State and the Lockdown of American Politics* (Princeton, N.J.: Princeton University Press, 2016), 220; Joseph Nevins, *Operation Gatekeeper and Beyond: The War on "Illegals" and the Remaking of the U.S.-Mexico Boundary* (New York: Routledge, 2010), 78–79.

15. Statement of Dan Stein in *Haitian Asylum Seekers: Hearing before the Subcommittee on International Law, Immigration, and Refugees of the Committee on the Judiciary, House of Representatives, 103rd Congress, 2nd Session, on H.R. 3663, H.R. 4114, and H.R. 4264, June 15, 1994* (Washington, D.C.: U.S. Government Printing Office, 1994), 221–222, 233.

16. Gottschalk, *Caught*, 220, 234.

17. Juliet P. Stumpf, "The Crimmigration Crisis: Immigrants, Crime, and Sovereign Power," in *Governing Immigration through Crime: A Reader*, edited by Julie A. Dowling and Jonathan Xavier Inda (Stanford, Calif.: Stanford University Press, 2013), 59–76.

18. Daniel Kanstroom, *Deportation Nation: Outsiders in American History* (Cambridge, Mass.: Harvard University Press, 2007), 227; Mark Dow, *American Gulag: Inside U.S. Immigration Prisons* (Berkeley: University of California Press, 2005), 164.

19. Patrisia Macías-Rojas, *From Deportation to Prison: The Politics of Immigration Enforcement in Post-Civil Rights America* (New York: New York University Press, 2016), 60.

20. Heather Ann Thompson, *Blood in the Water: The Attica Prison Uprising of 1971 and Its Legacy* (New York: Pantheon, 2016), 563.

21. Kanstroom, *Deportation Nation*, 227–228.

22. Jennifer M. Chacón, "The Security Myth," in *Governing Immigration through Crime: A Reader*, edited by Julie A. Dowling and Jonathan Xavier Inda (Stanford, Calif.: Stanford University Press, 2013), 83; David Manuel Hernández, "Pursuant to Deportation: Latinos and Immigrant Detention," in *Governing Immigration through Crime*, 210; Michael Welch, *Detained: Immigration Laws and the Expanding I.N.S. Jail Complex* (Philadelphia: Temple University Press, 2002), 73, 88; Austin T. Fragomen, "The Illegal Immigration Reform and Immigrant Responsibility Act of 1996: An Overview," *International Migration Review* 31, no. 2 (1997): 444–446, 453–454; Dow, *American Gulag*, 180; Daniel Wilsher, *Immigration Detention: Law, History, Politics* (Cambridge: Cambridge University Press, 2012), 69–70; Tanya Golash-Boza, *Due Process Denied: Detentions and Deportations in the United States* (New York: Routledge, 2012), 26–27.

23. Guttentag quoted in Welch, *Detained*, 68; "ACLU Joins 'Fix '96' Campaign for Justice for Immigrants," *ACLU*, press release, July 28, 1999, accessed November 22, 2016, https://www.aclu.org/news/aclu-joins-fix-96-campaign-justice-immigrants.

24. Golash-Boza, *Due Process Denied*, 26–27.

25. Fragomen, "The Illegal Immigration Reform and Immigrant Responsibility Act of 1996," 438.

26. The stories of Olufolake Olaleye and Garibaldy Mejia and many others affected by the 1996 laws are chronicled in Welch, *Detained*, 3, 35–36, 72–73.

27. Welch, *Detained*, 43.

28. Kanstroom, *Deportation Nation*, 228.

29. Kenneth Adams, "The Bull Market in Corrections," *The Prison Journal* 76, no. 4 (1996): 461–467.

30. Hernández, "Pursuant to Deportation," 201; Wilsher, *Immigration Detention*, 70.

31. Amnesty International, *United States of America: Lost in the Labyrinth: Detention of Asylum Seekers* (New York: Amnesty International, 1999), 4–5, 10, accessed February 2, 2017, file:///C:/Users/g00220413/Downloads/amr511151999en.pdf.

32. *Locked Away.*

33. Amnesty International, *United States of America: Lost in the Labyrinth*, 12.

34. *Locked Away*; Cheryl Little, "INS Detention in Florida," *University of Miami Inter-American Law Review* 30, no. 3 (1999): 572.

35. Women's Commission for Refugee Women and Children, *Behind Locked Doors*; Little, "INS Detention in Florida," 574.

36. Human Rights Watch, *Brutality Unchecked: Human Rights Abuses along the U.S. Border with Mexico* (New York: Human Rights Watch, 1992), 67–75.

37. Welch, *Detained*, 129.

38. Human Rights Watch Children's Project, *Slipping through the Cracks: Unaccompanied Children Detained by the U.S. Immigration and Naturalization Service* (New York: Human Rights Watch, 1997), 1, accessed December 29, 2017, https://www.hrw.org/sites/default/files/reports/us974.pdf.

39. Ibid., 4–5.

40. Welch, *Detained*, 140–142.

41. Wendy Young, testimony before the Senate Immigration Committee, September 16, 1998, box 46, folder House Subctte Hearing Torture Victims, 5/8/96; Women at Risk, Women's Refugee Commission Records.

42. Ibid.

43. Women's Commission for Refugee Women and Children, *Behind Locked Doors*, 5.

44. Cheryl Little, *Krome's Invisible Prisoners: Cycles of Abuse and Neglect* (Miami: Florida Immigrant Advocacy Center, 1996), 11, accessed December 29, 2017, http://d3n8a8pro7vhmx.cloudfront.net/aijustice/pages/264/attachments/original/1390424084/KromesInvisiblePrisoners.pdf?1390424084.

45. Letter quoted in Little, "INS Detention in Florida," 562.

46. Women's Commission for Refugee Women and Children, *Behind Locked Doors*, 7

47. Karl Ross, "Sexual Abuse Fears Reach beyond Krome," *Miami Herald*, January 7, 2001.

48. Little, *Krome's Invisible Prisoners*, 2–3; *Locked Away*; Dow, *American Gulag*, 111–116, 200–203.

49. Associated Press, "Detainees Take 2 Guards Hostage During Fracas," n.d., series 5, box 4, folder Haiti 1995, Alex and Carol Stepick Collection; Dow, *American Gulag*, 137; Welch, *Detained*, 103–105; Little, "INS Detention in Florida," 563.

50. Little, *Krome's Invisible Prisoners*, 130–132; *Locked Away*; "ACLU Joins 'Fix '96' Campaign for Justice for Immigrants"; Wendy Young, testimony before the Senate Immigration Committee.

Conclusion

1. Marie Jocelyn Ocean, testimony before the U.S. Senate Subcommittee on Immigration, October 1, 2002, box 46, folder 10/02 Senate Hearing, Women's Refugee Commission records.

2. Cheryl Little, testimony before the U.S. Senate Subcommittee on Immigration, October 1, 2002, box 46, folder FIAC Senate Test. 2002, Women's Refugee Commission Records.

3. Statement of Wendy Young at Briefing on US Policy Toward Haitian Refugees, Subcommittee on International Operations and Human Rights, October 1, 2002, box 46, folder Young Briefing 10/02, Women's Refugee Commission Records.

4. Statement of Wendy Young.

5. Cheryl Little, testimony before the U.S. Senate Subcommittee on Immigration, October 1, 2002, box 46, folder FIAC Senate Test 2002, Women's Refugee Commission Records; Brad Brown to John Ashcroft, April 16, 2002, box 46, folder 10/02 Senate Hearing, Women's Refugee Commission Records.

6. Amnesty International USA, *"Why Am I Here?" Children in Immigration Detention* (New York: Amnesty International USA, 2003), 58.

7. Ashcroft quoted in ibid.

8. Statement of John Hostettler, in U.S. Congress, House, Committee on the Judiciary, Subcommittee on Immigration, Border Security, and Claims, *War on Terrorism: Immigration Enforcement since September 11, 2001, Hearing before the Subcommittee on Immigration, Border Security, and Claims of the Committee on the Judiciary, 108th Congress, 1st Session, May 8, 2003* (Washington, D.C.: U.S. Government Printing Office, 2003), 1.

9. Statement of Michael Dougherty, in ibid., 12–13.

10. Statement of Laura Murphy, in ibid., 28.

11. David Cole, *Enemy Aliens: Double Standards and Constitutional Freedoms in the War on Terrorism* (New York: The New Press, 2003), 30–31; Michael Welch, *Detained: Immigration Laws and the Expanding I.N.S. Jail Complex* (Philadelphia: Temple University Press, 2002), 195–197.

12. Mary Bosworth and Emma Kaufman, "Foreigners in a Carceral Age: Immigration and Imprisonment in the United States," *Stanford Law and Policy Review* 22, no. 1 (2011): 438; Cole, *Enemy Aliens*, 24–26.

13. Tanya Golash-Boza, *Deported: Immigrant Policing, Disposable Labor, and Global Capitalism* (New York: New York University Press, 2015), 199.

14. Marie Gottschalk, *Caught: The Prison State and the Lockdown of American Politics* (Princeton, N.J.: Princeton University Press, 2016), 222–224; Julie A. Dowling and Jonathan Xavier Inda, "Introduction: Governing Migrant Illegality," in *Governing Immigration through Crime: A Reader*, edited by Julie A. Dowling and Jonathan Xavier Inda (Stanford, Calif.: Stanford University Press, 2013), 10.

15. Patrisia Macías-Rojas, *From Deportation to Prison: The Politics of Immigration Enforcement in Post–Civil Rights America* (New York: New York University Press, 2016), 73; Golash-Boza, *Deported*, 5.

16. Stephanie J. Silverman and Amy Nethery, "Understanding Immigration Detention and Its Human Impact," in *Immigration Detention: The Migration of a Policy and Its Human Impact*, edited by Amy Nethery and Stephanie J. Silverman (London: Routledge, 2017), 1; Deirdre Conlon and Nancy Hiemstra, "Introduction: Intimate Economies of Immigration Detention," in *Intimate Economies of Immigration Detention: Critical Perspectives*, edited by Deirdre Conlon and Nancy Hiemstra (New York: Routledge, 2017), 1–2; Lucy Fiske, *Human Rights, Refugee Protest, and Immigration Detention* (London: Palgrave Macmillan, 2016), 3, 191–193.

17. Fiske, *Human Rights, Refugee Protest and Immigration Detention*, 192–193; Silverman and Nethery, "Understanding Immigration Detention and Its Human Impact," 8.

18. Ibid.; Fiske, *Human Rights, Refugee Protest, and Immigration Detention*, 6.

19. Azadeh Dastyari, "Refugees on Guantanamo Bay: A Blue Print for Australia's 'Pacific Solution'?" *AQ: Australia Quarterly* 79 (2007), 4–8, 40; Azadeh Dastyari, ""Breaching International Law: Immigration Detention in Guantanamo Bay, Cuba," in *Immigration Detention: The Migration of a Policy and Its Human Impact*, edited by Amy Nethery and Stephanie J. Silverman (London: Routledge, 2017), 101–102.

20. Deborah Hardoon, Sophia Ayele, and Ricardo Fuentes-Nieva, "An Economy for the 1%: How Privilege and Power in the Economy Drive Extreme Inequality and How This Can Be Stopped," Oxfam International, January 2016, https://www.oxfam.org/sites/www.oxfam.org/files/file_attachments/bp210-economy-one-percent-tax-havens-180116-en_0.pdf.

21. Aristide R. Zolberg, *A Nation by Design: Immigration Policy in the Fashioning of America* (Cambridge, Mass.: Harvard University Press, 2008), 14.

22. Peter Andreas, *Border Games: Policing the U.S.-Mexico Divide* (Ithaca, N.Y.: Cornell University Press, 2009), 3. See also Wendy Brown, *Walled States, Waning Sovereignty* (New York: Zone Books, 2010), 8, 19; and Alexander C. Diener and Joshua Hagen, *Borders: A Very Short Introduction* (New York: Oxford University Press, 2012), 8–9.

23. Jenna M. Loyd, Matt Mitchelson, and Andrew Burridge, "Introduction: Borders, Prisons, and Abolitionist Visions," in *Beyond Walls and Cages: Prisons, Borders, and Global Crisis*, edited by Jenna M. Loyd, Matt Mitchelson, and Andrew Burridge (Athens: University of Georgia Press, 2012), 1.

24. Diener and Hagen, *Borders*, 7.

25. Galina Cornelisse, "Immigration Detention and the Territoriality of Universal Rights," in *The Deportation Regime: Sovereignty, Space and the Freedom of Movement*, edited by Nicholas De Genova and Nathalie Peutz (Durham, N.C.: Duke University Press, 2010), 101–102.

26. Torrie Hester, *Deportation: The Origins of U.S. Policy* (Philadelphia: University of Pennsylvania Press, 2017), 5; Kelly Lytle Hernández, Khalil Gibran Muhammad, and Heather Ann Thompson, "Introduction: Constructing the Carceral State," *Journal of American History* 102, no. 1 (2015): 20; Daniel Kanstroom, *Deportation Nation: Outsiders in American History* (Cambridge, Mass.: Harvard University Press, 2007), 16–17; Kunal M. Parker, *Making Foreigners: Immigration and Citizenship Law in America, 1600–2000* (Cambridge: Cambridge University Press, 2015), 187.

27. Cornelisse, "Immigration Detention and the Territoriality of Universal Rights," 103.

28. Rachel Ida Buff, "Introduction: Toward a Redefinition of Citizenship Rights," in *Immigrant Rights in the Shadows of Citizenship*, edited by Rachel Ida Buff (New York: New York University Press, 2008), 6.

29. Bryan Cohen, "Immigrant Detainees Resume Hunger Strike at Washington State Facility," *Reuters*, March 25, 2014, accessed March 20, 2017, http://www.reuters.com/article/us-usa-hungerstrike-immigrants-idUSBREA2P03X20140326; "Undocumented Immigrants Stage Hunger Strike at Tacoma Facility," *Democracy Now!*, July 31, 2014, accessed March 20, 2017, https://www.democracynow.org/2014/7/31/headlines/undocumented_immigrants_stage_hunger_strike_at_tacoma_facility.

30. "Immigrant Mothers in Detention Launch Second Hunger Strike Despite Retaliation," *Democracy Now!*, April 14, 2015, accessed March 10, 2017, https://www.democra-

cynow.org/2015/4/14/immigrant_mothers_in_detention_launch_second; "Dilley Protest & National Day of Action to #EndFamilyDetention," *Grassroots Leadership*, accessed March 18, 2017, http://grassrootsleadership.org/event/2015/dilley-protest-national-day-action-end-family-detention; Priscilla Mendoza, "SA to Dilley: Marching to End Immigrant Detention," *San Antonio Current*, May 3, 2015, accessed March 19, 2017, http://www.sacurrent.com/the-daily/archives/2015/05/03/sa-to-dilley-marching-to-end-immigrant-detention.

31. "Mothers Enter 2nd Week of Hunger Strike at PA Detention Facility," *Democracy Now!*, August 17, 2016, accessed March 22, 2017, https://www.democracynow.org/2016/8/17/headlines/mothers_enter_2nd_week_of_hunger_strike_at_pa_detention_center; Thom Senzee, "5 Arrested at California Rally to End Trans Immigration Detention," *Advocate*, May 28, 2015, accessed February 4, 2017, http://www.advocate.com/politics/transgender/2015/05/28/five-arrested-california-rally-end-trans-immigration-detention; Rossana Cambron, "Activists Begin Hunger Strike, Call for Halt to Detention of Transgender Immigrants," *People's World*, May 19, 2016, accessed, February 1, 2017, http://www.peoplesworld.org/article/activists-begin-hunger-strike-call-for-halt-to-detention-of-transgender-immigrants/; Brian Stauffer, "'Do You See How Much I'm Suffering Here?' Abuse against Transgender Women in U.S. Immigration Detention," *Human Rights Watch*, March 23, 2016, accessed January 12, 2017, https://www.hrw.org/report/2016/03/23/do-you-see-how-much-im-suffering-here/abuse-against-transgender-women-us.

32. "About Detention Watch Network," *Detention Watch Network*, accessed March 22, 2017, https://www.detentionwatchnetwork.org/about; Detention Watch Network and the Center for Constitutional Rights, *Banking on Detention: Local Lockup Quotas & the Immigrant Dragnet* ([Washington, D.C.]: Detention Watch Network, 2015), accessed January 9, 2017, https://www.detentionwatchnetwork.org/pressroom/reports/2015/banking-on-detention.

33. For example, the End Immigration Detention Network is a Canada-based organization with similar goals; see https://endimmigrationdetention.com/. The Global Detention Project tracks the detention of migrants and refugees around the world; see https://www.globaldetentionproject.org/. The United Nations Human Rights Council has brought together a coalition of human rights organizations to end the detention of immigrant children around the world; see http://endchilddetention.org/. Lucy Fiske has documented the global movement against immigration detention and the key role detained people are playing in resisting the system around the world; see Lucy Fiske, *Human Rights, Refugee Protest and Immigration Detention* (London: Palgrave Macmillan, 2016).

34. See, for example, Alison Parker, *A Costly Move: Far and Frequent Transfers Impede Hearings for Immigrant Detainees in the United States* (New York: Human Rights Watch, 2011), accessed December 22, 2017, https://www.hrw.org/report/2011/06/14/costly-move/far-and-frequent-transfers-impede-hearings-immigrant-detainees-united; "U.S. Deaths in Immigration Detention: Newly Released Records Suggest Dangerous Lapses in Medical Care," *Human Rights Watch*, July 7, 2016, accessed December 22, 2017, https://www.hrw.org/news/2016/07/07/us-deaths-immigration-detention; "Lost in Detention," episode of *Frontline*, aired on October 18, 2011, accessed December 22, 2017, https://www.pbs.org/wgbh/frontline/film/lost-in-detention/; Seth Freed Wessler, "'This Man Will Almost Certainly Die,'" *The Nation*, January 28, 2016.

35. "End Immigration Detention," *New York Times*, May 15, 2015, accessed December 12, 2016, https://www.nytimes.com/2015/05/15/opinion/end-immigration-detention.html?_r=2;

"Reform U.S. Immigration Detention System to End Unnecessary Detentions," *Seattle Times,*
May 19, 2015, accessed February 20, 2017, http://www.seattletimes.com/opinion/editorials/
reform-us-immigration-detention-system-2/; United States Conference of Catholic Bishops
and Center for Migration Services, *Unlocking Human Dignity: A Plan to Transform the U.S.
Immigrant Detention System* (New York: Center for Migration Studies, 2015), accessed January 17, 2017, http://www.usccb.org/about/migration-and-refugee-services/upload/unlocking-
human-dignity.pdf; Esther Yu Hsi Lee, "The Movement to End Immigrant Family Detention
Is Picking Up Steam. Here's Why," *Think Progress,* May 29, 2015, accessed February 18, 2017,
https://thinkprogress.org/the-movement-to-end-immigrant-family-detention-is-picking-
up-steam-heres-why-358bb28f0676#.lw3x5vrql.

36. "As Feds Close Prisons Run by Private Companies, Will They Do the Same for Immigrant Detention Centers?" *Democracy Now!,* August 19, 2016, accessed February 5, 2017,
https://www.democracynow.org/2016/8/19/as_feds_close_prisons_run_by.

37. Graham Lanktree, "New Trump Immigration Order Has Led to the Arrest of Hundreds of Undocumented Immigrants for Minor Crimes," *Newsweek,* April 11, 2017, accessed
October 2, 2017, http://www.newsweek.com/trumps-immigration-raids-round-367-us-ille-
gally-582489; Chris Hayes and Brian Montopoli, "Trump Administration Plans Expanded
Immigration Detention, Documents Say," *MSNBC,* March 3, 2017, accessed October 2, 2017,
http://www.msnbc.com/all-in/exclusive-trump-admin-plans-expanded-immigrant-deten-
tion; Julián Aguilar, "White House Greenlights a New Immigration-Detention Center in
Texas," *Texas Tribune,* April 14, 2017, accessed October 2, 2017, https://www.texastribune.
org/2017/04/14/white-house-green-lights-new-immigration-detention-center-texas/;
Roque Planas, "Private Prison Stocks Surge after Donald Trump Victory," *Huffington Post,*
November 9, 2016, accessed November 25, 2016, http://www.huffingtonpost.com/entry/
private-prison-stocks-trump_us_582336c5e4b0e80b02ce3287.

38. Heather Ann Thompson, *Blood in the Water: The Attica Prison Uprising of 1971 and Its
Legacy* (New York: Pantheon, 2016), 571.

39. Guy S. Goodwin-Gill, "International Law and the Detention of Refugees and Asylum
Seekers," *International Migration Review* 20, no. 2 (1986): 195.

Bibliography

Archival Collections

David M. Rubenstein Rare Book & Manuscript Library, Duke University
    Americans for Immigrant Justice Records
    Washington Office on Latin America Records
    Women's Refugee Commission Records
Florida International University, Miami
    Alex and Carol Stepick Collection
Schomburg Center for Research in Black Culture, New York Public Library
    Haiti/Dechoukaj Collection
    Haitian Refugee Collection
Ronald Reagan Presidential Library, Simi Valley, California
    Immigration Subject File
    James W. Cicconi Files
    Kate L. Moore Files
    Michael J. Luttig Files
William J. Clinton Presidential Library, Little Rock, Arkansas
    PRS-Presidential Records (Haiti and Lake)

Newspapers

Miami Herald, December 21–30, 1981
Miami News, December 21, 1981–January 1, 1982
San Juan Star, September 20–October 2, 1980

Published Sources

Adams, Kenneth. "The Bull Market in Corrections." *Prison Journal* 76, no. 4 (1996): 461–467.
Aleinikoff, Thomas, and David Martin. *Immigration: Process and Policy*. St. Paul, Minn.: West Publishing Co., 1985.
Aleinikoff, Thomas, David Martin, and Hiroshi Motomura. *Immigration: Process and Policy*. 3rd ed. St. Paul, Minn.: West Publishing Co., 1998.

American Civil Liberties Union. *Justice Detained: Conditions at the Varick Street Immigration Detention Center*. New York: American Civil Liberties Union, 1993.

Amnesty International. *United States of America: Lost in the Labyrinth: Detention of Asylum Seekers*. New York: Amnesty International, 1999.

Amnesty International USA. *"Why Am I Here?" Children in Immigration Detention*. New York: Amnesty International USA, 2003.

Andreas, Peter. *Border Games: Policing the U.S.-Mexico Divide*. Ithaca, N.Y.: Cornell University Press, 2009.

Bell, Beverly. *Walking on Fire: Haitian Women's Stories of Survival and Resistance*. Ithaca, N.Y.: Cornell University Press, 2001.

Bogre, Michelle. "Haitian Refugees: (Haiti's) Missing Persons." *Migration Today* 7, no. 4 (1979): 9.

Bosworth, Mary. *Inside Immigration Detention*. Oxford: Oxford University Press, 2014.

Bosworth, Mary, and Emma Kaufman. "Foreigners in a Carceral Age: Immigration and Imprisonment in the United States." *Stanford Law and Policy Review* 22, no. 1 (2011): 429–454.

Braziel, Jana Evans. "Haiti, Guantánamo, and the 'One Indispensable Nation': US Imperialism, 'Apparent States', and the Postcolonial Problematics of Sovereignty." *Cultural Critique* 64 (Autumn 2006): 127–160.

Brown, Wendy. *Walled States, Waning Sovereignty*. Brooklyn, N.Y.: Zone Books, 2010.

Buff, Rachel Ida, ed. *Immigrant Rights in the Shadows of Citizenship*. New York: New York University Press, 2008.

Bureau of Prisons and the U.S. Parole Commission. *Oversight Hearing before the Subcommittee on Courts, Civil Liberties, and the Administration of Justice of the Committee on the Judiciary, House of Representatives, 99th Congress, First Session on Bureau of Prisons and the U.S. Parole Commission, March 28, 1985*. Washington, D.C.: U.S. Government Printing Office, 1985. Accessed January 14, 2017. https://archive.org/stream/bureauofprisonsuoounit/bureauofprisonsuoounit_djvu.txt.

Castro, Max J. "The Politics of Language in Miami." In *Miami Now! Immigration, Ethnicity, and Social Change*, edited by Guillermo J. Grenier and Alex Stepick III, 109–132. Gainesville: University Press of Florida, 1992.

Chacon, Jennifer M. "The Security Myth." In *Governing Immigration through Crime: A Reader*, edited by Julie A. Dowling and Jonathan Xavier Inda, 77–94. Stanford, Calif.: Stanford University Press, 2013.

Charles, Carolle. "Political Refugees or Economic Immigrants? A New 'Old Debate' within the Haitian Immigrant Communities but with Contestations and Divisions." *Journal of American Ethnic History* 25, nos. 2–3 (2006): 190–208.

Chisholm, Shirley. "U.S. Policy and Black Refugees." *Issue: A Journal of Opinion* 12, nos. 1–2 (1982): 22–24.

Chomsky, Aviva. *Undocumented: How Immigration Became Illegal*. Boston: Beacon Press, 2014.

Churgin, Michael J. "Mass Exoduses: The Response of the United States." *International Migration Review* 30, no. 1 (1996): 310–324.

Cole, David. *Enemy Aliens: Double Standards and Constitutional Freedoms in the War on Terrorism*. New York: New Press, 2003.

Conlon, Dierdre, and Nancy Hiemstra. *Intimate Economies of Immigration Detention: Critical Perspectives.* London: Routledge, Taylor, and Francis Group, 2017.

——. "Introduction: Intimate Economies of Immigration Detention." In *Intimate Economies of Immigration Detention: Critical Perspectives,* edited by Deirdre Conlon and Nancy Hiemstra, 1–12. New York: Routledge, 2017.

Cornelisse, Galina. *Immigration Detention and Human Rights: Rethinking Territorial Sovereignty.* Leiden: Martinus Nijhoff Publishers, 2010.

——. "Immigration Detention and the Territoriality of Universal Rights." In *The Deportation Regime: Sovereignty, Space, and the Freedom of Movement,* edited by Nicholas De Genova and Nathalie Peutz, 101–122. Durham, N.C.: Duke University Press, 2010.

Curtin, Mary Ellen. "'Please Hear Our Cries': The Hidden History of Black Prisoners in America." In *The Punitive Turn: New Approaches to Race and Incarceration,* edited by Deborah E. McDowell, Claudrena N. Harold, and Juan Battle, 29–44. Charlottesville: University of Virginia Press, 2013.

Dastyari, Azadeh. "Breaching International Law: Immigration Detention in Guantanamo Bay, Cuba." In *Immigration Detention: The Migration of a Policy and Its Human Impact,* edited by Amy Nethery and Stephanie J. Silverman, 96–103. New York: Routledge, 2015.

——. "Refugees on Guantanamo Bay: A Blue Print for Australia's 'Pacific Solution'?" *AQ: Australia Quarterly* 79, no. 1 (2007): 4–8, 40.

——. *United States Migrant Interdiction and the Detention of Refugees in Guantánamo Bay.* Cambridge: Cambridge University Press, 2015.

De Genova, Nicholas, and Nathalie Peutz, eds. *The Deportation Regime: Sovereignty, Space, and the Freedom of Movement.* Durham, N.C.: Duke University Press, 2010.

DeWind, Josh, and David H. Kinley. *Aiding Migration: The Impact of International Development Assistance on Haiti.* Boulder, CO: Westview Press, 1988.

Diener, Alexander, and Joshua Hagen. *Borders: A Very Short Introduction.* New York: Oxford University Press, 2012.

Dow, Mark. *American Gulag: Inside U.S. Immigration Prisons.* Berkeley: University of California Press, 2005.

Dowling, Julie A., and Jonathan Xavier Inda, eds. *Governing Immigration through Crime: A Reader.* Stanford, Calif.: Stanford University Press, 2013.

Dunn, Timothy J. *The Militarization of the U.S.-Mexican Border, 1978–1992: Low-Intensity Conflict Doctrine Comes Home.* Austin: Center for Mexican American Studies, University of Texas, 1996.

Dupuy, Alex. *Haiti in the New World Order: The Limits of the Democratic Revolution.* Boulder, Colo.: Westview Press, 1997.

Ettinger, Patrick. *Imaginary Lines: Border Enforcement and the Origins of Undocumented Immigration, 1882–1930.* Austin: University of Texas Press, 2010.

Farmer, Paul. *AIDS and Accusation: Haiti and the Geography of Blame.* Berkeley: University of California Press, 1992.

——. *The Uses of Haiti.* Monroe, Maine: Common Courage Press, 2006.

Fiske, Lucy. *Human Rights, Refugee Protest, and Immigration Detention.* London: Palgrave Macmillan, 2016.

Fragomen, Austin T., Jr. "The Illegal Immigration Reform and Immigrant Responsibility Act of 1996: An Overview." *International Migration Review* 31, no. 2 (1997): 438–460.

Frelick, Bill. "The Back of the Hand: Bias and Restrictionism toward Central American Asylum Seekers in North America." Briefing paper prepared for the U.S. Committee for Refugees and Immigrants, Washington, D.C., 1988.

García, María Christina. *Havana USA: Cuban Exiles and Cuban Americans in South Florida, 1959–1994.* Berkeley: University of California Press, 1996.

———. *The Refugee Challenge in Post–Cold War America.* New York: Oxford University Press, 2017.

———. *Seeking Refuge: Central American Migration to Mexico, the United States, and Canada.* Berkeley: University of California Press, 2006.

García Hernández, César Cuauhtémoc. "Immigration Detention as Punishment." *UCLA Law Review* 61 (2014): 1346–1414.

Gatrell, Peter. *The Making of the Modern Refugee.* New York: Oxford University Press, 2015.

Ghoshal, Animesh, and Thomas M. Crowley. "Refugees and Immigrants: A Human Rights Dilemma." *Human Rights Quarterly* 5, no. 3 (1983): 327–347.

Gilbert, Jeffrey C., and Steven Kass. "*Jean v. Nelson*: A Stark Pattern of Discrimination." *University of Miami Law Review* 36 (1982): 1005–1038.

Golash-Boza, Tanya. *Deported: Immigrant Policing, Disposable Labor, and Global Capitalism.* New York: New York University Press, 2015.

———. *Due Process Denied: Detentions and Deportations in the United States.* New York: Routledge, 2012.

———. *Immigration Nation: Raids, Detentions, and Deportations in Post-9/11 America.* Boulder, CO: Paradigm Publishers, 2012.

Goldstein, Brandt, Rodger Citron, and Molly Beutz Land. *A Documentary Companion to Storming the Court.* Austen, Tex.: Wolters Kluwer Law & Business, 2009.

Goodwin-Gill, Guy S. "International Law and the Detention of Refugees and Asylum Seekers." *International Migration Review* 20, no. 2 (1986): 193–219.

Gottschalk, Marie. *Caught: The Prison State and the Lockdown of American Politics.* Princeton, N.J.: Princeton University Press, 2016.

Guia, Maria João, Robert Koulish, and Valsamis Mitsilegas, eds. *Immigration Detention, Risk and Human Rights: Studies on Immigration and Crime.* Heidelberg: Springer International, 2016.

Hahn, Richard F. "Constitutional Limits on the Power to Exclude Aliens." *Columbia Law Review* 82, no. 5 (1982): 957–997.

Haines, Christina Elefteriades, and Anil Kalyan. "Detention of Asylum Seekers En Masse: Immigration Detention in the United States." In *Immigration Detention: The Migration of a Policy and Its Human Impact,* edited by Amy Nethery and Stephanie J. Silverman, 69–78. New York: Routledge, 2015.

Hardoon, Deborah, Sophia Ayele and Ricardo Fuentes-Nieva. "An Economy for the 1%: How Privilege and Power in the Economy Drive Extreme Inequality and How This Can Be Stopped." Oxfam International, January 2016, https://www.oxfam.org/sites/www.oxfam.org/files/file_attachments/bp210-economy-one-percent-tax-havens-180116-en_0.pdf.

Helton, Arthur C. "The Legality of Detaining Refugees in the United States." *New York University Review of Law and Social Change* 353 (1986): 353–381.

———. "The Mandate of the U.S. Courts to Protect Aliens under International Human Rights Law." *Yale Law Journal* 100, no. 8 (1991): 2335–2346.

Hernandez, David Manuel. "Pursuant to Deportation: Latinos and Immigrant Detention." In *Governing Immigration through Crime: A Reader*, edited by Julie A. Dowling and Jonathan Xavier Inda, 199–216. Stanford, Calif.: Stanford University Press, 2013.

Hernandez, Kelly Lytle. *City of Inmates: Conquest, Rebellion, and the Rise of Human Caging in Los Angeles, 1771–1965*. Chapel Hill: University of North Carolina Press, 2017.

———. *Migra! A History of the U.S. Border Patrol*. Berkeley: University of California Press, 2010.

Hernández, Kelly Lytle, Khalil Gibran Muhammad, and Heather Ann Thompson, "Introduction: Constructing the Carceral State." *Journal of American History* 102, no. 1 (2015): 18–24.

Hester, Torrie. "Deportability and the Carceral State." *Journal of American History* 102, no. 2 (2015): 141–151.

———. *Deportation: The Origins of U.S. Policy*. Philadelphia: University of Pennsylvania Press, 2017.

Hinton, Elizabeth. *From the War on Poverty to the War on Crime: The Making of Mass Incarceration in America*. Cambridge, Mass.: Harvard University Press, 2016.

Human Rights Watch. *Brutality Unchecked: Human Rights Abuses along the U.S. Border with Mexico*. New York: Human Rights Watch, 1992.

———. "U.S. Deaths in Immigration Detention: Newly Released Records Suggest Dangerous Lapses in Medical Care." Human Rights Watch, July 7, 2016. https://www.hrw.org/news/2016/07/07/us-deaths-immigration-detention.

Human Rights Watch Children's Project. *Slipping through the Cracks: Unaccompanied Children Detained by the U.S. Immigration and Naturalization Service*. New York: Human Rights Watch, 1997. https://www.hrw.org/sites/default/files/reports/us974.pdf.

"The Indefinite Detention of Excluded Aliens: Statutory and Constitutional Justifications and Limitations." *Michigan Law Review* 82, no. 1 (1983): 61–89.

Jastram, Kate. "The Kids before Khadr: Haitian Refugee Children on Guantanamo [A Comment on Richard J. Wilson's *Omar Khadr: Domestic and Litigation Strategies for a Child in Armed Conflict Held at Guantanamo*]. *Santa Clara Journal of International Law* 11, no. 1 (2012): 83–98.

Kahn, Robert S. *Other People's Blood: U.S. Immigration Prisons in the Reagan Decade*. Boulder, Colo.: Westview Press, 1996.

Kanstroom, Daniel. *Deportation Nation: Outsiders in American History*. Cambridge, Mass.: Harvard University Press, 2007.

Kaplan, Amy. "Where Is Guantanamo?" *American Quarterly* 57, no. 3 (2005): 831–858.

Kendall, Wesley. *From Gulag to Guantanamo: Political, Social, and Economic Evolutions of Mass Incarceration*. New York: Rowman & Littlefield International, 2016.

Koh, Harold Hongju. "The 'Haiti Paradigm'" in United States Human Rights Policy." *Yale Law Journal* 103, no. 8 (1994): 2392–2435.

Kohler-Hausman, Julilly. *Getting Tough: Welfare and Imprisonment in 1970s America*. Princeton, N.J.: Princeton University Press, 2017.

Krajick, Kevin. "Prisons for Profit: The Private Alternative." *State Legislatures* 10 (April 1984): 9–14.

Kurzban, Ira J. "'Long and Perilous Journey' The Nelson Decision." *Human Rights* 11, no. 2 (1983): 41–43.

Laguerre, Michel S. *Diasporic Citizenship: Haitian Americans in Transnational America*. New York: St. Martin's Press, 1998.

LaPointe, Mary Jane. "Discrimination in Asylum Law: The Implications *of Jean v. Nelson*." *Indiana Law Journal* 62, no. 1 (1986): 127–149.

Lee, Erika. *The Making of Asian America: A History*. New York: Simon and Schuster, 2015.

Lee, Esther Yu Hsi. "The Movement to End Immigrant Family Detention Is Picking Up Steam. Here's Why." *Think Progress*, May 29, 2015. https://thinkprogress.org/the-movement-to-end-immigrant-family-detention-is-picking-up-steam-heres-why-358bb28f0676/.

Lindskoog, Carl. "Defending the Haitian Boat People: Origins and Development of a Movement." In *International Conference on Caribbean Studies. Selected Proceedings*, edited by Hector R. Romero, 185–199. Edinburgh, Tex.: University of Texas-Pan American, 2007.

———. "Refugees and Resistance: International Activism for Grassroots Democracy and Human Rights in New York, Miami, and Haiti, 1957 to 1994." PhD diss., City University of New York, 2013.

Lipman, Jana K. "'The Fish Trusts the Water, and It Is in the Water that It Is Cooked': The Caribbean Origins of the Krome Detention Center." *Radical History Review* 115 (2013): 115–141.

———. *Guantanamo: A Working-Class History between Empire and Revolution*. Berkeley: University of California Press, 2009.

Little, Cheryl. "INS Detention in Florida." *University of Miami Inter-American Law Review* 30, no. 3 (1999): 551–575.

———. *Krome's Invisible Prisoners: Cycles of Abuse and Neglect*. Miami: Florida Immigrant Advocacy Center, 1996.

———. *Not in Their Best Interest: A Report on the U.S. Government's Forcible Repatriation of Guantanamo's Unaccompanied Haitian Children*. Miami: Florida Rural Legal Services, 1995.

———. "United States Haitian Policy: A History of Discrimination." *New York Law School Journal of Human Rights* 10, part 2 (1993): 269–324.

Locked Away: Immigration Detainees in Jails in the United States. Special issue, *Human Rights Watch* 10, no. 1 (1998). https://www.hrw.org/legacy/reports98/us-immig/.

Loescher, Gilburt, and John Scanlan. *Calculated Kindness: Refugees and America's Half-Open Door 1945–Present*. New York: Free Press, 1986.

———. "Human Rights, U.S. Foreign Policy, and Haitian Refugees." *Journal of Interamerican Studies and World Affairs* 26, no. 3 (1983): 332–344.

Loyd, Jenna M., Matt Mitchelson, and Andrew Burridge, eds. *Beyond Walls and Cages: Prisons, Borders, and Global Crisis*. Athens: University of George Press, 2012.

Loyd, Jenna M., and Alison Mountz. *Boats, Borders, and Bases: Race, the Cold War, and the Rise of Migration Detention in the United States*. Berkeley: University of California Press, 2018.

Macías-Rojas, Patrisia. *From Deportation to Prison: The Politics of Immigration Enforcement in Post–Civil Rights America*. New York: New York University Press, 2016.

Maddux, Thomas R. "Ronald Reagan and the Task Force on Immigration, 1981." *Pacific Historical Review* 74, no. 2 (2005): 195–236.

Mattera, Philip, Mafruza Khan, and Stephen Nathan. *Corrections Corporation of America: A Critical Look at Its First 20 Years*. N.p.: Grassroots Leadership, 2003. Accessed October 19,

2016. http://grassrootsleadership.org/sites/default/files/uploads/CCAAnniversaryReport. pdf.

McDonald, Douglas C. "Private Penal Institutions." *Crime and Justice* 16 (1992): 361–419.

Mitchell, Christopher. "The Political Costs of State Power: U.S. Border Control in South Florida." In *The Wall around the West: State Borders and Immigration Controls in North America and Europe*, edited by Peter Andreas and Timothy Snyder, 81–98. Lanham, Md.: Rowman & Littlefield, 2000.

———. "U.S. Policy Toward Haitian Boat People, 1972–93." *Annals of the American Academy of Political and Social Science* 534, no. 1 (1994): 69–80.

Motomura, Hiroshi. *Americans in Waiting: The Lost Story of Immigration and Citizenship in the United States*. New York: Oxford University Press, 2006.

Muhammad, Khalil Gibran. *The Condemnation of Blackness: Race, Crime, and the Making of Modern Urban America*. Cambridge, Mass.: Harvard University Press, 2010.

Nethery, Amy, and Stephanie J. Silverman, eds. *Immigration Detention: The Migration of a Policy and Its Human Impact*. London: Routledge, 2017.

Nevins, Joseph. *Operation Gatekeeper and Beyond: The War on "Illegals" and the Remaking of the U.S.-Mexico Boundary*. New York: Routledge, 2010.

Ngai, Mae M. *Impossible Subjects: Illegal Aliens and the Making of Modern America*. Princeton, N.J.: Princeton University Press, 2004.

Paik, A. Naomi. *Rightlessness: Testimony and Redress in U.S. Prison Camps since World War II*. Chapel Hill: University of North Carolina Press, 2016.

Parker, Alison. *A Costly Move: Far and Frequent Transfers Impede Hearings for Immigrant Detainees in the United States*. New York: Human Rights Watch, 2011. Accessed December 22, 2017. https://www.hrw.org/report/2011/06/14/costly-move/far-and-frequent-transfers-impede-hearings-immigrant-detainees-united.

Parker, Kunal M. *Making Foreigners: Immigration and Citizenship Law in America, 1600–2000*. Cambridge: Cambridge University Press, 2015.

Peutz, Nathalie, and Nicholas De Genova. "Introduction." In *The Deportation Regime: Sovereignty, Space and the Freedom of Movement*, edited by Nicholas De Genova and Nathalie Peutz, 1–32. Durham, N.C.: Duke University Press, 2010.

Polyné, Millery. *From Douglass to Duvalier: U.S. African Americans, Haiti, and Pan Americanism, 1870–1964*. Gainesville: University Press of Florida, 2010.

Ratner, Michael. "How We Closed the Guantanamo HIV Camp: The Intersection of Politics and Litigation." *Harvard Human Rights Journal* 11 (1998): 187–220.

Regan, Margaret. *Detained and Deported: Stories of Immigrant Families under Fire*. Boston: Beacon Press, 2015.

Reimers, David M. *Unwelcome Strangers: American Identity and the Turn against Immigration*. New York: Columbia University Press, 1998.

Schuck, Peter H. "The Transformation of Immigration Law." *Columbia Law Review* 84, no. 1 (1984): 1–90.

Seller, Maxine S. "Historical Perspectives on American Immigration Policy: Case Studies and Current Implications." *Law and Contemporary Problems* 45, no. 2 (1982): 137–162.

Silk, James. *Despite a Generous Spirit: Denying Asylum in the United States*. Washington, D.C.: U.S. Committee for Refugees, 1986.

Silverman, Stephanie Jessica, and Amy Nethery. "Understanding Immigration Detention and

Its Human Impact." In *Immigration Detention: The Migration of a Policy and Its Human Impact*, edited by Amy Nethery and Stephanie J. Silverman, 1–12. London: Routledge, 2017.

Simon, Jonathan. "Refugees in a Carceral Age: The Rebirth of Immigration Prison in the United States." *Public Culture* 10, no. 3 (1998): 577–607.

St. John, Rachel. *Line in the Sand: A History of the Western U.S.-Mexico*. Princeton, N.J.: Princeton University Press, 2012.

Stepick, Alex. "Haitian Boat People: A Study in the Conflicting Forces Shaping U.S. Immigration Policy." *Law and Contemporary Problems* 45, no. 2 (1982): 163–196.

———. "The Refugees Nobody Wants: Haitians in Miami." In *Miami Now! Immigration, Ethnicity, and Social Change*, edited by Guillermo J. Grenier and Alex Stepick III, 57–82. Gainesville: University Press of Florida, 1992.

———. "Structural Determinants of the Haitian Refugee Movement: Different Interpretations." Occasional Papers Series, Dialogues #4, Latin American and Caribbean Center, Florida International University, 1981. http://digitalcommons.fiu.edu/laccopsd/60/.

Stumpf, Juliet P. "The Crimmigration Crisis: Immigrants, Crime, and Sovereign Power." In *Governing Immigration through Crime: A Reader*, edited by Julie A. Dowling and Jonathan Xavier Inda, 59–76. Stanford, Calif.: Stanford University Press, 2013.

The Africana Cultures and Policy Studies Institute: Zachery Williams, Robert Samuel Smith, Seneca Vaught, and Babacar M'Baye. "A History of Black Immigration into the United States through the Lens of the African American Civil and Human Rights Struggle." In *Immigrant Rights in the Shadows of Citizenship*, edited by Rachel Ida Buff, 159–179. New York: New York University Press, 2008.

Thompson, Heather Ann. *Blood in the Water: The Attica Prison Uprising of 1971 and Its Legacy*. New York: Pantheon, 2016.

———. "From Researching the Past to Reimagining the Future: Locating Carceral Crisis and the Key to Its End, in the Long Twentieth Century." In *The Punitive Turn: New Approaches to Race and Incarceration*, edited by Deborah E. McDowell, Claudrena N. Harold, and Juan Battle, 45–72. Charlottesville: University of Virginia Press, 2013.

———. "Why Mass Incarceration Matters: Rethinking Crisis, Decline, and Transformation in Postwar American History." *Journal of American History* 97, no. 3 (2010): 703–734.

Tichener, Daniel J. *Dividing Lines: The Politics of Immigration Control in America*. Princeton, N.J.: Princeton University Press, 2009.

Trouillot, Michel-Rolph. *Haiti, State against Nation: The Origins and Legacy of Duvalierism*. New York: Monthly Review Press, 1990.

United States Conference of Catholic Bishops and Center for Migration Services. *Unlocking Human Dignity: A Plan to Transform the U.S. Immigrant Detention System*. New York: Center for Migration Studies, 2015. Accessed January 17, 2017. http://www.usccb.org/about/migration-and-refugee-services/upload/unlocking-human-dignity.pdf.

U.S. Congress. House. Committee on Foreign Affairs. Subcommittee on Western Hemisphere Affairs and Subcommittee on International Operations. *U.S. Policy toward Haitian Refugees: Joint Hearing and Markup before the Subcommittees on Western Hemisphere Affairs and International Operations of the Committee on Foreign Affairs, House of Representatives, One Hundred Second Congress, Second Session, on H.R. 5360, June 11 and 17, 1992*. Washington, D.C.: United States Government Printing Office, 1992.

U.S. Congress. House. Committee on Government Operations. Legislation and National Security Subcommittee. *U.S. Human Rights Policy toward Haiti, Hearing before the Legisla-tion and National Security Subcommittee of the Committee on Government Operations, House of Representatives, One Hundred Second Congress, Second Session, April 9, 1992.* Washington, D.C.: U.S. Government Printing Office, 1993.

U.S. Congress. House. Committee on the Judiciary. *Detention of Aliens in Bureau of Prisons Facilities: Hearing before the Subcommittee on Courts, Civil Liberties and the Administra-tion of Justice, Ninety-Seventh Congress, Second Session, June 23, 1982.* Washington, D.C.: U.S. Government Printing Office, 1983.

U.S. Congress. House. Committee on the Judiciary. Subcommittee on International Law, Im-migration, and Refugees. *Cuban and Haitian Immigration: Hearing before the Subcom-mittee on International Law, Immigration, and Refugees of the Committee on the Judiciary, One Hundred Second Congress, First Session, November 20, 1991.* Washington, D.C.: U.S. Government Printing Office, 1992.

———. *Haitian Asylum Seekers: Hearing before the Subcommittee on International Law, Im-migration, and Refugees of the Committee on the Judiciary, House of Representatives, One Hundred Third Congress, Second Session, on H.R. 3663, H.R. 4114, and H.R. 4264, June 15, 1994.* Washington, D.C.: U.S. Government Printing Office, 1994.

———. *Haitian Detention and Interdiction: Hearing before the Subcommittee on Immigration, Refugees, and International Law of the Committee on the Judiciary, One Hundred First Con-gress, First Session, June 8, 1989.* Washington, D.C.: U.S. Government Printing Office, 1989.

———. *War on Terrorism: Immigration Enforcement since September 11, 2001, Hearing before the Subcommittee on Immigration, Border Security, and Claims of the Committee on the Judiciary, One Hundred Eighth Congress, First Session, May 8, 2003.* Washington, D.C.: U.S. Government Printing Office, 2003.

U.S. Congress. Senate. Committee on the Judiciary. *Caribbean Refugee Crisis: Cubans and Haitians: Hearing Before the Committee on the Judiciary, United States Senate, Ninety-Sixty Congress, Second Session, May 12, 1980.* Washington, D.C.: U.S. Government Printing Of-fice, 1980.

U.S. Congress. Senate. Committee on the Judiciary. Subcommittee on Immigration and Refu-gee Affairs. *Haitian Democracy and Refugees: Problems and Prospects: Staff Report.* Wash-ington, D.C.: U.S. Government Printing Office, 1992.

U.S. Congress. Senate. Committee on the Judiciary. Subcommittee on Immigration and Refu-gee Policy. *United States as a Country of Mass First Asylum: Hearing before the Subcommit-tee on Immigration and Refugee Policy, United States Senate, Ninety-Seventh Congress, First Session, July 31, 1981.* Washington, D.C.: U.S. Government Printing Office, 1982.

U.S. General Accounting Office. *Detention Policies Affecting Haitian Nationals.* Washington, D.C.: U.S. General Accounting Office, 1983.

Varma, Asim, and Craig M. Tateronis. *The Detention of Asylum Seekers in the United States: A Cruel and Questionable Policy: A Briefing Paper.* New York: Lawyers Committee for Human Rights, 1989.

Welch, Michael. *Detained: Immigration Laws and the Expanding I.N.S. Jail Complex.* Philadel-phia: Temple University Press, 2002.

Whelan, Daniel J. "Permanent Exile: The U.S. Exclusion of HIV-Positive Haitian Refugees—Public Health, Politics, and International Law." *Swords and Ploughshares* 2, no. 2 (1993): 8–11.

Wilsher, Daniel. *Immigration Detention: Law, History, Politics.* Cambridge: Cambridge University Press, 2012.

Women's Commission for Refugee Women and Children. *Behind Locked Doors: Abuse of Refugee Women at the Krome Detention Center.* New York: Women's Commission for Refugee Women and Children, 2000. http://www.womensrefugeecommission.org/images/zdocs/krome.pdf.

Wong, Tom K. *Rights, Deportation, and Detention in the Age of Immigration Control.* Stanford, Calif.: Stanford University Press, 2015.

Zolberg, Aristide R. *A Nation by Design: Immigration Policy in the Fashioning of America.* Cambridge, Mass.: Harvard University Press, 2008.

Zucker, Naomi Flink. "The Haitians versus the United States: The Courts as Last Resort." *Annals of the American Academy of Political and Social Science* 467 (May 1983): 151–162.

Zucker, Norman L., and Naomi Flink Zucker. *The Guarded Gate: The Reality of American Refugee Policy.* San Diego: Harcourt Brace Jovanovich, 1987.

Index

CARL LINDSKOOG is assistant professor of history at Raritan Valley Community College.